DEPARTMENT OF THE ENVIRONMENT

English House Condition Survey: 1986

LONDON: HER MAJESTY'S STATIONERY OFFICE

ISBN 0 11 752153 1

Contents

LIST OF FIGURES

Text

Appendices

LIST OF TABLES

Text

Appendices

Annex

1 Introduction

Background

1.1 The 1986 English House Condition Survey is the fifth in the quinquennial series undertaken by the Department of the Environment. These surveys provide the Department with the major source of information to assist in the development and monitoring of policies directed towards the repair and improvement of the housing stock.

1.2 The data presented in this report were collected through four separate but related surveys:

   i a survey of dwellings to provide a description of the stock and its present condition (the physical survey);

   ii interviews with households to determine their characteristics (including financial circumstances), to identify the improvement and repair works they have undertaken or intend to undertake, and to establish the effectiveness of heating arrangements in the home. The latter was supplemented by gas and electricity consumption data (the interview survey);

   iii a postal survey of local authorities, to identify the action they have taken or intend to take on either their own stock or that in the private sector (the postal survey);

   iv a survey of current market values to link property prices to condition (the valuation survey).

The survey forms used to collect these data are at Appendix A.

Conduct of the survey

1.3 Survey design, organisation and data analysis are the responsibility of staff at the Department of the Environment but a variety of other agencies and organisations were involved in the survey. The construction of the survey sample and the fieldwork monitoring system was undertaken by Services in Informatics and Analysis Ltd. The physical survey, which took place between September and December 1986, was carried out by 272 surveyors employed from local authorities and private surveying companies. National Opinion Polls Ltd conducted the interview survey between November 1986 and June 1987. The Electricity Boards and British Gas Regions supplied fuel consumption figures for a sample of households. The postal survey was organised by BJM Research and Consultancy Ltd and was undertaken between July and December 1987. District Valuers were responsible for providing current market values.

The survey method

1.4   Demands for better information have increased with each House Condition Survey. These demands have been met in the past by adapting the survey method previously used. However, to provide the more accurate and extensive range of data required for 1986 it was necessary to develop a new survey methodology. An explanation of the changes made and the reasons for these is at Appendix B.

1.5   Because the new survey used a different method of measurement, information provided by this method cannot be compared directly with that provided by previous surveys (see Appendix C). The 1986 survey was therefore divided into two parts. A sample of 22,473 dwellings was surveyed using the new method and the results are presented in Chapters 3–8 of this report. A sample of 8,213 dwellings which had been surveyed in 1981 were resurveyed in 1986 using the same (1981) method to measure change in the condition of the stock over this period. The results of this longitudinal survey are presented in Chapter 9.

The survey sample and rate of response

1.6   A sample of 30,686 dwellings was drawn for the survey and divided between the main and longitudinal surveys. Sub-samples of this main sample were drawn for the three other related surveys. A description of the sampling process and sample sizes is at Appendix D. Information was obtained for 81% of the dwellings included in the physical survey. With non-respondents from the latter already excluded, higher response rates were obtained in the other three surveys.

Interpretation of results

Sampling error

1.7   The results have been grossed up to the national level. The use of a sample survey to draw conclusions about the national stock introduces some uncertainty but, for ease of reading, the information is presented as single figures rather than ranges. A full explanation of these confidence limits is at Appendix D.

Measurement error

1.8   Errors are also associated with the methods of measurement. The implications of this for the interpretation of results are explained in the text where appropriate. A full account of the margins of error is at Appendices E and F.

Comparison of data from the two physical surveys

1.9   Because two survey methods have been used there are small differences in the number and proportions of dwellings unfit and without basic amenities reported in the main and longitudinal surveys. These differences are attributed to different methods of grossing the two samples. Grossing the longitudinal element of the survey overestimates the proportion of older dwellings in the stock which results in marginally higher estimates of the proportions of dwellings in poor condition. The longitudinal survey provides the most reliable estimate of change between 1981 and 1986. The main survey provides the most reliable estimate of the position in 1986 (Appendix C).

Measure of disrepair

1.10   The new survey method enables a range of measures of disrepair to be constructed which differ from those used in earlier surveys. The 1986 survey distinguishes repair which is urgent, in the sense that it is required to prevent the further rapid deterioration of the property. It also provides a measure of the more comprehensive repair, required to secure the property in the medium term, likely to be required as a condition of mortgage lending or a Home Improvement Grant (Appendix F).

Contents of report

1.11   This report includes the main results from all four surveys but does not report all the detailed information assembled. Further analysis of these surveys may be the subject of supplementary reports. A service will also be available for those who wish to purchase figures not otherwise published. The details are at Appendix G.

Layout of report

1.12   Abstracts of the data are presented in figures and tables throughout the text. Main tables are included in an annex at the end of the report. References to these tables have the prefix A, followed by the relevant chapter and table number.

2 Summary

2.1 In 1986 there were 18.8 million dwellings in England. Half of these were built before 1944 and one-quarter before 1919. One-quarter have been built since 1964 (Chapter 3).

2.2 Half the stock was in the form of detached or semi-detached houses, one-third terraced houses and the rest flats. Of the latter, around 70% were purpose-built flats mainly erected since the war, and 20% were provided by the sub-division of older property. On average, houses were 50% larger than flats. The great majority of owner-occupied properties were houses. About one-third of the dwellings provided by local authorities and private landlords and two-thirds those provided by Housing Associations were flats (Chapter 3).

2.3 Virtually all houses and flats had all standard amenities which include an indoor WC, a bath, sink and wash hand basin and hot and cold water supply to these. Only 2.5% did not have all these facilities, half of these were houses and flats built before 1900 and nearly one-third were vacant at the time of the survey (Chapter 4).

2.4 Almost three-quarters of all dwellings had some form of central heating. Nine out of ten had roof insulation and more than one in ten had additional wall insulation, or double glazing. However there remained almost one in ten dwellings which were judged to be inadequately heated. Around 1 million dwellings required rewiring (Chapter 4).

2.5 Repairs were reported to be required in around three-quarters of the stock. Many were not urgent in the sense that their neglect would affect the integrity of the building or present a risk to health or safety. Where urgent repairs were required many were modest and the cost was estimated to exceed £3,000 in less than 5% of all dwellings (Chapter 4).

2.6 Around 70% of the expenditure identified was for repairs to the external fabric, just over 20% for the internal fabric and the rest for repairs to amenities, services and fittings (Chapter 4).

2.7 Less than 5% of all houses and flats were unfit, as defined in section 604 of the Housing Act 1985. Three-quarters of these were houses and flats built before 1919 and one-quarter were vacant at the time of the survey. The main defects associated with unfitness were disrepair, dampness and inadequate facilities for food preparation (Chapters 4 and 5).

2.8 The proportion of dwellings lacking amenities or unfit was broadly the same whether these were owner occupied or rented from a local authority or Housing Association. The proportion of private-rented dwellings lacking amenities or unfit was five times higher than that in other sectors (Chapter 5).

2.9 The problems of disrepair varied substantially between tenures with the estimated cost of repair of private-rented dwellings more than twice that in any other sector. This was in part a function of the age of the private rented stock but not entirely. When properties of equivalent age were compared, those in the private rented sector were in the worst state of repair with properties owned by Housing Associations in the best state of repair. The cost of repair of the most recently built local authority owned properties was estimated to be almost twice that of owner-occupied properties of the same period (Chapter 4).

2.10 Over half the dwellings in poor condition had immediate neighbours which were in a similar or worse condition. This association of property in poor condition was more usual in local authority housing than in other tenures. Half of all local authority flats were affected by litter, graffiti or vandalism and this was reported to be extensive in 10% of these cases (Chapter 5).

2.11 There was a substantial difference in the condition of housing between urban and rural areas. Although the majority of dwellings in poor condition were in urban areas the proportion of such dwellings was much higher in rural areas. Owner occupiers in rural areas were one-and-a-half times more likely than those in urban areas to live in dwellings in poor condition (Chapter 5).

2.12 The proportion of housing in poor condition was higher in the North West, the West Midlands, Yorkshire and Humberside and the South West than in other regions (Chapter 5).

2.13 Poor housing was associated with low income. Half of all households lacking amenities and one-third of those in unfit housing had net annual incomes of less than £3,000. A high proportion of dwellings in poor condition were occupied by households whose head was aged 75 or over (Chapter 6).

2.14 Attitudes to the condition of their home differed between owners and tenants. Whatever the condition of the property reported by surveyors, local authority tenants were more likely than owner occupiers to see their home to be in a worse state of repair. The majority of owner occupiers believed the condition of their property had improved in recent years. The majority of tenants believed it had remained the same or had deteriorated (Chapter 6).

2.15 The value of works to repair and improve the stock, carried out in 1986, was estimated to be around £17bn with 80% of this contributed by the private sector. Approximately £6.5bn of this expenditure was related to repair and the provision of basic amenities (Chapter 7).

2.16 The value of work carried out by owner occupiers was, on average, twice that carried out by local authorities and other landlords. The most frequent works in the owner-occupied sector were internal decoration, improvements to kitchens and bathrooms, and the installation of central heating. The most frequent works on the local authority owned stock were to windows, heating, the provision of insulation and rewiring (Chapter 7).

2.17 Between 1981 and 1986 local authorities' action to improve and repair the private sector stock through area programmes, grant aid and the use of other powers included 1.6 million dwellings. Forty per cent of this action took place in the South East (including London) although this region included less than one-quarter of dwellings identified as unsatisfactory in the 1981 survey. In the same period 0.8 million local authority dwellings underwent major repairs or renovation, 0.5 million of these in estate programmes (Chapter 8).

2.18 Overall, the condition of the stock had improved between 1981 and 1986. There was a substantial fall in the number of dwellings lacking amenities, a small reduction in unfit dwellings but no significant change in the proportion of the stock in serious disrepair. The most substantial improvement in condition was found in the South East, there was modest improvement in the North but some deterioration in the Rest of England (in this analysis this includes East Anglia, the East and West Midlands and the South West) (Chapter 9).

3 The housing stock

3.1   At the end of 1986 there were 18.8 million dwellings in England. This number had increased from 16.1 million in 1971, 17.1 million in 1976 and 18.1 million in 1981. Half of the stock was built before 1944 and one-quarter before 1919.

Types of dwellings

Houses — types

3.2   Houses made up 80% of the stock and flats 20% (Figure 3.1). In 1986 there were 15.2 million houses in England but these showed substantial variation in type which was associated with different periods of house-building. Two-thirds of the houses built before 1919 were terraced, over half those built in the inter-war and post-war years were semi-detached and more than one-third of those built since 1964 were detached (Table A3.1).

Fig 3.1 Dwelling type by construction date

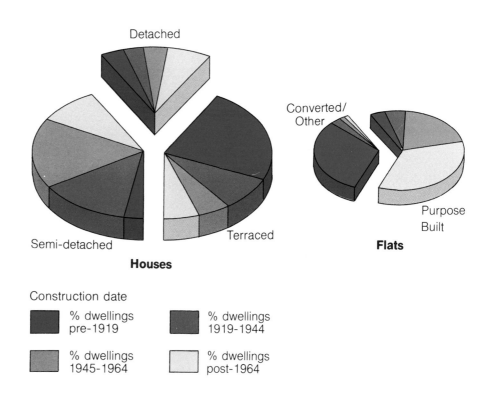

Detached

Semi-detached

Terraced

Houses

Converted/Other

Purpose Built

Flats

Construction date

% dwellings pre-1919

% dwellings 1919-1944

% dwellings 1945-1964

% dwellings post-1964

Houses — storey heights

3.3 As well as varying in type, houses varied in the number of storeys. Almost one-fifth of houses built before 1919 were of three or more storeys, while 20% of post-war housing were single storey (Table A3.2).

Flats — types

3.4 In 1986 there were 3.6 million flats in England, of which 21% were the result of the conversion of houses and 7% were flats associated with non-residential use[1] (Table A3.3). The remaining 72% were purpose built. Conversions occurred predominantly in pre-1919 houses. The construction of purpose-built flats in substantial numbers is a post-war phenomenon, with 61% of all flats in buildings constructed since 1945 and over one-third built since 1964.

Flats — storey heights

3.5 High rise flats (those of six storeys or more) represented a very small proportion of the stock. Only 16% of flats were in blocks of six or more storeys and only 7% in blocks of twelve or more storeys (Table A3.4).

Sizes of dwellings

3.6 Houses were, on average, 50% larger than flats. Dwellings of all types which survive from the last century were, on average, larger than those provided since 1919 (Table 3.1). The greatest variation in size was among detached houses. Those built after 1964 were, on average, 30% smaller than those built before 1919.

Table 3.1 Dwelling size by type and construction date

median internal floor area sqm

	Pre-1900	1900–1918	1919–1944	1945–1964	Post-1964	All Ages
Terraced Houses	79	81	69	73	74	74
Semi-Detached Houses	92	92	77	75	70	76
Detached Houses	138	138	100	95	96	101
Purpose-built Flats	59	64	49	50	44	47
Converted Flats	60	60	65	72	56	62
All Houses	87	86	76	76	77	78
All Flats	63	64	51	51	45	51

(See Table A.3.5)

Plot sizes

3.7 Plot size also varied with the age of the property. Houses built between 1919 and 1944 and those of early post-war construction had, on average, the largest plots. The oldest and most recently built dwellings had the smallest plots (Table A3.6). Over one-third of dwellings had no provision for off-street parking (Table A3.7).

[1.] Dwellings associated with non-residential use are typically flats over shops where the shop and the flat are rented as one unit. This category also includes residential accommodation associated with public houses and all cases where part of a dwelling is in commercial use.

Tenure

Changes 1971–86

3.8 Successive house condition surveys have revealed substantial changes in tenure patterns. Dwellings in owner occupation accounted for 63% of the stock in 1986 compared with 52% in 1971 (Figure 3.2). Much of this increase resulted from dwellings being transferred from both the private and public-rented sectors into owner occupation. In 1986 private-rented accommodation accounted for less than 7% of all dwellings, having declined from 18% in 1971. Local authority rented accommodation fell from 27% to 24% in the same period. Housing Association properties made up almost 3% of the stock in 1986. The remaining 4% of the stock was vacant.

Fig 3.2 Tenure change 1971 to 1986

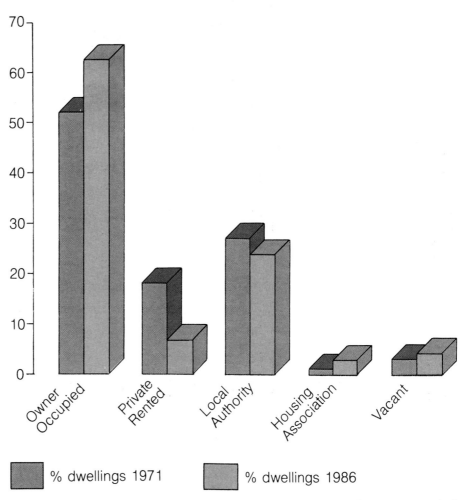

☐ % dwellings 1971   ☐ % dwellings 1986

Variations with construction date

3.9 The age and type of property varied with tenure. Owner-occupied dwellings were relatively evenly distributed across the whole age range (Table 3.2). Private-rented dwellings were most heavily concentrated in the older stock, with 70% of this group built before 1919. The local authority stock is of relatively recent construction with only one-quarter of local authority dwellings built before 1945. The Housing Association stock included the oldest and most recent dwellings.

Table 3.2   Construction date by tenure

thousands/% dwellings

	Pre-1919	1919–1944	1945–1964	Post-1964	All Ages
Owner Occupied	3,374 (29)	2,645 (22)	2,356 (20)	3,445 (29)	11,820 (100)
Private Rented	861 (69)	186 (15)	142 (11)	56 (5)	1,244 (100)
Local Authority/New Town	166 (4)	956 (21)	1,864 (42)	1,504 (33)	4,490 (100)
Housing Association	166 (35)	48 (10)	5 (1)	254 (54)	473 (100)
Vacant Dwellings	429 (53)	128 (13)	109 (13)	146 (18)	812 (100)
All Tenures	4,996 (26)	3,963 (21)	4,476 (24)	5,404 (29)	18,839 (100)

Variation in dwelling types

3.10   The majority of dwellings in all tenures were houses, except in Housing Associations where 65% of the dwellings were flats. Of these, most were purpose built (Table A3.8). Over 90% of owner-occupied dwellings were houses, the greatest proportion of which were semi-detached (Table A3.9). Most private-rented dwellings (68%) were houses, and the majority of these were terraced. Private-rented flats were mainly provided by the conversion of older houses. About two-thirds of local authority dwellings were houses and most of these were terraced. One-third of local authority dwellings were flats, half of which had been built since 1964. High-rise flats (those of six storeys or more) were almost all (85%) owned by local authorities, but they made up only 20% of all local authority flats (Table A3.10).

Variation in size

3.11   Owner-occupied dwellings were, on average, substantially larger than those owned by local authorities and occupied larger plots (Tables 3.3, A3.11, A3.12).

Table 3.3   Dwelling size by type and tenure

median internal floor area — sqm

	Owner Occupied	Private Rented	Local Authority/ New Town	Housing Association	All Occupied Dwellings
House	83	76	71	77	78
Flat	61	56	46	45	51
All Dwelling Types	82	70	65	57	75

(See Table A.3.11)

Vacant dwellings

3.12 Over 4% of the stock were vacant[2]. Of these dwellings, 36% appeared to have become vacant only recently, 23% were for sale or were already sold and awaiting occupation, 19% were in the process of modernisation, a further 2% were about to be demolished and 3% were empty but no longer in use as dwellings; 16% appeared to have been vacant for a considerable period.

Variation with construction date

3.13 Just over half the vacant dwellings were built before 1919 (Figure 3.3). Almost one-fifth of this group were long-term vacants. A further fifth of these were for sale and one-quarter were in the process of modernisation. The most recent dwellings which were empty had either become vacant only recently or were for sale.

Fig 3.3   Vacant dwellings: construction date by type of vacancy

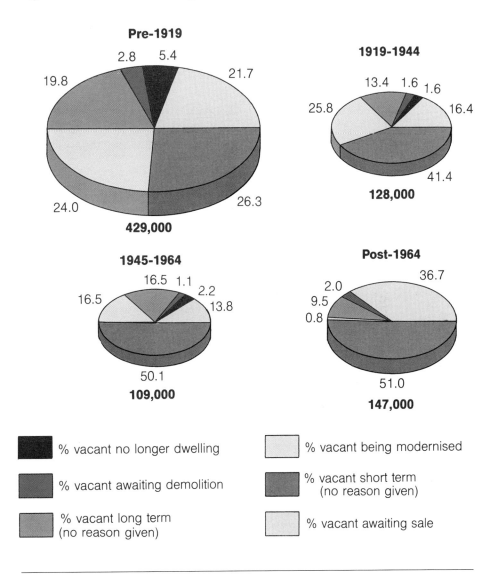

% vacant no longer dwelling

% vacant being modernised

% vacant awaiting demolition

% vacant short term (no reason given)

% vacant long term (no reason given)

% vacant awaiting sale

[2.] Vacant dwellings were divided into six categories:

(1) For sale — for sale/sold notice outside.
(2) Awaiting demolition — in block where demolition work is in progress or no sign of activity but a demolition notice on the dwelling.
(3) Being modernised — an empty dwelling with building works in progress.
(4) Vacant short term (no reason given).
(5) Vacant long term (no reason given).
(6) Vacant — no longer dwelling. Still rated as dwelling but used for non-residential purpose.

Variation with ownership

3.14   Only 16% of vacant dwellings were owned by local authorities. This sector had a lower vacancy rate (2.7%) than the private sector (4.8%) (Figure 3.4).

Figure 3.4   Vacant dwellings: tenure by type of vacancy

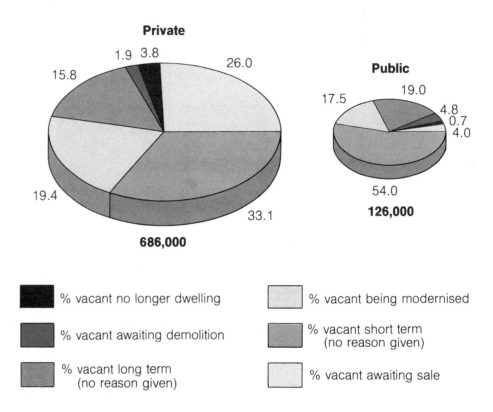

Private

1.9 3.8
15.8
26.0
19.4
33.1
686,000

Public

17.5
19.0
4.8
0.7
4.0
54.0
126,000

■ % vacant no longer dwelling	☐ % vacant being modernised
■ % vacant awaiting demolition	▨ % vacant short term (no reason given)
▨ % vacant long term (no reason given)	☐ % vacant awaiting sale

Houses in multiple occupation[3]

3.15   A very small proportion of dwellings (1.1%) were occupied by more than one household. Dwellings providing this type of accommodation were usually in the older stock. Over half of the houses in multiple occupation were occupied by only two households, but one-quarter were much larger, providing accommodation for more than seven households (Table A3.13).

Construction type

3.16   The great majority of houses and flats were of masonry construction, that is, built of bricks or blocks. A small proportion (9%) were of frame or panel construction, in timber, steel or reinforced concrete. The survey identified around 800,000 of these non-traditional houses and a similar number of non-traditional flats (Table A3.14). Sixty-one per cent of dwellings of non-traditional construction were in local authority ownership (Table A3.15).

---

3. A dwelling is multi-occupied if it contains more than one household. A household is:
— a single person living alone, or
— a group of people (who may or may not be related) living at the same address with common housekeeping (sharing at least one meal a day) or sharing a living or sitting room.

Market value

3.17   In November 1986 the average vacant possession market value of all dwellings, regardless of tenure, was £42,000 implying a value of £800 bn for the stock as a whole (Table A3.16). Values varied considerably with tenure; owner-occupied dwellings had the highest average value at £49,500 which was almost twice the value of dwellings in the public sector (Figure 3.5). Vacant dwellings had a surprisingly high average value at £37,000.

Fig 3.5   Mean market value by tenure

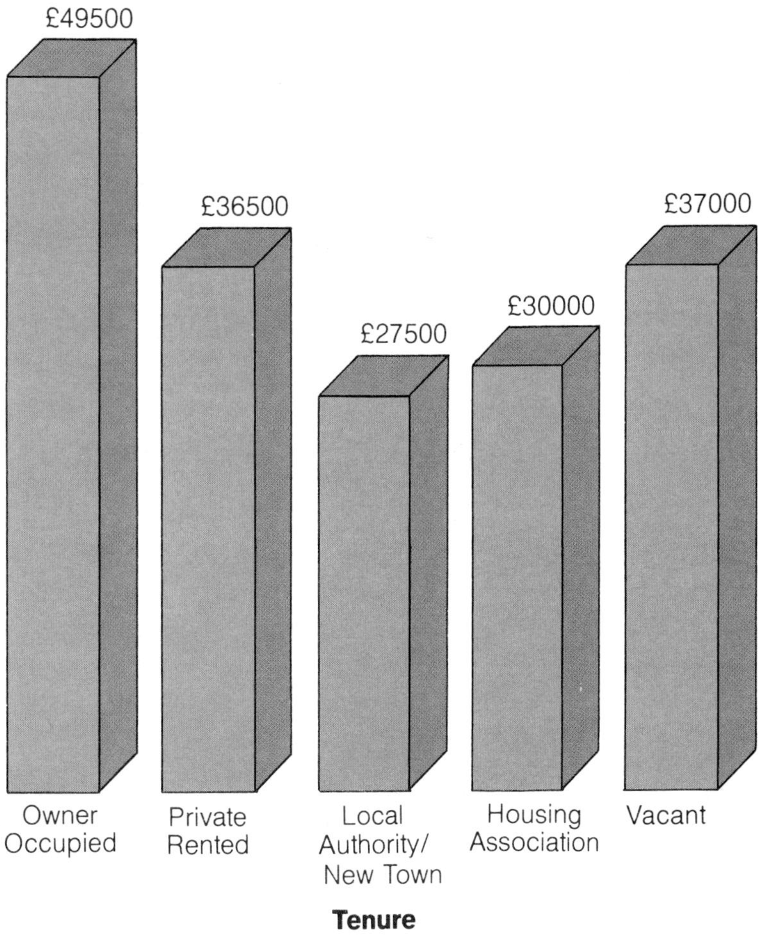

Variation with dwelling type

3.18   Market value varied with dwelling type. Detached houses had almost twice the value of any other form of dwelling. Purpose-built flats had the lowest average values. A similar relationship between value and dwelling type applied to all tenures (Table A3.17).

Regional Distribution
Construction date

3.19   The composition of the dwelling stock varied across the country. Inner London had by far the highest proportion of older dwellings with 49% of its stock built before 1919. The North West and South West also had higher than average proportions of pre-1919 dwellings (Figure 3.6). The greatest growth in housing during the inter-war years was in Outer London, where 43% of the stock was built in this period. The early post-war years saw relatively high levels of house building in the Northern region, the West Midlands and the Rest of the South East. East Anglia had the highest proportion of dwellings (39%) built since 1964. The South East (excluding London), the East Midlands and the South West also had a higher than average proportion of their stock built in this period.

Fig 3.6 Construction date and tenure by region

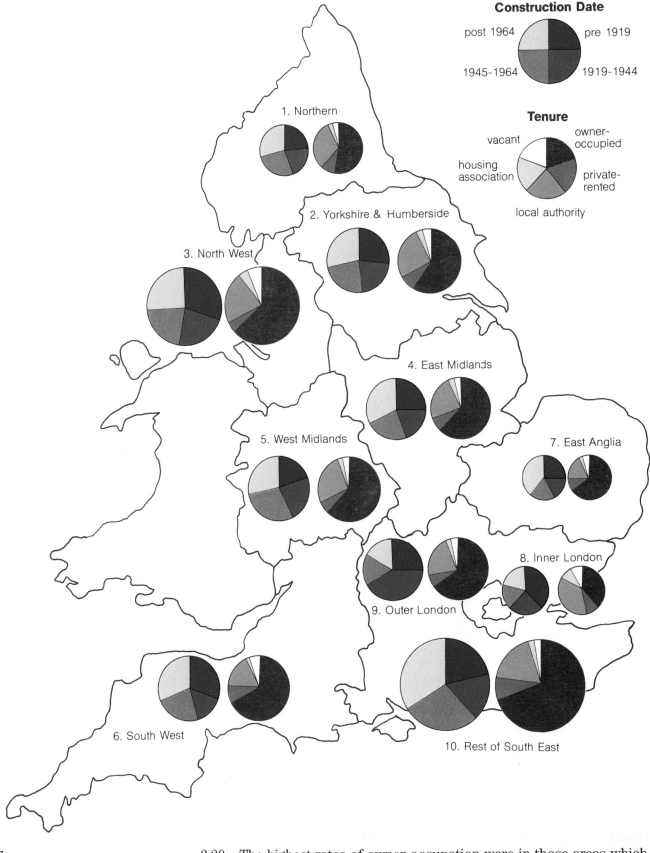

Construction Date

post 1964   pre 1919

1945-1964   1919-1944

Tenure

vacant   owner-occupied

housing association   private-rented

local authority

1. Northern

2. Yorkshire & Humberside

3. North West

4. East Midlands

5. West Midlands

6. South West

7. East Anglia

8. Inner London

9. Outer London

10. Rest of South East

Tenure

3.20   The highest rates of owner occupation were in those areas which had seen the most recent growth in housing: the South East, South West and East Anglia (Figure 3.6). Here owner occupation represented 70%, 68% and 66% of the stock respectively. Private renting was most common in Inner London, East Anglia and the South West, with these two largely rural regions having 8% and 9% of their stock in this tenure. Local

16

authority housing was most common in the Northern region and Inner London, where it accounted for one-third of all housing. The highest proportions of Housing Association properties were found in Inner London and the North West.

Market values

3.21   Market values varied substantially between regions. Average values ranged from £22,500 in the North to £72,000 in Inner London (Figure 3.7). More substantial variations were found within particular tenures. The value of private-rented accommodation in Inner London was over five times that of private-rented accommodation in the North West whereas the differential in the public-rented sector was much less, with Inner London values only three times those of Northern regions. Vacant dwellings had the highest regional differential, values in Inner London being nearly five-and-a-half times higher than those in the North West (Table A3.16).

Fig 3.7   Mean market value by region

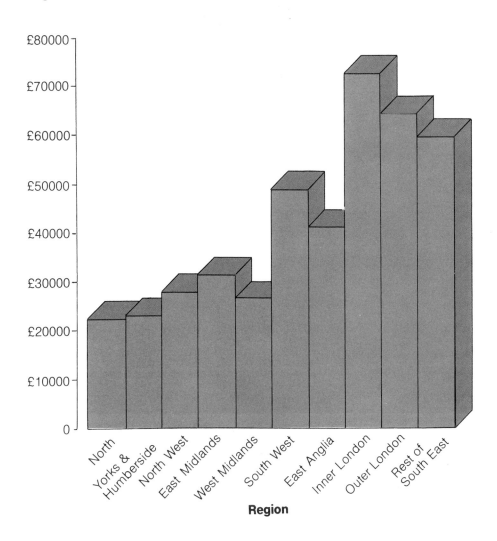

Houses in multiple occupation and vacant dwellings

3.22   Regional variation was apparent in the proportion of houses in multiple occupation (HMOs) and vacant dwellings. Inner London had the highest concentration of HMOs which made up 2.2% of its dwelling stock, although the largest number of HMOs were in the South East (Table A3.18). The highest proportion of vacant dwellings was found in Inner London, where 7.6% of the stock was vacant. The North West had the second highest vacancy rate at 5.2% (Table A3.19).

4 The condition of the housing stock in 1986

4.1   Previous house condition surveys have described the condition of the stock in terms of three basic measures: the presence of basic amenities, disrepair and fitness for human habitation as defined in section 604 of the Housing Act 1985. These are maintained but extended in this survey to provide further information on fittings and equipment, extended measures of disrepair and the matters which determine fitness.

Provision of amenities and services

Availability of basic amenities

4.2   The survey recorded the provision of basic amenities[1] and information on heating and hot water systems, insulation, space standards in kitchens and bathrooms, drainage and electrical systems.

4.3   The vast majority of dwellings had all five basic amenities; 2.5% did not (Figure 4.1). Of the 463,000 dwellings which lacked one or more of

Fig 4.1   Dwellings lacking basic amenities

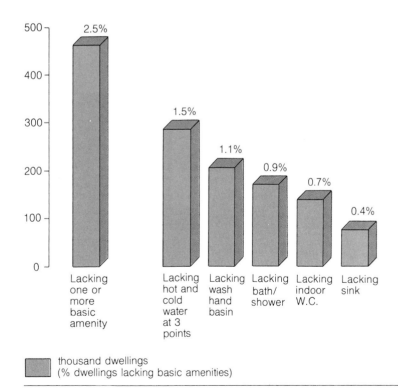

thousand dwellings
(% dwellings lacking basic amenities)

---

[1] Basic amenities are those which qualify for a mandatory grant under the present Home Improvement Grant system. They are a kitchen sink, a bath or shower in a bathroom, a wash hand basin, hot and cold water provided to each of these and an indoor WC.

the basic amenities 286,000 dwellings did not have hot and cold water at three points. This was associated with the absence of a bath or shower in 170,000 dwellings and a wash hand basin in 206,000 cases; 139,000 homes had no indoor WC. A small proportion (16%) of dwellings lacking amenities did so because they were in the process of modernisation. If these are excluded from the count of dwellings lacking amenities the proportion falls to 2.1% (396,000 dwellings).

Variations with tenure

4.4   Almost one-third of dwellings lacking amenities were vacant but 39% of these were in the course of renovation (Table 4.1). A further third of dwellings lacking amenities were owner occupied but the highest concentration in occupied dwellings was found in the private-rented sector where 8% of the stock lacked at least one basic amenity.

Table 4.1   Dwellings lacking basic amenities by tenure

thousands/% dwellings

	Owner Occupied	Private Rented	Local Authority /New Town	Housing Association	Vacant	All Dwellings
Dwellings Lacking 1 or More Amenity	144 (31.1) (1.2)	102 (22.0) (8.2)	72 (15.5) (1.6)	5 (1.1) (1.1)	140 (30.3) (17.2)	463 (100) (2.5)

(see Table A4.1)

Variations with dwelling age

4.5   The older stock included the highest proportion of dwellings lacking basic amenities (Table 4.2). Most of the post-war dwellings lacking amenities were purpose-built flats which provided shared accommodation, particularly for the elderly.

Table 4.2   Dwellings lacking basic amenities by construction date

thousands/% dwellings

	Pre- 1900	1900- 1918	1919- 1944	1945- 1964	Post- 1964	All Dwellings
Dwellings Lacking 1 or More Amenity	234 (50.5) (6.3)	69 (14.9) (5.3)	94 (20.3) (2.4)	22 (4.8) (0.5)	44 (9.5) (0.8)	463 (100) (2.5)

Hot water systems

4.6   There were only 151,000 dwellings with no hot water, representing less than 1% of the stock (Table A4.2), and a further 135,000 dwellings where the hot water did not serve three points. Almost all dwellings where hot water was provided were served from a central system[2], only 1.3% of dwellings having individual hot water heaters. Nearly all hot water systems were in good order with only 1% requiring repair or replacement.

---

2. Central systems are those which have a hot water cylinder or a central multi-point water heater serving one or more points.

Space standards in bathrooms and kitchens[3]

4.7 Even though dwellings were provided with bathroom and kitchen amenities the rooms in which they were located were, in some cases, so small that their effective use was inhibited. Lack of space in kitchens and bathrooms was a problem, in each case, for only 2% of dwellings (Table A4.3). Lack of space in the kitchen was associated with the private-rented sector where 6% of dwellings were affected.

Drainage

4.8 Most dwellings were served by mains drainage. Overall only 3.4% of properties had some other provision. In rural areas almost one-quarter had no mains drainage with the highest proportion being in the private-rented sector (Table A4.4).

Heating

Provision

4.9 Almost three-quarters of all dwellings had central heating[4], and in four out of five cases the system extended to more than 60% of the dwelling (Table A4.5). The most common form of central heating was the independent gas-fired boiler feeding a water-borne distribution system (Table A4.6). This was installed in 50% of centrally heated dwellings. A further 18% of such dwellings had a water-borne system fed by a back boiler, associated with a gas fire or convector heater. Properties without the benefit of central heating relied primarily on open gas fires or gas convector heaters (64%) or solid fuel fires or stoves (21%). 5% of dwellings with no central heating had no fixed heating appliance (Table A4.7).

Adequacy

4.10 During the survey a judgement was made on whether the heating system was adequate to maintain a comfortable temperature throughout the dwelling[5]. Approximately 1.7 million dwellings (9%) were considered inadequate in this respect. Nearly nine out of ten of these had no fixed central heating (Table A4.5). Post-1964 properties had the most effective provision for heating and pre-1900 dwellings the least effective, with respectively 4% and 13% judged inadequate. Adequacy of heating also varied with tenure. Only 5% of owner-occupied dwellings were considered inadequate compared with 17% of the local authority stock and 24% of privately rented dwellings (Table A4.8).

Insulation

4.11 Only 11% of all dwellings were without loft insulation and these were mainly built before 1919 (Table A4.9). Wall insulation was less common, with only 14% of dwellings insulated in this way. Full double glazing had been installed in 14% of dwellings. Full double glazing was present in 14% of dwellings.

---

[3] Kitchens with inadequate space are defined as those which are less than 1.6m wide. A bathroom has inadequate space if it is too small or the wrong shape to accommodate and use comfortably a fixed bath, wash hand basin and WC, or a bath and wash hand basin only where the WC is nearby.

[4] Central heating is defined as heating provided from a central system where the heat is provided through radiators or ducted air vents. Also included is underfloor or ceiling heating and individual off-peak storage heaters where they are the main or only form of heating.

[5] Heating was judged inadequate if fixed heating appliances did not appear to be able to maintain a temperature of 18°c in the main living rooms and 13°c elsewhere when outside temperatures are −1°c.

| **Electrical systems** | 4.12 An estimated 2.15 million dwellings (11.4% of the stock) had electrical systems which were defective or inadequate. Almost half of these dwellings required complete rewiring. The condition of electrical systems was related to the age of the property, with 9% of pre-1919 dwellings needing rewiring, and to tenure with 16% of privately rented dwellings needing rewiring compared with 5% or less in other tenures (Table A4.8). |

Amenities and services — a summary

4.13 Lack of basic amenities is now a relatively minor problem for the housing stock with less than 400,000 dwellings without provision, if dwellings undergoing modernisation are excluded from the analysis. Many dwellings without amenities may be considered to be marginal to the stock as they have been vacant for some time. Lack of adequate heating and inadequate or defective electrical systems affect many more dwellings, the greatest problems being found in private-rented housing. But the problem of inadequate heating is not insubstantial in the public sector.

State of repair

4.14 A convenient way of representing the scale of disrepair in a dwelling is in terms of the cost of carrying out the required repair based on standard rates[6] for labour and materials. In practice the price paid for building work will vary substantially from any standard rate depending on the scale of the job and the way it is commissioned and financed. Therefore the repair costs generated by the application of standard rates in this survey are used to provide an index of the repair work required but not necessarily the sum of money which would need to be spent to carry out the work.

Definition of repair

4.15 An assessment of repair required to any dwelling can vary considerably depending on the objectives to be achieved. This survey provides three measures:

> *urgent repair* is that which needs to be done to prevent immediate rapid deterioration in other parts of the building, or to remove a threat to the health, safety, security or comfort of the occupant.

> *repair* includes the above and all other repairs which are economically effective, in that, if they were postponed the cost of the works would be disproportionately increased.[7]

> *comprehensive repair* includes all the above, plus work necessary to secure the property in the medium term, likely to be required as a condition of mortgage lending or Home Improvement Grant.

Need for repair

4.16 The state of repair of the stock, expressed in terms of the estimated cost of urgent repair, repair and comprehensive repair, is described in Table 4.3. This shows that for the majority of the stock the estimated cost of repair was modest. For example, for half the stock, the cost of urgent repair was no more than £170 per dwelling. But a small proportion of the stock required more substantial work with 5% requiring £2,900 or more to be spent on urgent repairs. The greater the extent of disrepair in a dwelling, the higher was the proportion of urgent repairs.

---

6. The standard rates used in this survey are based on the PSA schedule of rates (1986). The costs are generated through the application of a cost model which is described in Appendix F. The costs include those for all repairs/replacements which the surveyor identified. They do not include VAT.

7. In practice surveyors classified work to a dwelling in this category if, by postponing the work for five years, one-third more work would be required.

In the 5% of the stock which required most repair that which was urgent represented at least three-quarters of the cost of these repairs and one-half of the cost of comprehensive repair.

Table 4.3   Distribution of estimated cost of repairs

£

% Dwellings	Urgent Repair	Repair	Comprehensive Repair
2	4,750	5,900	8,800
5	2,900	3,900	6,100
10	1,750	2,600	4,400
25	730	1,200	2,200
50	170	350	660
75	0	10	30

Variation with age and tenure

4.17   The estimated cost of repair varied with the age and tenure of the property. The variation with age was substantial, with the mean estimated cost of repair for dwellings built before 1919 approximately ten times that for dwellings built after 1964 (Table 4.4); 10% of dwellings built before 1900 had estimated costs of repair of £5,400 or more (Table A4.10).

Table 4.4   Estimated cost of repair by construction date and tenure

mean cost £

	Pre-1919	1919-1944	1945-1964	Post-1964	All Ages
Owner Occupied	1,920	940	480	170	900
Private Rented	2,570	1,720	880	300	2,030
Local Authority/New Town	1,600	970	730	300	670
Housing Association	940	830	780	110	480
Vacant	2,970	1,550	770	410	1,980
All Dwellings	2,090	1,010	600	210	950

4.18   There were very large differences between tenures in terms of the estimated mean cost of repair. The mean cost for private-rented dwellings was twice that for the owner-occupied stock and about the same as that for vacant properties (Table 4.4). A small proportion of private sector dwellings (5%) had estimated costs of repair of at least £6,800 showing that in this sector there were some dwellings requiring extensive repairs. Of vacant dwellings 2% had estimated costs of repair of £12,500 or more (Table A4.11).

4.19   The estimated mean cost of repair of dwellings of different ages varied with tenure. The mean cost of older property (pre-1944) was substantially higher in the private-rented sector than in other tenures. The mean cost of repair of the inter-war local authority stock was similar to that of the owner-occupied stock of the same period, but for the post-war stock it was almost twice that of the owner-occupied stock.

Building elements

Extent of disrepair

4.20   The need for repair varied between different elements of the building as illustrated in Table A4.12. Thirty per cent of dwellings required repairs to windows or the pointing or rendering of walls. One-quarter of all roofs required some repair. The elements requiring work varied with the age of dwellings. Almost half of all dwellings built before 1919 required repair and pointing or rendering of chimneys and walls. External joinery had deteriorated relatively rapidly in dwellings of more recent construction and 14% of dwellings built since 1964 required repairs to windows.

4.21 Dwellings of non-traditional construction showed particular defects. Spalling of concrete frames which required urgent attention affected 45,000 dwellings and spalling of concrete panels affected 33,000 dwellings. Defective fixings of panels were found in approximately 15,000 dwellings. Private balconies in dwellings of non-traditional construction required urgent repairs in about 30,000 cases (Table A4.13).

Repair cost by element

4.22 The total estimated repair cost can be apportioned to different elements of the buildings. Roofs (18%), walls (18%) and windows and doors (16%) accounted for the highest proportion of costs (Figure 4.2).

Fig 4.2 Repair costs by construction date and building elements

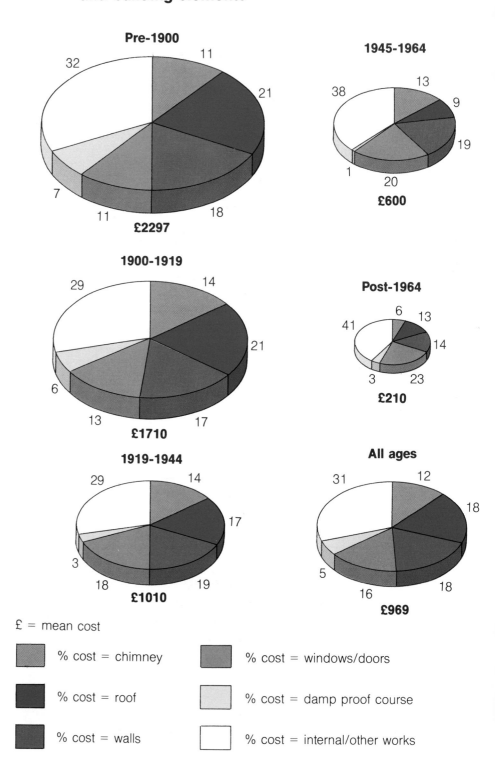

£ = mean cost

- % cost = chimney
- % cost = roof
- % cost = walls
- % cost = windows/doors
- % cost = damp proof course
- % cost = internal/other works

Overall, 71% of the average estimated repair cost was attributable to the external fabric of the building, 23% to the internal fabric and 6% to the amenities and services. These proportions were surprisingly constant for dwellings of different ages (Table A4.14).

Houses and flats compared

4.23 The balance in estimated repair costs between the interior and exterior of the dwellings was different for houses compared with flats. Estimated external repair costs represented over 70% of the total costs in the former but were less than 50% in the latter when the costs of work to the exterior were shared between flats (Table A4.15). There was an additional cost to individual flats for repairs to communal areas and accessways within the building but this amounted, on average, to no more than 8% of total costs.

4.24 The average estimated repair cost varied with the type of construction. For houses built between 1945 and 1964 the average repair cost was almost twice as high for houses of non-traditional construction than for those of traditional construction. For flats of the same period the average repair cost for those of non-traditional construction was only 20% higher than those of traditional construction (Table A4.15). The average estimated repair cost of both non-traditional flats and houses built since 1964 was more than twice that of flats and houses of traditional construction of the same period.

Unfit dwellings
Definition

4.25 An unfit dwelling is one which is unsuitable for human habitation as defined in section 604 of the Housing Act 1985. To be classed as unfit a dwelling has to be so far defective in one or more of nine specified matters[8] as to be unsuitable for occupation. One-quarter of the stock (4.7 million dwellings) was defective in some respect but only 4.8% (0.9 million dwellings) were reported to be unfit.

Distribution of defects

Defects by age

4.26 The 'matters' most frequently reported defective were repair, the provision of facilities for the preparation and cooking of food and disposal of waste water, freedom from damp and internal arrangement (Figure 4.3). Some of these problems such as internal arrangement, natural lighting and freedom from damp resulted from design faults in the original building. Properties built before 1919 were at least three times more likely to be defective in these matters than properties built after this date (Table A4.16).

Defects by tenure

4.27 Defective matters were not equally distributed between tenures (Table A4.17). Dwellings which were defective in natural lighting, internal arrangement and ventilation were primarily found in the private-rented sector. This may be partly a result of the conversion of dwellings into flats where inappropriate building works have impaired ventilation, blocked natural light or resulted in bad arrangement of rooms.

---

8. The nine matters on which unfitness is determined are: repair; stability; freedom from damp; internal arrangement; natural lighting; ventilation; water supply; drainage and sanitary conveniences; facilities for the preparation and cooking of food and for the disposal of waste water.

Fig 4.3 Dwellings with defective items

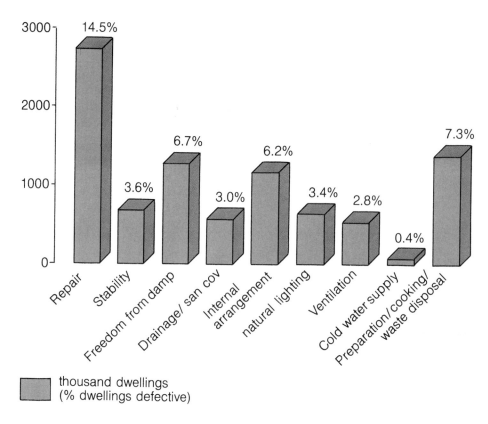

thousand dwellings
(% dwellings defective)

The relationship between defects and fitness

4.28 Dwellings reported unfit were generally defective on more than one of the nine specified matters; 90% were defective on at least two matters and 10% on at least six matters (Figure 4.4).

Fig 4.4 Unfit dwellings: number and proportion of items defective

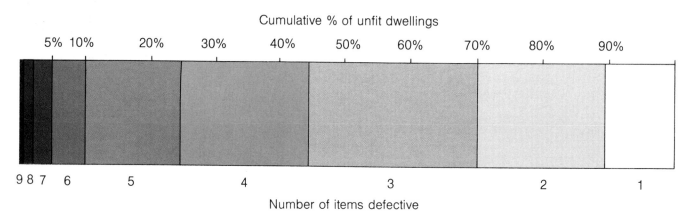

4.29 Unfit dwellings were associated with particular defects (Table 4.5). An unfit dwelling was more likely to be defective in repair than to suffer any of the other defects. Certain defects were particularly associated with unfitness. Dwellings with a defective cold water supply or defective drainage and sanitary conveniences had a more than even chance of being classed as unfit.

4.30 Some defects were considered not to be remediable since the cost was prohibitive or an effective solution could not be found. Defects in natural lighting and internal arrangement were the most difficult to remedy (Table 4.5). However, if a dwelling were classed as unfit because of a combination of defects, some of which could be remedied, then the treatment of just these might be sufficient to make the dwelling fit.

Table 4.5 Relationships between defects in a dwelling and the assessment of fitness

	% Unfit Dwellings With Given Defect	% Defective Which Were Unfit	% Unfit Which Were Remediable
Repair	78	26	98
Stability	29	38	91
Freedom from Damp	52	37	97
Drainage/Sanitary Convenience	35	56	98
Internal Arrangement	40	31	73
Natural Lighting	24	34	68
Ventilation	19	31	93
Cold Water Supply	7	74	92
Cooking & Waste Disposal	47	31	95

Condition of the environment
Definition

4.31   In addition to assessing the condition of the dwellings, surveyors were asked to record their impressions of the environment in which the dwelling was located. They were asked to judge whether action was needed to repair roads or pavements; to repair fences, gardens and common areas around dwellings; to improve lighting, tree planting or landscaping; to clear or improve vacant or derelict sites; to provide public green space; to provide private gardens; to tackle intrusive industry or traffic. A dwelling was considered to be located in a poor environment if action was required on four or more of these items.

Distribution of poor environments

4.32   Some 2 million dwellings (10.6%) were considered to be located in poor environments but they were not evenly distributed throughout the country. Inner London was judged to contain the highest proportion of dwellings in poor environments with one-quarter of its dwellings located in such areas. The North West, Outer London and Yorkshire and Humberside had higher than average proportions (respectively 15%, 13% and 13%) of their dwellings in poor environments (Table A4.18).

5 Dwellings in poor condition

Definition of poor condition

5.1   The indicators of poor condition which have provided the focus for earlier surveys are 'unfitness', 'the lack of basic amenities' and 'serious' disrepair. The first two of these relate to the statutory measures which have been defined in paragraphs 4.2 and 4.25. 'Disrepair' has no such statutory basis. It is a measure of the condition of the fabric of a dwelling with some threshold set to designate those deemed to be in the worst state of repair. In this report, dwellings in a poor state of repair are taken to be those where urgent repairs to the external fabric of the property are estimated to cost more than £1,000. These are referred to as dwellings in poor repair.

Fig 5.1   Dwellings in poor condition

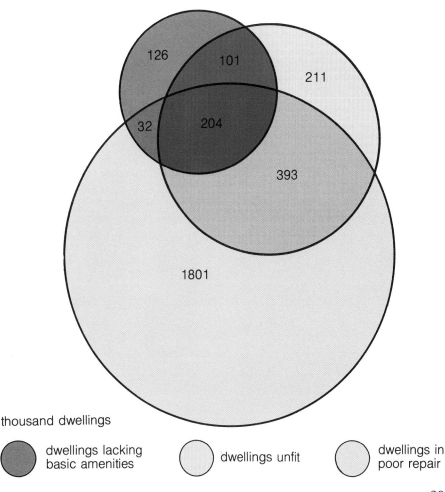

thousand dwellings

⬤ dwellings lacking basic amenities   ◯ dwellings unfit   ◯ dwellings in poor repair

The incidence of poor condition

5.2 It is estimated that 909,000 dwellings were unfit in 1986 (4.8% of the total stock), 463,000 lacked one or more of the basic amenities (2.5%) and 2.4 million were in poor repair (12.9%). Just over 200,000 (1.1%) failed on all three criteria and 730,000 (3.9%) failed on two or more (Figure 5.1). In total nearly 2.9 million dwellings (15% of the stock) failed on one or more criteria.

5.3 Dwellings which lacked basic amenities were also likely to be unfit and/or be in poor repair. Only just over one-quarter of dwellings which lacked basic amenities were neither unfit nor in poor repair. Most unfit dwellings (66%) were also in poor repair.

Variation with construction date

5.4 The oldest stock was in the worst condition. Over 40% of the dwellings built before 1870 were in poor condition compared with only 2.6% of the most recently built stock (Figure 5.2). Any dwelling built before 1919 was at least three times more likely than any other dwelling to be unfit and at least twice as likely to lack amenities or to be in poor repair (Table A5.1).

Fig 5.2   Construction date by condition

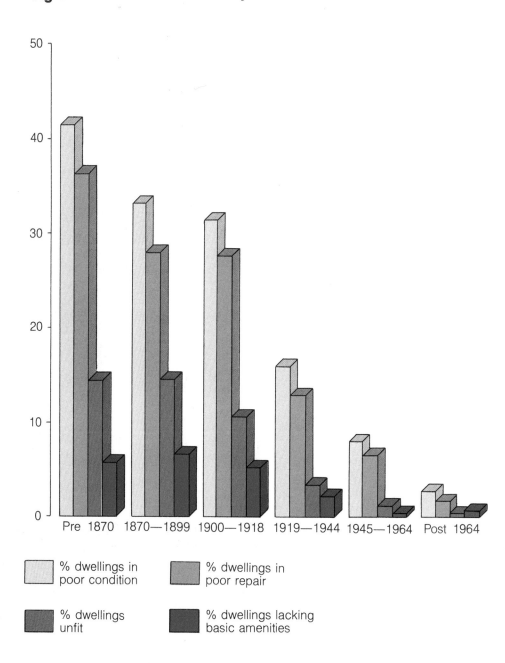

□ % dwellings in poor condition

▨ % dwellings in poor repair

▩ % dwellings unfit

■ % dwellings lacking basic amenities

5.5 Over 80% of the older stock had undergone improvement, at some time, but this had had a variable affect on the overall condition of these dwellings (Table A5.2). Improvement clearly reduced the number of older dwellings which lacked amenities and far fewer of the "improved" dwellings were unfit compared with those which had not been improved. But improvement had less effect on the present state of repair. For example, 54% of the pre-1870 dwellings which had not been improved were in poor repair, compared with 43% of improved dwellings in the same age group (Table A5.3).

Variation with tenure

5.6 The relationship between condition and tenure can be described in terms of the proportion of dwellings within any particular tenure which fails on one or more of the three condition criteria. On this basis 42% of dwellings in the private-rented sector, 13% of owner-occupied dwellings, 11% of those owned by local authorities and only 7% of dwellings owned by Housing Associations were in poor condition (Figure 5.3).

Fig 5.3 Tenure by condition

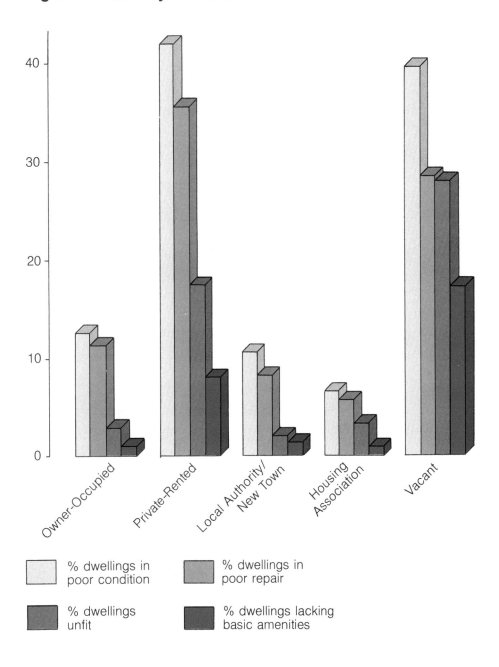

5.7   This simple relationship between condition and tenure changes if dwellings of different ages are considered (Table 5.1). For all tenures, the strong relationship between age and condition was maintained. Regardless of age, the private-rented sector was proportionately in the poorest condition compared with other tenures. But local authorities owned over half the dwellings in poor condition built after 1944.

Table 5.1   Dwellings in poor condition by tenure and construction date

thousands/% dwellings in poor condition

	Owner Occupied	Private Rented	Local Authority/ New Town	Housing Association	Vacant	All Dwellings
Pre-1900	773 (31.3)	313 (48.3)	38 (32.4)	16 (10.1)	198 (57.5)	1,338 (36.2)
1901–1918	237 (26.4)	114 (43.6)	10 (19.9)	1 (12.1)	45 (53.2)	407 (31.3)
1919–1944	344 (12.9)	60 (32.3)	169 (17.6)	8 (16.6)	45 (35.2)	626 (15.8)
Post-1964	162 (2.8)	36 (18.3)	258 (7.7)	6 (2.3)	35 (13.7)	497 (5.0)
All Dwellings	1,516 (12.8)	523 (42.0)	475 (10.6)	31 (6.6)	323 (39.8)	2,868 (15.2)

Vacant dwellings

5.8   Over one-third of all vacant dwellings were in poor condition and 90% of these were in private ownership. Dwellings which had been empty for a long period, including those undergoing modernisation and those about to be demolished, were in particularly poor condition. Almost one-third of these were without amenities and nearly one-half were unfit. However, nearly one-half of these poor condition long term vacants were being improved (Table 5.2).

Table 5.2   Condition of vacant dwellings

th   ᴺnds/% dwellings affected

	Long Term Vacant	Short Term Vacant	All Vacant Dwellings	All Occupied Dwellings
⌐ ᴺking Amenities	122 (36.5)	27 (5.6)	140 (17.2)	323 (1.8)
Unfit	167 (50.0)	61 (12.8)	228 (28.1)	680 (3.7)
In Poor Repair	138 (41.3)	94 (19.7)	232 (28.6)	2,198 (12.2)
Failing One or More of the Above Criteria	211 (63.2)	113 (23.6)	323 (39.8)	2,544 (14.1)
All Dwellings	334	478	812	18,027

(See Also Table A5.3)

The impact of condition on market values

5.9   The values of properties in poor condition were, predictably, lower than those of other dwellings. The value of unfit dwellings was, on average, 37% lower than that of fit dwellings and the value of those lacking amenities 30% lower than those which had all amenities (Table 5.3). The difference for dwellings in poor repair was much less at 5%.

Table 5.3 Average market value of dwellings by condition

	Average Market Value
All Dwellings	£42,200
Fit Dwellings	£43,000
Unfit Dwellings	£27,200
Dwellings with All Amenities	£42,600
Dwellings Lacking Amenities	£29,700
In Good Repair	£42,500
In Poor Repair	£40,200
Fit, Private, Pre-1919 Terrace	£36,500
Unfit, Private, Pre-1919 Terrace	£22,000

5.10 Such differences were unlikely to be solely attributable to condition, as dwellings in poor condition were of a type which would command relatively low market values or were in areas where values were depressed. But when values for a common type of dwelling, for example pre-1919 terraced houses, were compared unfit dwellings were even lower in value (40%) than fit dwellings in the same group.

The distribution of dwellings in poor condition

5.11 The majority of the stock (16.3m dwellings) was in urban areas[1]. However, the proportion of dwellings in poor condition was higher in rural areas with 22% of rural housing in this category compared with 14% of housing in urban areas (Figure 5.4).

Fig 5.4 Dwellings in urban and rural areas by condition

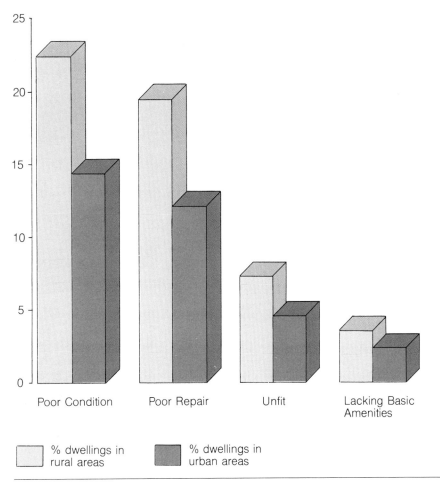

[1]. Urban areas include inner cities, suburbs and small towns. Rural areas include isolated dwellings and those in villages of up to 1,000 dwellings.

33

Differences in condition between urban and rural areas

5.12   The greater concentration of poor condition dwellings in rural areas can in part be explained by the higher proportion of older houses in these areas. Almost 40% of dwellings in rural areas in were built before 1919 compared with only one-quarter of the urban stock. However this does not account for the whole difference. The older rural stock itself was in worse condition than the older urban stock with 41% of pre-1919 rural dwellings being in poor condition compared with 33% of urban dwellings (Table A5.4).

5.13   Owner occupiers in rural areas were one-and-a-half times more likely than their urban counterparts to live in dwellings in poor condition (Table A5.5). There was less difference between urban and rural areas for households in the private-rented and local authority sectors.

Regional differences in condition

5.14   There were differences between the numbers of dwellings in poor condition in different regions (Figure 5.5). Overall, the North West had the highest proportion of dwellings in poor condition. Yorkshire and Humberside, the West Midlands and the South West also had significantly higher than average proportions of such dwellings. Within this overall picture different problems were apparent in different regions (Figure 5.6). The West Midlands had the highest proportion of unfit dwellings, Inner London the highest proportion lacking amenities and the North West the highest proportion of dwellings in poor repair.

Fig 5.5 The distribution of dwellings in poor condition between regions

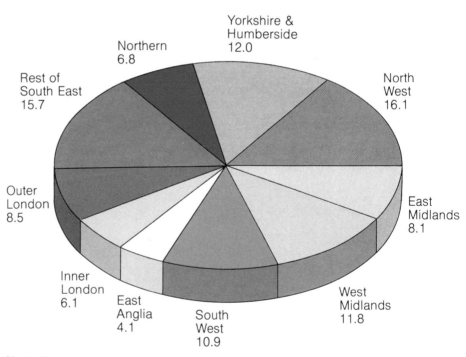

% dwellings

34

Fig 5.6 Dwelling condition in each region

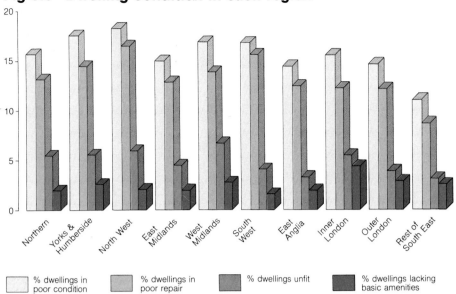

% dwellings in poor condition | % dwellings in poor repair | % dwellings unfit | % dwellings lacking basic amenities

5.15   These differences between regions were in part a reflection of differences in the age and tenure of the stock. The areas which had the highest proportions of poor condition housing were generally those with the highest proportions of older dwellings (Chapter 3, Figure 3.5). But within particular age and tenure groups the proportion of dwellings in poor condition varied between regions. On this basis, the highest proportion of older private sector dwellings in poor condition was found in the West Midlands (Figure 5.7).

Fig 5.7   Condition of pre-1919 private sector dwellings in each region

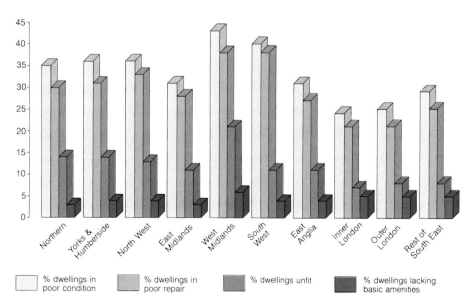

% dwellings in poor condition | % dwellings in poor repair | % dwellings unfit | % dwellings lacking basic amenities

5.16 The condition of the local authority stock followed a similar pattern to the older private sector stock. The West Midlands again had the highest proportion of its public sector housing in poor condition (15%) while the lowest figures were in Inner London, East Anglia and the Rest of the South East (Figure 5.8).

Fig 5.8 Condition of local authority dwellings in each region

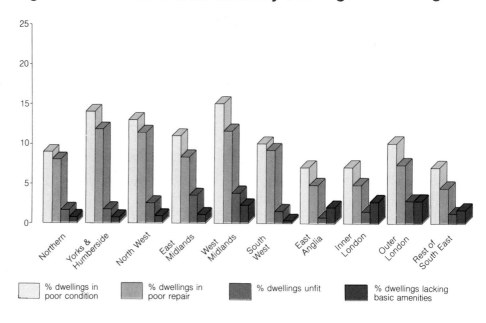

Regional variations in market value

5.17 Differences between the market values of dwellings in poor condition and the rest of the stock varied between regions. The most marked differences were between property in good condition and that which was unfit. Differences were lowest in the North and Yorkshire and Humberside and highest in the Rest of South East (Figure 5.9)[2]. This in part reflected the different stock in different regions, but if values are compared for only pre-1919 owner-occupied terraced houses there was still a greater difference between the value of unfit properties and those in good condition in the 'Southern' regions compared with the regions of the 'North' and 'Midlands'.

[2.] The small difference in Inner London is probably explained by the type of dwellings which were likely to be unfit; these were large older houses which, because of the housing demand in London, commanded high prices.

Fig 5.9   Regional variations in market value by fitness

(a) All dwellings

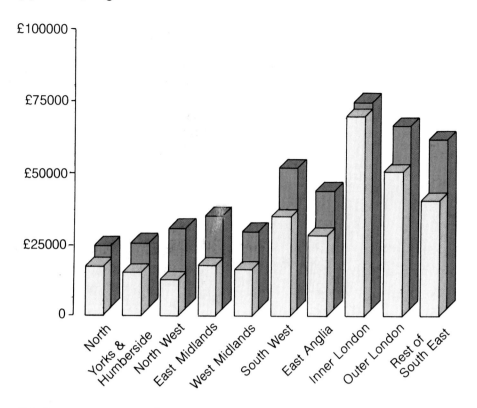

(b) Pre-1919 owner-occupied terraced houses

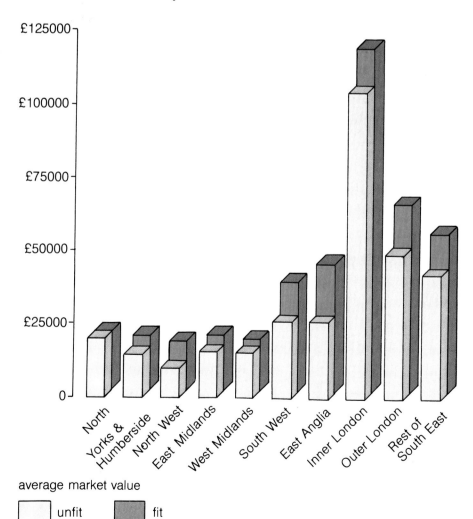

average market value

☐ unfit   ▨ fit

Distribution of dwellings in poor condition at the local level

The condition of blocks of property in which dwellings in poor condition were found

5.18   The likely future of dwellings in poor condition will be influenced by, among other factors, the condition of dwellings in the same block, the condition of other dwellings in the surrounding area and by the nature of the local environment.

5.19   Almost 60% of the dwellings in poor condition (excluding detached houses) had immediate neighbours which were in similar or worse condition (Figure 5.10). This grouping together of dwellings in poor condition was more prevalent in local authority housing than in other tenures (Figure 5.10). Almost three-quarters of the poor condition local authority stock was in blocks of property in similar condition compared with 60% of owner-occupied housing.

Fig 5.10 Dwellings in poor condition – whether they are found in blocks of similar dwellings – by tenure

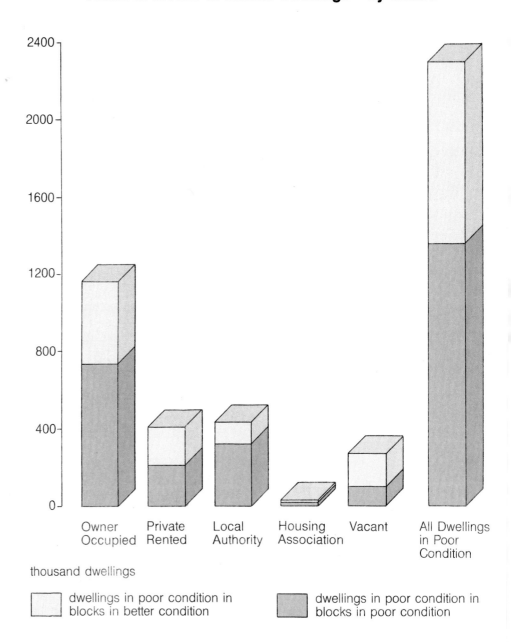

thousand dwellings

dwellings in poor condition in blocks in better condition

dwellings in poor condition in blocks in poor condition

5.20 As well as conventional measures of condition, the incidence of vandalism, graffiti, litter and the dumping of rubbish in the common areas of blocks of flats was recorded. Some 6% of flats generally were affected, but half of all local authority flats were affected and in 10% of the latter vandalism, graffiti, litter and dumped rubbish was extensive (Figure 5.11).

Fig 5.11 Misuse of common areas in blocks of flats

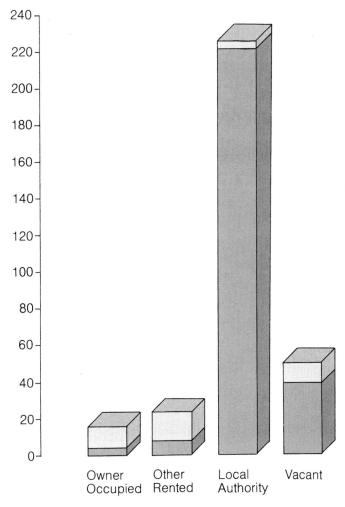

Number of flats in blocks which suffer from extensive vandalism, graffiti, litter and dumped rubbish common areas: thousand dwellings

Dwellings in poor condition — types of areas in which they are found

5.21 The majority of dwellings in poor condition were found in areas where the rest of the housing was in generally good condition. Only 11% of the stock in poor condition fell in areas where the majority of the housing was run down[3]. Poor condition dwellings were more likely to be in association with other dwellings in poor condition in areas of older property, in areas of flats rather than houses and in areas where the majority of the property was owned by the local authority. The association between individual dwellings in poor condition and areas of run down housing also varied between regions (Figure 5.12).

[3.] An area of run down housing is one which required comprehensive repair/improvement or clearance, or selective repair/improvements and clearance.

Fig 5.12 The likelihood of dwellings in poor condition being located in run down areas

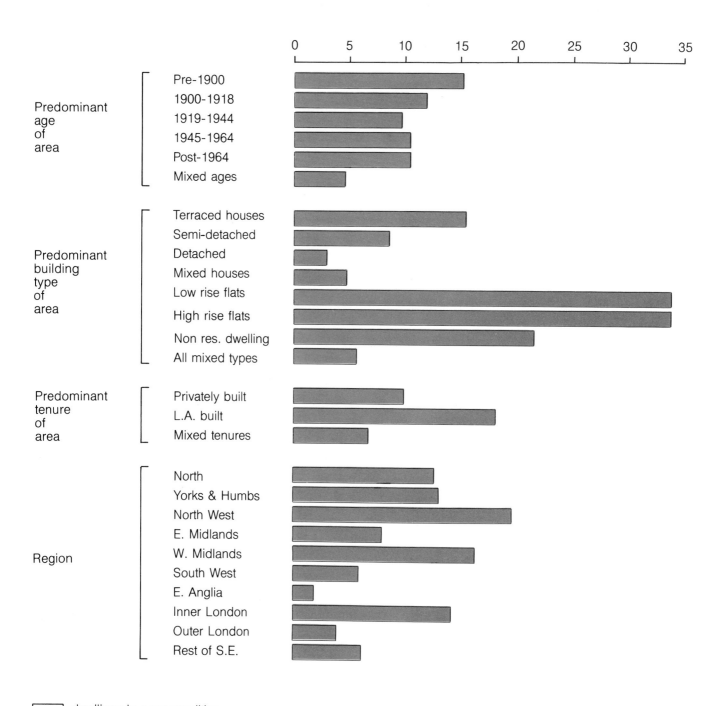

dwellings in poor condition:
% in run down areas

Poor condition dwellings and poor environments[4]

5.22 Not surprisingly there was some association between dwellings in poor condition and poor environments. Almost one-third of unfit dwellings, over one-quarter lacking amenities and one-fifth of dwellings in poor repair were in poor environments. Nevertheless, the majority of dwellings in poor condition were not found in poor environments (Table A5.6).

---

4. Poor environments are defined in Chapter 4, para 4.31.

6 People who live in housing in poor condition

Housing conditions and household groups

6.1   Housing in poor condition is not uniformly distributed throughout the population but is associated with a variety of social, demographic and economic factors. In broad terms, the elderly, single people, those on low incomes and tenants of private landlords were the worst housed.

Age of head of household
Variation by construction date

6.2   For convenience, households were divided into three roughly equal groups based on the age of the head of household: 17–39, 40–59 and 60 and over. This latter group was further divided between those aged 60–74 and those aged 75 and over. These groups were not evenly distributed throughout the dwelling stock (Table A6.1). The youngest group was concentrated in the oldest and most recent housing. Households of middle age were proportionately the largest group in inter-war housing, with households aged between 60–74 heavily concentrated in the early post-war stock. Those aged 75 and over were evenly distributed in housing of all ages. As well as the movement of households over the years this pattern reflects the choice of tenure.

Variation by tenure

6.3   Middle-aged households were most likely to own their homes, with three-quarters of them in this position (Table A6.2). Younger households were also predominantly owner occupiers (64%), even though they made up the largest single class in the private-rented sector. Half of all elderly households rented their accommodation. In particular, almost two-thirds of those aged 75 and over were tenants with 50% of these renting from the local authority.

6.4   Households aged 75 and over were more likely than other groups to have homes which were unfit or lacked amenities. Although they made up only 10% of all households they occupied almost one-third of dwellings lacking amenities and 16% of unfit dwellings. Otherwise the condition of dwellings varied very little between households of different ages (Figure 6.1. Table A6.3).

Household type

6.5   Elderly persons living alone were more likely to occupy housing in poor condition than elderly couples or similarly aged people in larger households. Nineteen per cent of single pensioners had houses which were in poor condition compared with 14% of pensioner households of more than one person (Table A6.4). The worst housed, however, were single people below retirement age, 23% of whom lived in dwellings which were in poor condition. This was associated with a high proportion of this group living in private-rented accommodation.

Fig 6.1 Age of head of household by provision of basic amenities, fitness and repair

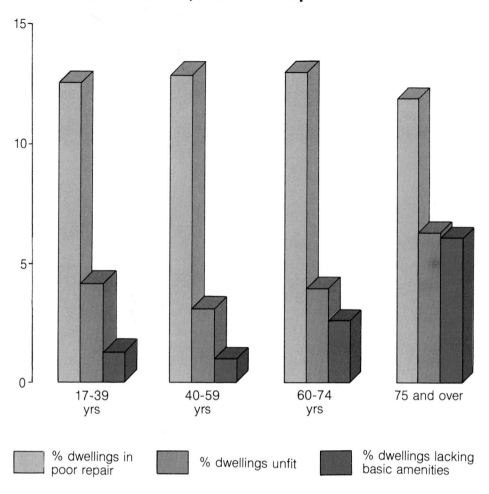

% dwellings in poor repair

% dwellings unfit

% dwellings lacking basic amenities

Length of residence

6.6   One-fifth of all households had lived in their homes for more than twenty years. One-quarter of these long-term residents lived in poor housing compared with 15% of the population as a whole (Figure 6.2). The majority of long-term residents were elderly (Table A6.5) and within this group they occupied a disproportionately large share of housing which lacked basic amenities, was unfit, or was in poor repair (Table 6.1).

Table 6.1   Long-term residents in housing in poor condition by age of head of household

% households in each age group in dwellings in poor condition

	Lacking Basic Amenities	Unfit	In Poor Repair	All Households Resident 20 Years and Over
Aged 17–39	2.5	2.0	1.3	0.7
Aged 40–59	12.9	18.5	24.8	27.2
Aged 60–74	38.4	41.4	46.9	52.6
Aged 75 and Over	46.2	38.1	27.0	19.5
All Households Resident 20 Years and Over	100	100	100	100

Fig 6.2 Length of residence by proportion of households in dwellings in poor condition

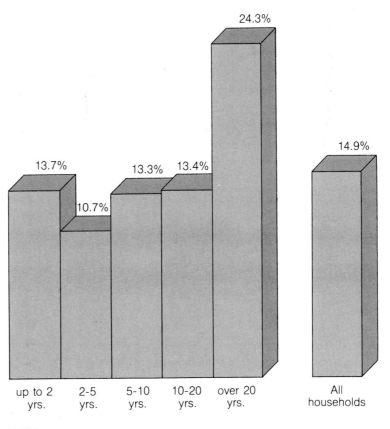

% households

Economic circumstances

6.7 Poor housing was also associated with unemployment. Where the head of household was unemployed 22% of these households lived in dwellings which were in poor condition, compared with 15% of all households (Figure 6.3), while 11% of unemployed households lived in unfit housing, compared with 4% of all households.

Ethnic origin

6.8 The survey determined ethnic origin by identifying the birthplace of the head of household. A higher proportion of those households whose head identified themselves as being born in the New Commonwealth or Pakistan lived in housing in poor condition compared with all other households (Table 6.2). In particular, the proportion living in unfit housing was two-and-a-half times higher than that of other households.

Table 6.2 Ethnic origin of head of households living in dwellings in poor condition

% households in dwellings in poor condition

	Lacking Basic Amenities	Unfit	In Poor Repair	All Households
Birthplace of Household Head				
United Kingdom	2.0	3.8	12.5	91.3
Other Europe	1.2	2.6	11.3	2.7
New Commonwealth and Pakistan	2.5	9.3	21.9	4.9
Other	0.9	2.3	13.3	1.1
All Households	2.0	4.0	13.1	100

Fig 6.3 Employment status of head of household by proportion of households in unfit dwellings and dwellings in poor condition

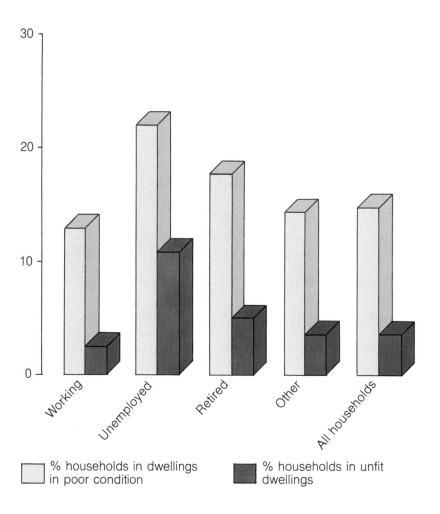

% households in dwellings in poor condition

% households in unfit dwellings

Household income

6.9   Poor housing was related, above all, to income[1]. Half of all households lacking amenities, one-third of those in unfit housing and 27% of those whose homes were in poor repair had net incomes of less than £3,000 (Table A6.6). The majority of these households lived in rented accommodation (Table A6.7).

Regional distribution of households in dwellings in poor condition

6.10   The association between household characteristics and housing in poor condition has been analysed geographically. Three areas were used, broadly classified as the 'North', the 'Rest of England' and the 'South East'[2].

---

[1] Household income is defined as net annual income of household head and partner. An imputed income from savings is not included. The figures presented here are 20% lower than those quoted by the Family Expenditure Survey (FES), the closest comparable source. The FES includes income from all household members and imputes income from savings.

[2] *North* — including the Northern, North West, and Yorkshire and Humberside regions. *Rest of England* — including the West Midlands, East Midlands, East Anglia and the South West.

South East — including London and the South East. Because of the size of the sample, reliable information based on interviews with households cannot be provided at a lower level of disaggregation.

6.11 The condition of the stock varied between regions (see Chapter 5). So too did the population in terms of age, income and other characteristics. The North had the highest proportion of local authority tenants and households on low income, the Rest of England had the highest proportion of households aged 75 and over. The South East had the highest proportion of households under 40, households in work, and owner occupiers (Tables A6.8–6.12). Because these groups had different distributions between the regions it would be expected that there would be regional differences in the proportions of particular household groups occupying housing in poor condition.

6.12 Households headed by someone aged 75 and over have already been shown to occupy a disproportionate share of dwellings in poor condition (para 6.4). Nationally they were three times more likely than other households to live in dwellings lacking basic amenities and one-and-a-half times more likely to live in unfit dwellings. At the regional level higher proportions of households aged 75 and over lived in poor condition dwellings in the North and Rest of England compared with the South East (Table A6.13). But this is explained by the South East having lower proportions of this group of households and dwellings in poor condition than the other two regions. After controlling for these differences the probability of households aged 75 and over living in housing in poor condition, when compared with other households, was the same in each region.

6.13 One-fifth of the unemployed lived in housing in poor condition and they were 50% more likely to live in such housing compared with all households at the national level. But this picture showed great variation at the regional level (Table A6.14). Over one-quarter of the unemployed in the North lived in poor condition housing compared with only 12% of the unemployed in the South East (Table 6.3). This difference was not only attributable to the higher proportion of unemployed in the North. In this region they were 60% more likely than all households to live in housing in poor condition whereas in the South East they were as likely as other households to do so. In part this is explained by many of the unemployed in the South East being tenants of the local authority whose stock, on average, is in better condition than that of the private sector.

Table 6.3 Regional differences in those groups of households which have a high probability of living in poor condition housing

% households in housing in poor condition (probability of households living in poor condition housing compared with all other households in their region)

	North	Rest of England	South East	All Regions
Aged 75 and Over	21.9 (1.3)	20.2 (1.3)	16.7 (1.3)	19.5 (1.3)
Unemployed	27.4 (1.6)	23.6 (1.5)	12.2 (1.0)	21.7 (1.5)
Income Less Than £3,000	22.0 (1.3)	20.0 (1.3)	13.6 (1.1)	18.3 (1.2)

6.14 Low-income households lived in better condition housing in the South East than in other regions (Table A6.15). Only 14% of households with incomes less than £3,000 lived in housing in poor condition in the South East compared with 22% in the North. At national level this group was 20% more likely to live in poor condition housing whereas in the North and Rest of England they were 30% more likely to do so (Table A6.2).

Attitudes to housing condition

Perception of poor condition

Tenure

6.15 Housing in poor condition has been shown to be closely associated with low income and there are obvious reasons for this. But there are other factors, such as lack of perception of the problems and lack of motivation, which may affect the housing circumstances of some groups.

6.16 The biggest variation in the perception of poor condition occurred between local authority tenants and households in the private sector. Tenants of local authority owned properties reported their homes to be in a significantly worse state of repair than did the surveyors. The reverse was the case for owner-occupied and private-rented dwellings (Figure 6.4).

Fig 6.4 Household's view of state of repair compared with surveyor's view of state of repair – by tenure

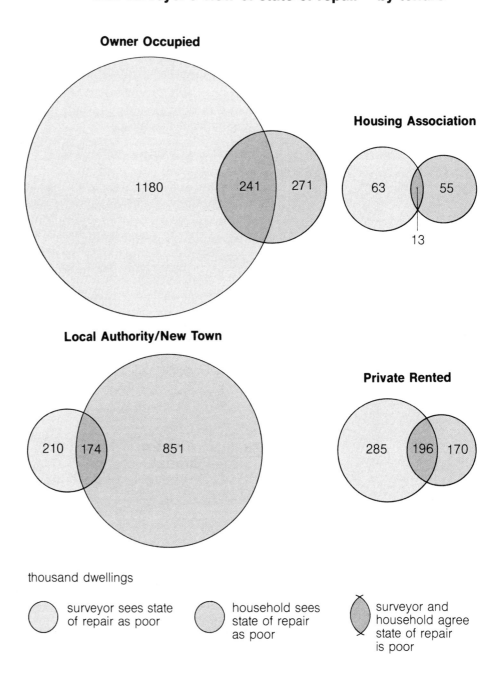

thousand dwellings

○ surveyor sees state of repair as poor

○ household sees state of repair as poor

◉ surveyor and household agree state of repair is poor

6.17 Some households were more able than others to recognise the need for repair. Where the surveyor had said that a dwelling was in poor repair this view was more often supported by younger households than by the elderly (Figure 6.5). Households on low incomes and unemployed

Fig 6.5 Number of households in dwellings in poor repair: attitude to state of repair by age of head of household

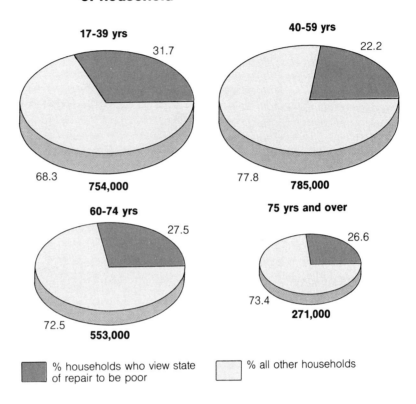

households were more likely to report that repairs were required than those on higher incomes and those in work (Figures 6.6 and 6.7). However, the majority of these low income and unemployed households were local authority tenants who, as a whole, appeared more critical of poor condition than owner occupiers or tenants of private landlords.

Fig 6.6 Number of households in dwellings in poor repair: attitude of state of repair by employment status of head of household

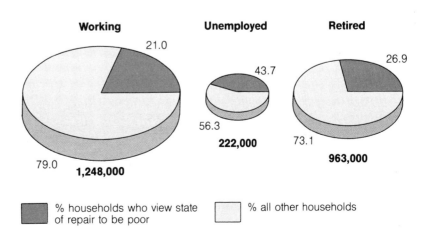

Fig 6.7 Number of households in dwellings in poor repair: attitude to state of repair by household income

£0-2,999
37.2
62.8
639,000

£3,000-5,999
25.9
74.1
645,000

£6,000-8,999
25.6
74.4
476,000

£9,000-11,999
22.0
78.0
313,000

£12,000-14,999
12.9
87.1
186,000

£15,000 and over
17.5
82.5
97,000

■ % households who view state of repair to be poor   □ % all other households

Attitudes to carrying out work

6.18   Tenants rarely have responsibility for carrying out work to their home and their views on this topic were, not surprisingly, different to those of owner occupiers. Tenants and owner occupiers are therefore considered separately.

Owner-occupiers

6.19   The majority of owner occupiers (63%) had a positive attitude to repair work. They said they were either constantly carrying out jobs on their home or that they tackled jobs promptly to prevent problems arising. A further 31% did only those jobs which they felt to be essential whilst 6% said that they put off jobs or were not bothered about them. Households aged 75 and over were less positive and were most likely to tackle only those jobs which they considered essential. Attitudes to repair varied surprisingly little with income (Table A6.16).

Attitudes to work in relation to the state of repair

6.20   The state of repair of the dwelling reflected to a degree the householder's attitude to repair and maintenance. Of the dwellings in poor condition 13% were owned by those who tended to get behind with maintenance to their home or were not bothered about the condition of their home (Table A6.17). This compares with only 5% of households living in good condition dwellings who had this attitude. But over half of poor condition property was owned by those who reported a positive attitude to carrying out repairs.

Tenants

6.21   Although tenants generally do not have the responsibility for repairing and maintaining their home many nevertheless said they did undertake such work. One-third of local authority tenants reported that they acted promptly to tackle jobs which needed to be done and a further third said they undertook essential maintenance (Table A6.18). As with owner occupiers it was people aged 75 and over and those on lowest incomes who were least likely to carry out work to their homes. Tenants in the private rented sector, and particularly those under 40, were even less inclined to take on themselves any repairs or maintenance (Table A6.19).

6.22   Few tenants living in dwellings in poor condition became involved with repairs or maintenance work. Only half of this group said they either carried out jobs promptly or at least undertook essential maintenance compared with two-thirds of those tenants living in property in good condition (Table A6.17).

Occupants' views on changing conditions

Owner occupiers

6.23   The majority of owner occupiers considered that the state of repair of their home had changed in the previous five years. Around 60% felt their homes to be in a better state of repair whilst 7% thought them to be worse. Overall, of the 4% of owner occupiers who considered their homes to be in poor condition half felt they were now in a worse state of repair than five years ago (Table A6.20).

Changing condition and attitudes to repair

6.24   Those owner occupiers who considered the state of their home to have deteriorated were least likely to be actively concerned with its maintenance. In this group 16% either put off maintenance or could not be bothered to carry it out compared with only 2% of all owner occupiers (Table A6.16). Of those who felt the condition of their home had deteriorated 20% said that they were about to tackle the problem. But the majority had done nothing because they said they lacked the money to do so (Table A6.22).

Tenants

6.25   Tenants were less inclined than owner occupiers to think that the condition of their home had improved. Over one-fifth of private-rented sector tenants thought the condition of their home had got worse since 1981 compared with 15% of local authority tenants. However, where tenants felt their home to be in poor condition 18% of those in the private sector believed there had been some deterioration over the last five years compared with 38% of local authority tenants (Table A6.20).

Changing condition and attitudes to repair

6.26   Tenants who considered the condition of their home had deteriorated were much less likely than other tenants to have undertaken any repair and maintenance work. This was particularly true of those from the private rented sector (Table A6.21).

7 Improvement and repair of the stock

7.1 The survey collected information on action to repair and improve the stock from two separate sources. Householders were asked what works they, or their landlords, had carried out in the last five years. Local authorities were asked what work they had undertaken as landlords and what action they had taken to support improvement and repair in the private sector in the same period. In addition, developers make a contribution to improvement and remedial activity and an estimate has been made of the extent of their expenditure. This chapter identifies the amount and type of work undertaken in 1986; the associated expenditure, the extent to which work carried out has contributed to the repair of the stock and the characteristics and motivations of those people who have undertaken work.

Incidence of Work Undertaken

Work undertaken by owner occupiers and landlords

7.2 Three-quarters of all dwellings had some work carried out on them during 1986 (Table 7.1). Much of the work was relatively minor[1], and over half of all dwellings had nothing more than minor works undertaken (Table 7.1). Major works[2] were carried out on 19% of the stock. Owner

Table 7.1   Work reported by occupants in 1986

thousands/% households

	Owner Occupied	Private Rented	Local Authority(3) New Town	Housing Association (4)
No Works	2,680 (22)	443 (34)	1,330 (27)	99 (20)
Minor Works by Occupant	6,483 (56)	219 (17)	1,022 (21)	51 (10)
Minor Works by Landlord		226 (18)	1,101 (22)	66 (13)
Minor Works by Occupant and Landlord		127 (10)	763 (15)	215 (44)
Major Works by Occupant	2,392 (21)	55 (4)	128 (3)	4 (1)
Major Works by Landlord		216 (17)	598 (12)	59 (12)

1. Minor works are defined as those which cost less than £400 or would have cost less than this if undertaken by a contractor.
2. Major works are defined as those which cost more than £400 or would have done so if undertaken by a contractor.
3. These figures relate to work by local authorities as reported by tenants. They will include work from both revenue and capital expenditure.
4. Housing Association figures can be provided at this general level but more detailed analysis is not possible due to small sample sizes.

occupiers were most likely to have carried out major works, over one-fifth having done so. Landlords undertook major work on between 12% and 17% of their stock. Tenants carried out few major jobs, and only 2% of local authority tenants and 5% of private tenants had done so.

7.3 Owner occupiers who lived in inter-war housing carried out the most work (Table A7.1). If major jobs alone are considered, it was owner occupiers of pre-1919 and inter-war dwellings that undertook the most work (Table A7.2).

7.4 Private landlords were less likely than owner occupiers to carry out work (Table A7.1). Work was only undertaken on less than half the stock owned by private landlords and less than one-fifth undertook major work (Table A7.2).

7.5 In comparison with private landlords local authorities carried out more work to their stock, but undertook less than owner occupiers. There was little variation in the amount of work undertaken to local authority dwellings of different ages. Local authorities carried out proportionately more work on their houses than flats, and more work was undertaken on dwellings of non-traditional construction (Table 7.2); 21% of the latter had major work undertaken compared with 17% of dwellings of traditional construction.

Table 7.2 Major repairs and improvement[5] 1981–1986 reported by local authorities on their stock by construction type

% dwellings

	Houses	Flats	Traditional	Non-traditional	All Dwellings
Work Undertaken	20.0	15.4	17.4	21.2	16.6
No Work Undertaken	80.0	86.6	82.6	78.8	83.4

Work undertaken by tenants

7.6 Tenants rarely had contractual responsibility for the repair and improvement of their homes, although the 1980 Housing Act enabled local authority tenants to undertake work, and be reimbursed by the local authority, and Home Improvement Grants were made available to private sector tenants. These initiatives have had little take-up. The age of the dwelling made some difference to the work tenants undertook (Table A7.2). Within the private-rented sector a greater proportion of tenants in pre-1919 dwellings did work to their home than those who lived in dwellings of other ages (Tables A7.1–2).

Value of work undertaken

7.7 It is estimated that in carrying out both major and minor works a total of £14.5bn was spent in 1986. Much of the work undertaken by households did not use paid labour and therefore underestimated the real value of the work carried out. If a notional cost for unpaid labour[6] is included then the total value of all work carried out increases to £17.3bn (Table 7.3). Eighty per cent of this was in the private sector.

[5.] These relate to capital works only as reported by local authorities.
[6.] Value of DIY work was estimated as twice the actual expenditure; where work was a mixture of DIY and contracted labour the value of the work was established by multiplying expenditure by 1.5.

Table 7.3 Value of work undertaken on repair and improvement of dwellings in 1986

(£bn)

	Owner Occupied	Private Rented	Local Authority/ New Town	Housing (4) Association	All Tenures
Source of Finance					
Occupants	12.1	0.3	0.6	0.1	13.1
Grants	0.3	0.1			0.4
Landlord		0.6***	2.6**	0.4**	3.6
Developer	0.2*				0.2
All Sources	12.6	1.0	3.2	0.5	17.3

Notes * Estimated from 1981 EHCS
      ** Estimated from official statistics
      *** Estimated from information provided by tenant

Variation with tenure

7.8   The average value of work undertaken in 1986 was £937 per dwelling (Table 7.4). This figure reflects the relatively small number of dwellings having substantial sums spent on them. Compared with the owner-occupied dwellings the value of work undertaken on private-rented dwellings was, on average, some 30% less, and for local authority dwellings 40% less.

Table 7.4 Average value of all work undertaken in 1986 by both occupants and landlords

£ mean values

	Owner Occupied	Private Rented	Local Authority	Housing Association	All Tenures
Occupants	1,074	258	111	97	—
Landlords	—	500	532	337	—
All dwellings	1,074	758	643	434	937

7.9   In those dwellings where major work was undertaken the expenditure was often considerable (Table 7.5). The average value of major work undertaken by owner occupiers was twice that carried out by private landlords and two-and-a-half times the value of major work undertaken by local authorities.

Table 7.5 Average value of major work undertaken in 1986 by occupants (7) and landlords who undertook work

£ mean values where work undertaken

Owner Occupiers	Private Landlords	Local Authorities
3,315	1,616	1,319

Variation with age of dwelling

7.10   The value of works, whether major works or minor, tended to be greater the older the property; this holds true for all tenures. The average value of work undertaken on the pre-1919 stock was at least twice that of work on post-1964 dwellings (Figure 7.1). The average value of work undertaken by owner occupiers on the pre-1919 stock was over twice that of work carried out by landlords.

---

7. Owner occupiers only, as the sample size for tenants was too small to allow analysis.

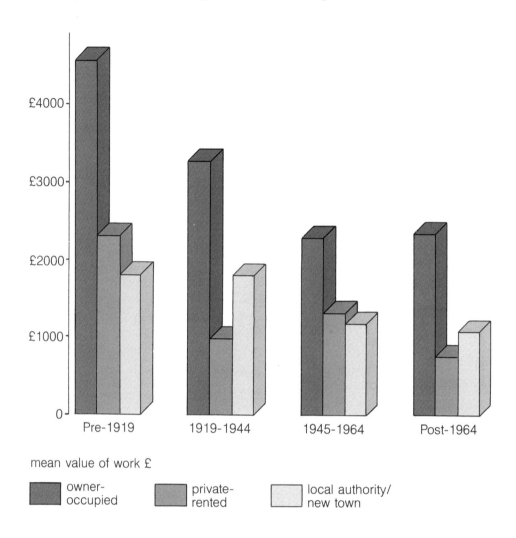

Fig. 7.1 Mean value of work undertaken by tenure and age of dwelling: expenditure by owners/landlords

mean value of work £

☐ owner-occupied   ☐ private-rented   ☐ local authority/new town

Type of work undertaken

Variation with region

7.11   The value of work varied between regions. For the owner-occupied stock as a whole the average value of work undertaken in the North was 20–30% higher than in the South East and Rest of England; but, if only the oldest owner-occupied stock is considered, more was spent in the South East. The average value of work undertaken in the private-rented sector was also highest in the South East. For local authority housing the average value of works carried out was higher in the North than in other regions (Table 7.6).

Table 7.6   Average value of work undertaken by region and tenure

£ mean value

	North	Rest of England	South
Owner-Occupied–All Dwellings	1,061	818	881
Owner-Occupied–Pre-1919 Dwellings	1,066	906	1,283
Private-Rented	259	665	738
Local Authority	643	483	473

Variation with tenure

7.12   Overall, owner occupiers paid more attention to improving the quality and services of their homes than repairing the fabric. The five jobs most frequently undertaken were internal decoration, improvement of kitchens and bathrooms, installing central heating and work to windows (Table A7.3). The profile of work by local authorities was rather different. Their five most common jobs were work to windows, heating, rewiring, installation of insulation and work to external doors. Private landlords were more likely to carry out repairs on the external fabric of the dwelling. Work to roofs, gutters and downpipes, external painting, rewiring and central heating were their most frequent jobs.

Variation with age of dwelling

7.13 The overall emphasis on improvement rather than repair in the owner-occupied sector stemmed from the considerable amount of work to modern dwellings which were essentially in good condition. Owner occupiers in pre-1919 dwellings were more likely to undertake repair to the fabric of the property. Work to roofs and windows were two of the five most common jobs (Table A7.4). However improvements still featured in the work to dwellings of this age with installation of kitchen fittings and central heating being particularly common. Works carried out by private landlords were predominantly repairs and included little improvement work (Table A7.4). In the local authority stock the range of jobs undertaken was less influenced by the age of the dwelling although there were some differences in the frequency with which jobs were undertaken (Table A7.4). Work to heating accounted for a higher proportion of jobs in housing built since 1964 than in inter-war housing, and works to remedy problems of condensation were featured substantially in dwellings built since 1964.

Impact of work undertaken

7.14 To try and identify the effect on the stock of the type of work which was carried out, work done has been divided into that classed as 'necessary' and that which was 'discretionary'. 'Necessary' works were those which maintained the fabric of the stock and provided essential facilities and included external painting, provision of basic amenities for the first time, installation of insulation and work to services (this includes the electrical system, hot water systems etc). 'Discretionary' works were those associated with replacement of bathroom or kitchen fitments, building extensions, installation of double glazing or central heating and internal decoration. For owner-occupied dwellings the proportion of the total value of the work attributed to 'necessary' and 'discretionary' expenditure was 41% and 59% respectively (Table 7.7). The balance towards 'discretionary' was reversed in the local authority and private-rented sectors. Fifty-eight per cent of the value of local authority work and 65% of the value of work by private landlords was associated with 'necessary' works.

Table 7.7 Value of 'necessary' and 'discretionary' expenditure by owner occupiers and landlords

% of total value of work

	Owner Occupiers	Private Landlords	Local Authorities
Necessary Expenditure			
Amenities (first-time)	2.3	—	0.2
Repairs to Fabric	29.1	45.1	39.6
Services	6.4	11.7	8.6
Insulation	0.7	0.1	5.6
External Decoration	2.3	8.0	3.5
Total Necessary Expenditure	40.8	64.9	57.5
Discretionary Expenditure			
Internal Decoration	6.5	—	1.2
Extensions	11.4	3.5	1.4
Amenities/Fitments/CH	24.5	24.6	33.7
Double Glazing	14.1	4.0	3.8
Other (Porches etc)	2.7	3.1	2.4
Total Discretionary Expenditure	59.2	35.2	42.5

Household characteristics and work undertaken

7.15 The nature of work carried out was influenced by the resources, characteristics and motivation of the occupants. (The survey obtained no information on the motivations of landlords, whether local authority or private sector). Because responsibilities for repair and maintenance of homes differ between owner occupiers and tenants they are considered separately.

Owner occupiers
Characteristics of owner-occupiers

7.16 Households whose incomes were less than £3,000 were the least likely to have carried out any work (Table 7.8). Above this threshold the

Table 7.8   Income of owner occupiers undertaking major works

% owner-occupied households

	£0–£2,999	£3,000–£5,999	£6,000–£8,999	£9,000–£11,999	£12,000 and Over
Owner Occupiers Undertaking Work	9.4	16.6	24.3	23.7	26.0
All Owner Occupiers	14.3	19.2	24.2	20.0	22.3

proportion of households doing such work increased slightly with income. However, the value of the work undertaken increased progressively with income. Where work was undertaken, the average value was £840 for households whose incomes were less than £3,000 compared with an average value of £2,100 where incomes were over £12,000 (Figure 7.2).

Fig 7.2   Owner occupiers: income by mean value of major work where work undertaken in 1986

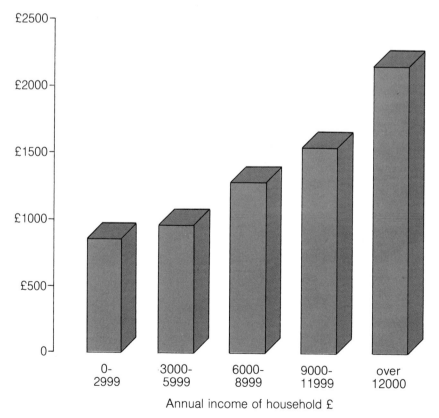

Annual income of household £

☐ £ mean value of work

7.17 Those households with heads aged under 40 were most likely to carry out major work to their homes (Table 7.9). But it was middle-aged households who, on average, spent the most (Figure 7.3).

Table 7.9   Age of head of owner-occupied households undertaking major works

% owner-occupied households

	17–39 Years	40–59 Years	60–74 Years	75 years and Over
Owner Occupiers Undertaking Work	37.8	39.1	20.5	2.6
All Owner Occupiers	33.4	39.2	21.7	5.7

Fig 7.3   Owner occupiers: age of head of household by mean value of all work where work undertaken in 1986

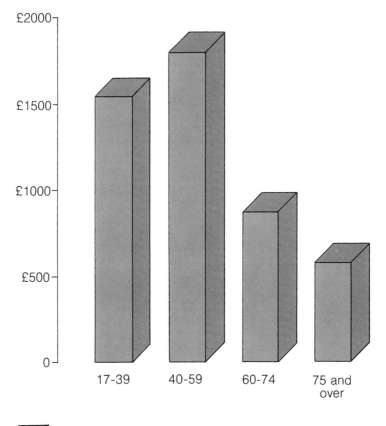

£ mean value of work.

7.18   The most important period for carrying out work to their homes appears to be between two and ten years after a household moves in (Table 7.10). During 1986 the average value for work undertaken was

Table 7.10   Length of residence of owner occupiers undertaking major works

% owner-occupied households

	0–2 Years	2–5 Years	5–10 Years	10–20 Years	20 Years and Over
Owner Occupiers Undertaking Work	12.0	28.5	23.9	21.4	14.3
All Owner Occupiers	18.4	24.6	18.3	20.8	17.9

highest for households who had lived in their homes for between two and five years (Figure 7.4).

Fig 7.4 Owner occupiers – length of residence by mean value of all work where work undertaken in 1986

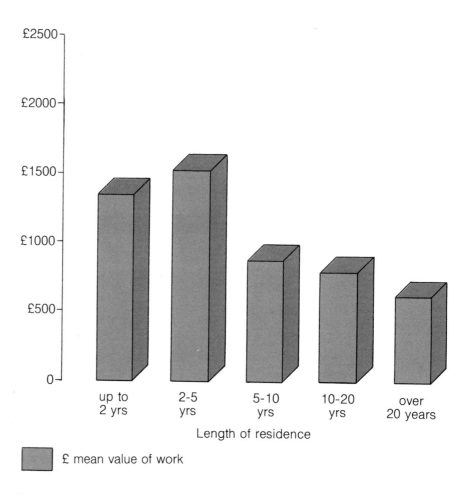

£ mean value of work

Use of paid labour and DIY

7.19 Just over one-fifth of all jobs undertaken were carried out by the occupants themselves or possibly with unpaid assistance, and a further 5% involved both DIY and a paid contractor. Lack of money alone did not appear to be the main reason for the owners' involvement and, indeed, it was those households with incomes between £9–£12,000 which were the most likely to resort to DIY. Of this group 31% undertook the work themselves compared with 16% of households whose incomes were less than £3,000 (Table A7.5). Ability to do the work was equally important: 31% of the jobs undertaken by households under 40 were DIY compared with 12% of the jobs undertaken by those over 60.

Reasons for work

7.20 Half of the owner occupiers who carried out works said that they did so to increase the comfort or enhance the appearance of their homes. One third did works to repair the property (Table A7.6). This distribution is consistent with the type of work undertaken, with over half of the work undertaken classed as improvement and only 30% of the work classed as repair. Very little of the work undertaken was at the sole instigation of a bank or building society as a condition of mortgage lending. Only 1.4% of jobs were carried out for this reason (Table A7.6).

7.21 The nature of the work and reasons for carrying it out varied with the resources available to the household. Those who were less well off were the most likely to carry out repairs. Forty-five per cent of jobs done by households with incomes of less than £3,000 were carried out for this reason compared with around 30% of jobs undertaken by all other income groups. For those with higher incomes and those aged under 40 the intention of increasing the value of their property figured prominently in the reasons given. Elderly households sought to increase the comfort or appearance of their homes compared with younger households (Table A7.6).

Resources for undertaking the work

7.22 A household's savings appeared to be the most important source of funding: 71% of the jobs carried out were funded from savings only and a further 3% relied on savings together with another source of finance. An increase to the mortgage or a bank or building society loan was used by 19% of owner occupiers who undertook work (Table A7.7).

Tenants
Characteristics of tenants

7.23 Very few tenants undertook repair or improvement of their homes. Where work was carried out it was more likely to be undertaken by the better-off tenants than those on low incomes. Those under 40 were the most likely to carry out work and they also spent the most money in doing so (Table A7.8).

Reasons for doing work

7.24 Over 70% of the jobs undertaken by tenants were directed at increasing the comfort and enhancing the appearance of their home. The longer tenants had been resident the more likely they were to carry out a job for this reason. Those who had recently moved into their home tended to carry out needed repairs (Table A7.9).

Persuasion of landlords

7.25 Although tenants carried out little work themselves, many had pointed out to their landlords that work needed doing. In the private-rented sector 42% of the jobs carried out by private landlords had been initiated by tenants (Table A7.10). Most private landlords were reported to have carried out jobs when requested: in only 16% of cases did the tenant experience difficulty in getting the work done. Problems were greater for local authority tenants. In half the cases where the local authority had been asked to carry out a job the tenant experienced difficulty in getting the work done.

8 Improvement and repair activity organised by local authorities

8.1   Some improvement and repair of property in the private sector is grant aided by local authorities; some stems from their use of compulsory powers or their block repair and enveloping schemes. Local authorities can also encourage repair and improvement activity through area action programmes. Authorities are, of course, responsible for the renovation and maintenance of their own stock. This chapter describes local authorities' involvement in instigating and coordinating improvement and repair and identifies which dwellings were targeted by authorities.

Private sector stock

8.2   Between 1981 and 1986 local authority action on the private sector stock involved a total of 1.6m dwellings; of this, 1.2m dwellings were the subject of individual action and 897,000 dwellings were included in area schemes[1]. Both area schemes and individual action involved a high proportion of private-rented housing, this accounted for 22% of all dwellings included (Figure 8.1).

Fig 8.1   Current and completed action in the private sector: 1981-86

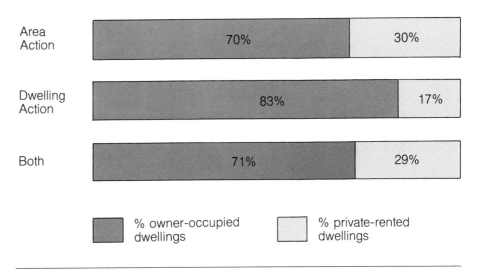

1. Individual action refers to that which is specific to particular dwellings or blocks containing them. By comparison with national statistics local authorities in this survey have under-reported their activity in the private sector. For specific activities, such as provision of home improvement grants and area action, it is possible to adjust the reported figures to known national estimates. But for aggregate measures (which contain more than one type of local authority action) such as reported here it is not possible to make adjustments for known individual figures because of the overlap between categories. Therefore these aggregate figures are likely to be lower than the true picture.

Home improvement grants

8.3 In the five years between the 1981 and 1986 surveys 791,000 Home Improvement Grants[2] and 1.58 million Homes Insulation Grants were given (Table A8.1). The majority of Home Improvement Grants went to owner occupiers (82%) with only 15% being given to landlords and 3% to tenants. Home Improvement Grants were primarily given for dwellings built before 1919 although one-quarter of intermediate grants were given on inter-war dwellings (Table A8.2). Homes Insulation Grants were distributed more evenly between dwellings of different ages with inter-war dwellings receiving the highest proportion (42%).

Grants to owner occupiers

8.4 Two-thirds of Home Improvement Grants were given to owner occupiers with net household incomes below £9,000 per year (Table A8.3). People aged 75 and over were the least likely to obtain grants; only 3% of grants went to people in this age group (Table A8.4). Grant take-up was greatest a few years after households had moved into their homes (Table A8.5).

Effectiveness of grants

8.5 Just over two-thirds of all Home Improvement Grants went to dwellings which the 1981 survey had identified as unsatisfactory [3]. Intermediate and improvement grants were more likely than repairs grants to be given to dwellings in the worst condition[4] (Table A8.6). One-quarter and one-fifth of these grants respectively went to the worst housing.

Regional distribution

8.6 The use of Home Improvement Grants was not equally distributed between the regions[5] with a slightly higher proportion of grants being given in the South East than in the other two regions (Table 8.1). The effective use of grants differed between regions. A higher proportion of dwellings identified as being unsatisfactory in 1981 were provided with grants in the South East and North compared with the Rest of England (Table A8.7).

Table 8.1   Distribution of Home Improvement Grants by region

thousands/% dwellings

	North	Rest of England	South East	All Regions
Grant	205 (25.9) (5.4)	264 (33.4) (5.4)	322 (40.7) (6.1)	791 (100) (5.7)
No Grant	3,576 (27.3) (94.6)	4,618 (35.2) (94.6)	4,919 (37.5) (93.9)	13,113 (100) (94.3)
All Private Sector Dwellings	3,781 (27.1) (100)	4,882 (35.2) (100)	5,241 (37.7) (100)	13,904 (100) (100)

[2] Home Improvement Grants include improvement grants, intermediate grants, repairs grants and special grants.

[3] Unsatisfactory dwellings were those which lacked amenities, were unfit or required repairs over £2,500 in 1981.

[4] Dwellings in the worst condition were those which, in 1981, were unfit, in serious disrepair and lacked amenities.

[5] The regions used here are North, Rest of England and South East as defined in Chapter 6, para 6.10. These broad regions are used because of sample size.

Compulsory powers and notices

8.7   Between 1981 and 1986 local authorities used their powers[6] to initiate action on 229,000 private sector dwellings. Most commonly the dwellings were subject to compulsory renovation (34%), or cleared or closed (18%). In over half the cases these powers were directed at the private-rented stock reflecting the higher proportion of poor condition dwellings in this sector compared with owner-occupied housing (Figure 8.2). Of this local authority intervention 82% was directed at dwellings built before 1919 (Table A8.8). In addition, 14,000 dwellings in local authority ownership were closed or cleared.

Fig 8.2   Power used on individual dwellings in the private sector: 1981-1986

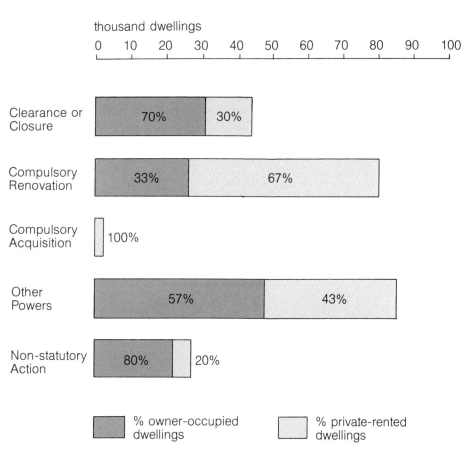

Effectiveness of powers

8.8   The use of these powers made only a relatively small contribution to reducing the numbers of dwellings in poor condition. Only 5% of the dwellings which were unsatisfactory in 1981 had been the subject of the use of local authority powers by 1986. However, of the very worst housing 10% were subject to local authority powers (Table A8.9).

Regional distribution

8.9   Overall, 46% of the dwellings where local authorities instigated action were in the South East (Table A8.10) although this region had only 23% of the dwellings which were reported unsatisfactory in 1981. Powers were used differentially between the regions. Compulsory renovation was hardly used in the North, this region using its powers primarily for clearance. The South East and Rest of England were more likely to use compulsory renovation and the South East also used other powers to a significant extent.

---

6. Powers included in this definition are (i) 1985 Housing Act; Part IX (Clearance and Closure/demolition); Part VI (repairs notices); Part VII(improvement notices); Part VI (works to houses in multiple occupation); Part II (Acquisition) and Part VIII (Acquisition). (ii) other powers Planning or Public Health acts, and (iii) informal notices by the local authority.

Block and group schemes

8.10   Local authorities instigated some repair and improvement in the private sector through organising, and in some cases providing 100% funding for, work to whole blocks of dwellings; 152,000 dwellings were included in block repair, enveloping and similar schemes[7]. Owner occupied, rather than private-rented dwellings were more likely to be included in such schemes; 59% compared with 20% (Figure 8.3). Block schemes in the private sector as a whole varied in size from less than ten dwellings to large schemes of over 300 dwellings. Over half the schemes included more than 300 dwellings (Table 8.2).

Fig 8.3   Private sector dwellings in completed and current block or group repairs schemes

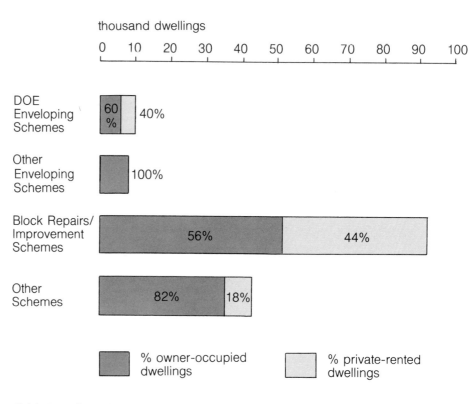

thousand dwellings

| 0 | 10 | 20 | 30 | 40 | 50 | 60 | 70 | 80 | 90 | 100 |

DOE Enveloping Schemes — 60% / 40%

Other Enveloping Schemes — 100%

Block Repairs/ Improvement Schemes — 56% / 44%

Other Schemes — 82% / 18%

◼ % owner-occupied dwellings   ▢ % private-rented dwellings

Table 8.2   Size of block or group schemes

% dwellings

<10	11–49	50–149	150–299	300 and over
0	1.4	12.5	19.4	66.7

Effectiveness of block schemes and regional distribution

8.11   Local authorities' block schemes had less impact than their use of compulsory powers with 2.8% of the unsatisfactory stock in 1981 included in block schemes by 1986 (Table A8.11). The impact of block schemes on the very worst housing was limited with only 5.1% of dwellings in this group being the subject of block action. Block action was least frequent in the South East which accounted for only 27% of all dwellings in such schemes. The Rest of England had the highest proportion at 41% (Table 8.12).

[7.] Group schemes are those with a number of dwellings which, although not necessarily in the same block, are dealt with under the same contract or programme.

Area-based action by local authorities

8.12 Area-based programmes have long been an important part of improvement policy. Between 1981 and 1986 897,000 private sector dwellings[8] were included in Housing Action Areas (HAAs), General Improvement Areas (GIAs) or "non-statutory" area schemes[9] devised by the local authority (Figure 8.4). These area-based programmes included a further 47,000 public sector dwellings in GIAs and HAAs which were properties acquired by local authorities, or small pockets of purpose built local authority stock incorporated to provide logical boundaries to an area.

Fig 8.4 Current and completed area activity involving private sector dwellings

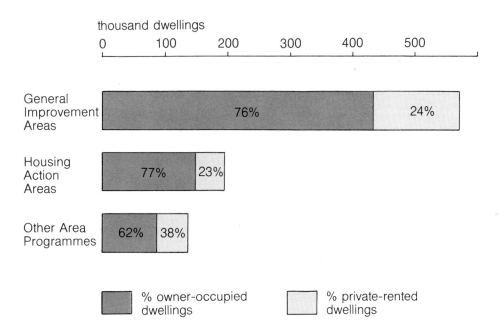

8.13 GIAs were the most common form of area action and accounted for 63% of all private sector dwellings in area-based programmes. Both GIAs and HAAs included a high proportion (20%) of privately rented dwellings (Figure 8.4). Area-based action in the private sector was undertaken almost exclusively on pre-1919 dwellings with only 5% of dwellings built after this date being included (Table A8.13). The size of the area-based schemes varied, with HAAs being generally smaller than GIAs; 41% of HAAs included fewer than 300 dwellings compared with 36% of GIAs and 29% of "other" schemes (Table A8.14).

Regional distribution of area action

8.14 Area-based activity was concentrated in the North; almost half of all dwellings included in GIAs and HAAs were in this region (Figure 8.5). In the South East "other" area schemes predominated with 70% of all dwellings in such schemes being in this region.

---

8. The figures cover all dwellings included in schemes between 1981–1986 regardless of whether the scheme had started before 1981, was completed by 1986 or was still in operation.
9. Non-statutory schemes were areas declared by local authorities which do not benefit from specific legislative provision.

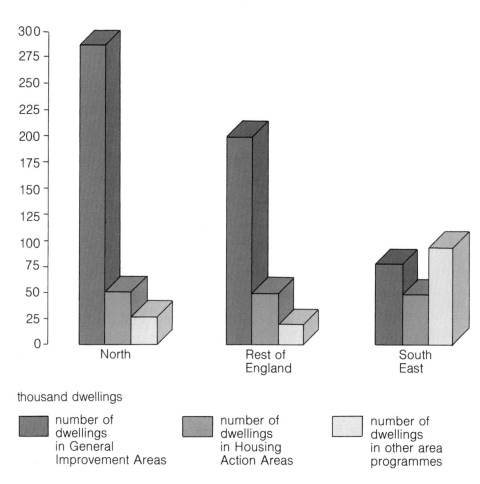

Fig 8.5 Current and completed area activity in the private sector by region: 1981-1986

thousand dwellings

- number of dwellings in General Improvement Areas
- number of dwellings in Housing Action Areas
- number of dwellings in other area programmes

Characteristics of households in area action programmes

8.15 The population in designated action areas tended to be long standing residents or very recent movers. Over one-third of residents of area schemes had lived in their homes for less than five years and one-quarter had been resident for more than twenty. HAAs demonstrated this pattern more clearly than GIAs (Table A8.15). Households in HAAs would appear to have higher incomes than households in GIAs; 61% of residents of GIAs had incomes of less than £6,000 compared with 25% of households in HAAs (Table A8.16).

Action on dwellings within area-based programmes

8.16 Over one-third of dwellings in area-based programmes were subject to some kind of specific action relating to the individual dwelling, or as part of a block scheme. The proportion of dwellings receiving attention was highest in HAAs (Table A8.17). The level of grant aid in both HAAs and GIAs was also high, being around one-third in each case. Home Improvement Grants given to dwellings in HAAs or GIAs accounted for 19% of all grants given between 1981 and 1986. Compulsory Action was undertaken on almost one-fifth of dwellings in HAAs and on the same proportion of dwellings included in "non-statutory" areas defined by authorities (Table A8.18).

Effectiveness of area-based programmes

8.17 Area-based programmes contained both satisfactory and unsatis-factory dwellings. Over half of the dwellings included in area-based programmes between 1981 and 1986 were in an unsatisfactory condition in 1981 (Table A8.19). HAAs had the highest proportion of unsatisfactory dwellings at 66%. However, the overall extent to which area-based action contributed to improving housing conditions was relatively small as these programmes took in only 12% of the private sector stock which was unsatisfactory in 1981. The effectiveness of these area-based program-mes varied substantially between regions. The North included three times as many unsatisfactory dwellings in its area-based programmes as did the South East (Table A8.20).

8.18   The potential scope for area-based action was much greater than the level of activity suggests (Table A8.21). In the 1981 EHCS surveyors considered that 1.78 million private sector dwellings were suitable for inclusion in either GIAs or HAAs. Of these only 541,000 had been included in some form of area-based action by 1986; they represented 60% of all dwellings included in such schemes.

Estate-based action on the authorities' own stock

8.19   Between 1981 and 1986 local authorities included 699,000 of their own dwellings in estate-based programmes. Within these programmes 523,000 dwellings had work done, either on an individual basis or as part of a block. Outside these estate programmes, a further 295,000 dwellings were repaired or renovated[10].

Renovation of blocks of dwellings

8.20   Of the 818,000 local authority dwellings that were being repaired or renovated during the period, 84% (686,000 dwellings) were dealt with as part of a block or group. In turn, the work on many of these blocks was undertaken as part of an estate programme which usually involved both works to dwellings and works to the surrounding environment. Two-thirds of all dwellings being renovated in blocks were being renovated as part of an estate wide programme.

8.21   In addition to the 686,000 local authority dwellings being renovated in blocks a further 33,000 dwellings had been originally included in these programmes but had since been transferred to the private sector. Local authority action on its own stock comprised mainly larger schemes with 80% of all block renovation being on groups of fifty or more dwellings (Table A8.22). Block renovation was most prevalent in the inter-war and immediate post-war stock (Table 8.3).

Table 8.3   Renovation of blocks in local authority stock by age of dwelling

	Pre-1919	1919–1944	1945–1964	Post-1964	All Dwellings
Dwellings in Block Renovation	10 (1.5) (6.4)	207 (30.2) (17.2)	326 (47.5) (15.3)	143 (20.8) (9.8)	686 (100) (13.9)
All Dwellings	156 (3.2)	1,202 (24.4)	2,125 (43.1)	1,453 (29.4)	4,935 (100)

Effectiveness of block renovation

8.22   The renovation of blocks of local authority dwellings included 23% of dwellings which the 1981 survey found to be in an unsatisfactory condition (Table A8.23). However, over two-thirds of dwellings included in these schemes had been classed as satisfactory, reflecting the fact that a substantial proportion of work related to the modernisation or replanning of dwellings.

---

10. These figures only include major capital works.

Work in estate based programmes

8.23   Nearly three-quarters of all activity on the local authority stock was undertaken as part of an estate-based programme. Such programmes included estates of inter-war and post-war housing as well as the more recent estates which consisted mainly of flats. Also included in estate-based programmes were 89,000 privately owned dwellings, these having been subsequently purchased by tenants.

8.24   As well as the renovation of blocks described above, work was undertaken to individual dwellings, common areas, and to the environment of estates. Improvements and major repairs to dwellings were the most common activity (Figure 8.6). Estate programmes were most likely to include the inter-war stock and to include flats rather than houses (Table A8.24). Local authorities in the North were more likely to undertake estate-based programmes compared with those in the other two regions (Table A8.25). Estate based programmes varied in size. Large schemes predominated with 50% including 300 or more dwellings (Table A8.26).

Fig 8.6   Action on public sector dwellings in estate-based schemes

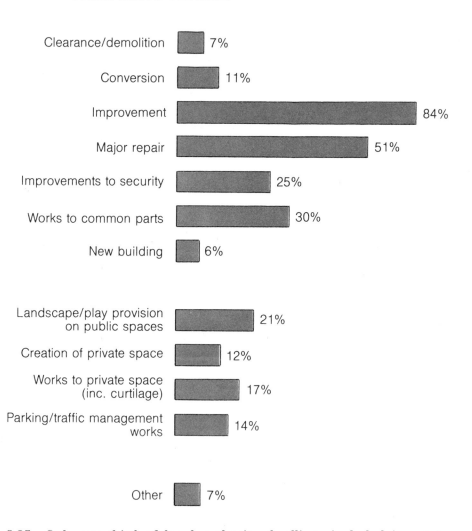

Effectiveness of estate based schemes

8.25   Only one-third of local authority dwellings included in estate-based action schemes were reported to be in unsatisfactory condition in the 1981 survey (Table A8.27). But, as already noted, much of local authority action on its own stock is concerned with modernisation. Overall, 31% of unsatisfactory dwellings owned by local authorities were included in estate-based programmes.

Condition of dwellings following local authority activity

Private sector

8.26   One measure of the effectiveness of local authority activity is the condition of dwellings where action has been completed. This can be assessed by using the surveyors' judgement of condition in 1986 for those dwellings where action was completed in the period 1981–1986, or where dwellings were in areas where the programme had been completed. In completed area programmes, 20% of dwellings were in poor condition in 1986 (Table A8.28). There are two possible explanations: either these particular dwellings did not receive specific attention during the area programme, or there was specific action on the dwellings but they had subsequently fallen back into poor condition. The latter must provide part of the explanation as 20% of dwellings in area programmes which had been the subject of action were in poor condition in 1986.

8.27   Outside completed area programmes, 27% of dwellings which had received attention in the period were in poor condition in 1986. Taking all dwellings where work had been completed, and dwellings in areas where the programme had been completed, 25% of these were in poor condition in 1986. This raises questions about the type and standard of work being carried out and the suitability of the dwellings for the action undertaken.

Public sector

8.28   Of the estate-based programmes which had been completed since 1981, 12% were in poor condition in 1986 (Table A8.29). Overall, 16% of local authority dwellings which had had work done, or been included in completed estate programmes, were in poor condition in 1986. This is a lower level than in the private sector. This must in part be a reflection of the relative overall condition of the stock in the different tenures and also the nature of the works undertaken.

9 Changes in the condition of the stock: 1981–86

9.1   The previous chapters have shown that, between 1981 and 1986, there was substantial investment in the improvement and repair of the housing stock. The extent to which this has brought about a change in the condition of the stock is examined in this chapter. Changes are looked at first in terms of the processes which have effected them, secondly in terms of the types of dwellings affected and the geographical impact of change, and finally in relation to different household groups.

Measuring change
Method

9.2   To measure change, the dwellings surveyed in 1981 were surveyed again in 1986. A comparable survey method was used, but it was still necessary to ensure that similar standards of assessment were employed in the two surveys. How this was achieved and its impact on the results is explained in Appendices E and F.

Indicators used

9.3   Changes in condition are assessed using the three measures used in the 1981 survey. These are the lack of basic amenities, fitness and disrepair. Basic amenities and fitness are precisely those measures used in the previous chapters to describe the condition of the stock in 1986 and they have already been defined in the report (chapter 4, paras 4.2 and 4.25)[1]. The measure of disrepair that is used in this chapter is not that developed for the main 1986 survey, rather it is the measure used in the 1981 survey. (The differences between the two methods are described in Appendices B, C and F.)

Net change

9.4   There was an overall improvement in housing conditions between 1981 and 1986. Within the existing stock repair and improvement activity broadly kept pace with deterioration and the overall improvement was largely the result of the demolition or change of use of those dwellings in the worst condition coupled with new building. Overall, the proportion of dwellings lacking basic amenities fell from 5.0% to 2.9% (Table 9.1). The proportion of unfit dwellings fell from 6.3% to 5.6% and dwellings in "serious" disrepair[2] fell from 6.5% to 5.9%. The proportion of dwellings which were either unfit, lacked basic amenities or were in "serious" disrepair fell from 11.4% to 9% between 1981 and 1986.

---

[1] Although the measures are the same there are small differences in the numbers produced. These are explained in Appendix C.
[2] "Serious" disrepair is defined as those dwellings requiring over £7,000 of work at 1981 prices.

Table 9.1   The condition of the stock: 1981 and 1986 compared

thousands/% dwellings

	1981		1986	
	No	%	No	%
Total Dwellings	18,067	100.0	18,954	100.0
Lacking Amenities	905	5.0	543	2.9
Unfit	1,138	6.3	1,053	5.6
"Serious" Disrepair	1,178	6.5	1,113	5.9

Components of change

Improvement/repair and deterioration

9.5   Four processes contribute to the overall change: improvement and repair, deterioration, demolition and the construction of new dwellings. Their impacts are identified separately.

9.6   For those dwellings which existed in both 1981 and 1986, improvement and repair activity broadly kept pace with the rate of deterioration. In terms of fitness and "serious" disrepair the stock remained in a steady state (Table 9.2). However, improvement activity made inroads into those dwellings lacking basic amenities, causing a net increase of 293,000 dwellings provided with exclusive use of basic amenities.

Table 9.2   Changes[3] in condition in a constant population of dwellings (dwellings in existence in both 1981 and 1986)

thousands/% dwellings

	1981		1986	
	No	%	No	%
Total Dwellings	17,886	100.0[4]	18,132	100.0
Lacking Basic Amenities	836	4.7	543	3.0
Unfit	1,037	5.8	1,053	5.8
"Serious" Disrepair	1,102	6.2	1,113	6.1

Demolitions

9.7   Between 1981 and 1986 111,000 dwellings were demolished and 70,000 were transferred to non-residential use. About half the dwellings which were demolished, and over one third of those taken out of residential use, were in poor condition in 1981 (Table 9.3).

---

[3] Measurement of change has a degree of error associated with it which results from different interpretations of standards between survey years. This has been allowed for in the results and is explained in Appendices C and F.

[4] The difference in these constant population figures is due to conversions where single dwellings in 1981 were converted into more than one dwelling by 1986.

Table 9.3 Condition of dwellings demolished or taken out of residential use between 1981 and 1986

thousand dwellings

	Demolitions	No Longer Dwellings
Total Dwellings	111	70
Lacking Basic Amenities	49	20
Unfit	57	22
"Serious" Disrepair	48	28

9.8   Inclusion of dwellings lost to the stock in the calculation of change in condition brings about a further fall in the proportion of dwellings lacking basic amenities, and a marginal reduction in the proportion of dwellings unfit, but no significant change in the proportion in "serious" disrepair compared with 1981 (Table 9.4).

Table 9.4 Changes in condition 1981–1986, including the effect of demolitions and changes of use

thousands/% dwellings

	1981		1986	
	No	%	No	%
Total Dwellings	18,067	100.0	18,132	100.0
Lacking Basic Amenities	905	5.0	543	3.0
Unfit	1,138	6.3	1,053	5.8
"Serious" Disrepair	1,178	6.5	1,113	6.1

New build

9.9   Between 1981 and 1986 822,000 dwellings were added to the stock. This reduced the proportion of dwellings which lacked amenities, were unfit or in "serious" disrepair to 2.9%, 5.6% and 5.9% respectively. Overall there was a 40% reduction in dwellings lacking amenities between 1981 and 1986 and a small reduction of 8% in dwellings which were unfit[5] (Table 9.1).

Long term trends

9.10   As similar surveys were carried out in 1971, 1976 and 1981 an indication of the change in the condition of the stock between 1971 and 1986 can be provided. The number of dwellings which lacked basic amenities continued its dramatic decline but the rate of fall slowed between 1981 and 1986 as the total number of dwellings without basic amenities became very small (Figure 9.1). The number of unfit dwellings changed little in 15 years. There were minor fluctuations in the number of dwellings in "serious" disrepair throughout the period but, in broad terms the number remained relatively stable[6].

[5.] The change in unfit dwellings is just statistically significant when both sampling error and measurement error are taken into account (Appendix E). The change in serious disrepair is not significant when the errors are taken into account (Appendix F).

[6.] This conclusion differs from that presented in the 1981 report, see Appendix F.

Fig 9.1 Trends 1971-1986: dwellings lacking basic amenities, dwellings unfit, dwellings in serious disrepair

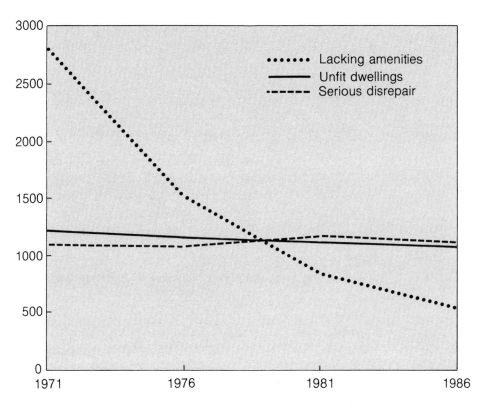

Distribution of change

Variation between dwellings of different ages

9.11 These broad changes conceal greater variations which have occurred between dwellings of different ages, types, tenures and between dwellings in different parts of the country.

9.12 The highest proportions of dwellings lacking amenities, unfit or in "serious" disrepair were still found in the pre-1919 stock but there had been a substantial improvement in the condition of this older sector. The proportion of pre-1919 dwellings lacking basic amenities had fallen from 12.3% to 7.0% (Figure 9.2). Three-quarters of this net change resulted from dwellings being provided with amenities and one-quarter from demolitions and dwellings being taken out of domestic use. One-quarter of the net reduction in the proportion of unfit pre-1919 dwellings and those in "serious" disrepair resulted from improvement and repair activity and three-quarters was a result of demolitions and change of use (Table A9.1).

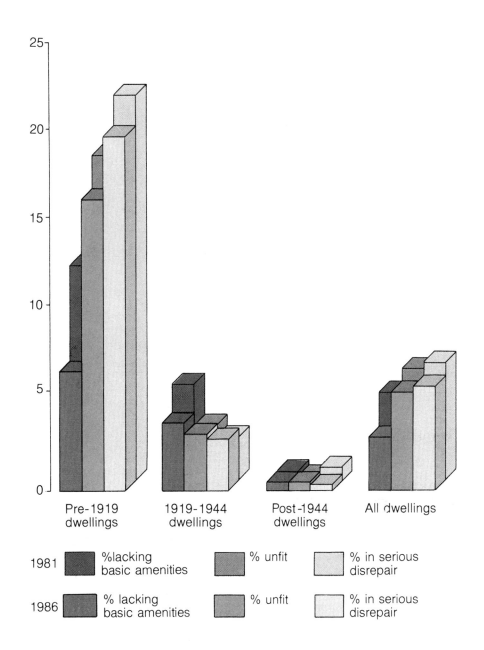

Fig 9.2 Differences in dwelling condition 1981-1986 by construction date

1981	%lacking basic amenities	% unfit
	% in serious disrepair	
1986	% lacking basic amenities	% unfit
	% in serious disrepair	

9.13 Inter-war dwellings presented a different picture. There is evidence that this sector continued the deterioration shown by the 1981 survey with a small increase in the proportion of dwellings which were unfit or were in "serious" disrepair (Figure 9.2). However, unfit dwellings or those in "serious" disrepair still only accounted for a very small proportion of the inter-war stock.

Changes in condition in different tenures

9.14 Overall, changes in condition within different tenures resulted both from physical change in condition and from dwellings changing tenure. Some 14% of the stock moved from one tenure to another between 1981 and 1986. Amongst those dwellings which did not change tenure there had been a marked improvement in the proportion of dwellings lacking basic amenities; the improvement affected all tenures but the greatest improvement was in owner-occupied housing (Figure 9.3). There was little change in the proportion of dwellings, which were unfit or in "serious" disrepair in any tenure.

Fig 9.3 Differences in dwelling condition 1981-1986 by tenure

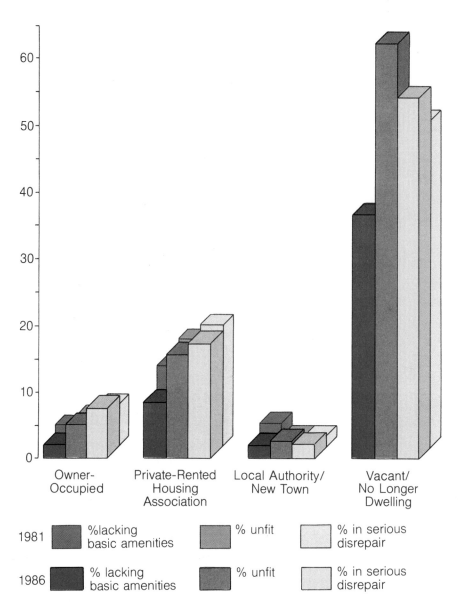

1981	%lacking basic amenities	% unfit
		% in serious disrepair
1986	% lacking basic amenities	% unfit
		% in serious disrepair

9.15   The greatest changes occurred in those dwellings which were vacant in both 1981 and 1986, and presumably during the intervening period. There was a large increase in the proportion which was unfit, from 38% to 62% (Figure 9.3). There were also increases in the proportions which lacked basic amenities or which were in "serious" disrepair.

Regional differences

9.16   Changes in housing conditions had not occurred uniformly across the country. Of the three broad regions[7] the greatest reduction in dwellings lacking amenities was in the North where the number fell by almost half (Figure 9.4). The change was largely a result of improvements to dwellings; demolitions and dwellings falling out of domestic use accounted for less than one-quarter of this change.

---

7. Broad regions are: *North* — including the North West, Northern and Yorkshire and Humberside regions.
Rest of England — including the East Midlands, West Midlands, Eastern and South West regions.
South East — including Greater London and South East regions. This broad regional grouping is used as sample sizes do not permit a finer breakdown.

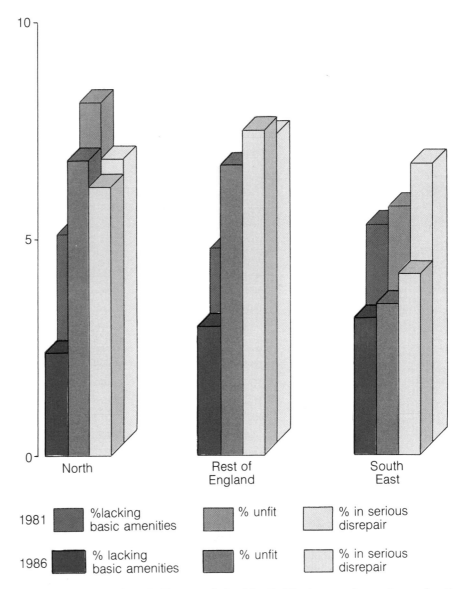

Fig 9.4   Differences in dwelling condition 1981-1986 by region

Legend:

1981
- %lacking basic amenities
- % unfit
- % in serious disrepair

1986
- % lacking basic amenities
- % unfit
- % in serious disrepair

9.17   Both the South East and the North West experienced a reduction in dwellings which were unfit or which were in "serious" disrepair, with the greatest reduction in the South East (Figure 9.4). Over 80% of the change in the South East was a result of improvement and repair activity. By contrast, the proportion of dwellings which were unfit or were in "serious" disrepair in the Rest of England increased (Table A9.1).

Changing conditions related to local authority activity in the private sector

9.18   These different patterns of change show some correspondence to local authority action in the private sector. Both the North and the South East tackled higher proportions of their unsatisfactory stock through the Home Improvement Grant System compared with the Rest of England (Table A8.7). This was a result of more effective targeting rather than higher proportions of grants being provided in these two regions. The highest proportion of clearance was undertaken in the North whilst over half of the compulsory renovation undertaken in England was carried out in the South East (Table A8.10).

Changing conditions related to expenditure on the stock

9.19　Expenditure on the stock has also been shown to have the same regional variation, with the Rest of England having the lowest average value of work done by owner occupiers. This was particularly true for the oldest stock where the value of work undertaken on the pre-1919 stock was 40% higher in the South East than in with the Rest of England.

Household characteristics

9.20　Chapter 6 showed that some types of household were more likely than others to live in housing in poor condition. Since 1981 housing conditions had improved[8] for the majority of household groups but the relative positions of groups had changed (Tables A9.2–6).

Groups whose housing conditions had substantially improved

9.21　The greatest improvement in conditions was in dwellings occupied by people aged 75 and over (Table 9.5). In 1981 they were over two-and-a-half times more likely than other groups to lack basic amenities, twice as likely to live in unfit houses and 1.8 times as likely to live in houses in "serious" disrepair. Five years later, again compared with other households, they were twice as likely to lack basic amenities, less than one-and-a-half times as likely to live in an unfit house and 1.3 times as likely to live in houses in "serious" disrepair.

9.22　Other groups whose housing conditions had improved were pensioner households including two or more people, recent movers, those on low incomes and, to a certain extent, the unemployed. In 1981 pensioner households were one-and-a-half times more likely than other groups to live in dwellings lacking amenities. By 1986, their relative position had substantially improved, so that they were less likely to occupy such housing than other groups. Recent movers in 1981 were already relatively well housed. By 1986, their position had improved further. For those on low incomes housing conditions also improved. The unemployed in 1986 were much less likely to live in unfit dwellings or dwellings in "serious" disrepair than this group in 1981. However they were more likely to lack basic amenities (Table 9.5).

Table 9.5　Households whose housing conditions had improved: 1981–1986

	1981			1986		
	Lacking Basic Amenities	Unfit	"Serious" Disrepair	Lacking Basic Amenities	Unfit	"Serious" Disrepair
75 Years and Over	2.7	2.0	1.8	2.0	1.4	1.3
Pensioners (2+ Persons)	1.4	1.4	0.9	0.7	0.6	0.8
Recent Movers	0.9	0.9	0.8	0.4	0.9	0.5
Households with Incomes in Lowest 25%	2.0	1.6	1.5	1.6	1.1	1.1
Unemployed	1.2	1.5	1.4	1.4	1.0	0.8

Numbers represent the likelihood of households living in dwellings in poor condition in comparison with their expected position. The expected position = 1.0 (see also Tables A 9.2–6).

8.　A change in housing conditions for different household groups is measured in terms of their relative share of dwellings in poor condition. This compares the proportion of any particular group in dwellings which are unfit, in "serious" disrepair, or which lack basic amenities with the proportion that group represents of all households. A value of 1.0 means the household group occupies its expected share of dwellings in a particular condition. Values of more than 1.0 represent more than the expected share and values of less than 1.0 are the converse.

Groups whose housing conditions had substantially declined

9.23 Single parent families, families with one or two children, long term residents and those who had lived in their home for between five and ten years, were the groups most likely to have experienced some deterioration in their housing conditions (Table 9.6). In particular, households with one or two children occupied in 1981 substantially less than their expected share of dwellings which were unfit or in "serious" disrepair, but by 1986 this position had reversed. For people who had lived in their homes for between five and ten years the changes between 1981 and 1986 were even greater.

Table 9.6   Households whose housing conditions had deteriorated since 1981

	1981			1986		
	Lacking Basic Amenities	Unfit	"Serious" Disrepair	Lacking Basic Amenities	Unfit	"Serious" Disrepair
Single Parent Families	0.2	0.5	0.5	—	2.0	1.2
Small Families	0.6	0.6	0.5	0.9	1.5	1.3
5–10 Year Residents	0.5	0.6	0.6	0.9	1.3	1.4
20 Years + Residents	1.9	1.7	1.6	2.2	1.6	1.9

Numbers represent likelihood of households living in dwellings in poor condition, in comparison with their expected position. (see also Tables A9.2–6).

Annex Tables

Table A 3.1 Type of house by construction date

thousands/% dwellings

	Pre-1900	1900–1918	1919–1944	1945–1964	Post-1964	All Ages
Terraced	1,826 (31.9) (63.8)	746 (13.1) (68.0)	993 (17.4) (27.5)	876 (15.3) (24.3)	1,273 (22.3) (31.2)	5,714 (100) (37.5)
Semi-Detached	482 (8.3) (16.8)	224 (3.9) (20.4)	1,950 (33.5) (54.0)	1,906 (32.8) (53.0)	1,251 (21.5) (30.7)	5,813 (100) (38.1)
Detached	554 (15.1) (19.4)	127 (3.5) (11.6)	667 (18.2) (18.5)	810 (22.1) (22.5)	1,500 (41.1) (36.8)	3,658 (100) (24.0)
Temporary	1 (1.6) —	—	2 (3.3) —	7 (11.5) (0.2)	51 (83.6) (1.3)	61 (100) (0.4)
All Types	2,863 (18.8) (100)	1,097 (7.2) (100)	3,612 (23.7) (100)	3,599 (23.6) (100)	4,075 (26.7) (100)	15,246 (100) (100)

Sample: PHY2

Table A 3.2 Storey height of houses by construction date

thousands/% dwellings

	Pre-1900	1900–1918	1919–1944	1945–1964	Post-1964	All Ages
1	58 (3.0) (2.0)	17 (0.9) (1.6)	302 (15.9) (8.4)	698 (36.7) (19.4)	828 (43.5) (20.3)	1,903 (100) (12.5)
2	2,266 (18.3) (79.1)	927 (7.5) (84.5)	3,251 (26.2) (90.0)	2,848 (22.9) (79.2)	3,121 (25.1) (76.6)	12,413 (100) (81.4)
3	452 (55.0) (15.8)	142 (17.3) (12.9)	58 (7.1) (1.6)	51 (6.2) (1.4)	118 (14.4) (2.9)	821 (100) (5.4)
4	71 (82.6) (2.5)	9 (10.5) (0.8)	— —	1 (1.1) —	5 (5.8) (0.1)	86 (100) (0.6)
5 or more	16 (69.6) (0.6)	2 (8.7) (0.2)	1 (4.3) —	1 (4.3) —	3 (13.1) (0.1)	23 (100) (0.1)
All Houses	2,863 (18.8) (100)	1,097 (7.2) (100)	3,612 (23.7) (100)	3,599 (23.6) (100)	4,075 (26.7) (100)	15,246 (100) (100)

Sample: PHY2

Table A 3.3 Type of flat by construction date

thousands/% dwelling

	Pre-1900	1900–1918	1919–1944	1945–1964	Post-1964	All Ages
Purpose-built	120 (4.7) (14.5)	49 (1.9) (23.8)	276 (10.8) (78.6)	822 (32.1) (93.8)	1,297 (50.5) (97.5)	2,564 (100) (71.4)
Converted	578 (75.1) (69.6)	112 (14.5) (54.4)	41 (5.3) (11.7)	17 (2.2) (1.9)	22 (2.9) (1.7)	770 (100) (21.4)
Non-residential With Dwelling	132 (50.9) (15.9)	45 (17.4) (21.8)	34 (13.1) (9.7)	38 (14.7) (4.3)	10 (3.9) (0.8)	259 (100) (7.2)
All Types	830 (23.1) (100)	206 (5.7) (100)	351 (9.8) (100)	877 (24.4) (100)	1,329 (37.0) (100)	3,593 (100) (100)

Sample: PHY3

Table A 3.4 Purpose-built flats: storey height by construction date

thousands/% dwellings

	Pre-1919	1919–1944	1945–1964	Post-1964	All Ages
1–5	150 (6.9) (88.8)	251 (11.6) (90.9)	699 (32.3) (85.0)	1,064 (49.2) (82.0)	2,164 (100) (84.5)
6–11	19 (8.4) (11.2)	25 (11.1) (9.1)	90 (40.0) (11.0)	91 (40.5) (7.0)	225 (100) (8.8)
12 or more	—	—	33 (18.9) (4.0)	142 (81.1) (11.0)	175 (100) (6.7)
All Flats	169 (6.6) (100)	276 (10.8) (100)	822 (32.0) (100)	1,297 (50.6) (100)	2,564 (100) (100)

Sample: PHY15

Table A 3.5 Dwelling size: type[1] by construction date

thousand dwellings
median internal floor area (sq m)
median number of habitable rooms

	Terraced Houses	Semi-detached Houses	Detached Houses	Purpose-built Flats	Converted Flats	Non-Residential with Dwelling	All Houses	All Flats
Pre-1900	1,826	482	554	120	578	132	2,862	830
	78.6	92.3	137.5	58.8	60.3	82.5	87.3	63.2
	6	6	7	5	4	5	6	5
1900–1918	746	224	127	49	112	45	1,097	206
	80.8	92.2	137.7	64.4	60.2	68.1	85.9	63.9
	6	6	8	5	4	5	6	5
1919–1944	993	1,950	667	276	41	34	3,610	351
	68.7	76.6	100.4	49.1	65.3	81.4	76.4	51.4
	5	6	6	4	4	5	6	4
1945–1964	876	1,906	810	822	17	38	3,592	877
	72.8	75.1	95.1	49.5	72.0	67.1	76.0	50.5
	5	6	6	4	4	5	5	4
Post-1964	1,273	1,251	1,500	1,297	22	10	4,024	1,329
	73.5	70.1	95.8	44.0	56.4	56.8	77.3	44.8
	5	5	6	4	4	4	5	4
All Ages	5,714	5,813	3,658	2,564	770	259	15,185	3,593
	74.4	75.7	100.5	46.8	61.6	70.2	78.4	50.9
	5	6	6	4	4	5	6	4

Sample: PHY1

[1] Excludes temporary dwellings

Table A 3.6 Plot size of houses by construction date

thousands/% dwellings

Plot Size	Pre-1900	1900–1918	1919–1944	1945–1964	Post-1964	All Ages
1–200m²	1,597 (27.3) (55.8)	679 (11.6) (61.9)	945 (16.2) (26.2)	858 (14.7) (23.8)	1,765 (30.2) (43.3)	5,844 (100) (38.3)
200–500m²	676 (9.2) (23.6)	330 (4.5) (30.1)	2,159 (29.2) (59.7)	2,261 (30.6) (62.8)	1,960 (26.5) (48.1)	7,386 (100) (48.5)
500–700m²	416 (30.3) (14.5)	46 (3.4) (4.2)	343 (25.0) (9.5)	308 (22.4) (8.6)	259 (18.9) (6.4)	1,372 (100) (9.0)
700–1,000m²	34 (11.2) (1.2)	17 (5.6) (1.5)	93 (30.6) (2.6)	105 (34.5) (2.9)	55 (18.1) (1.3)	304 (100) (2.0)
Over 1,000m²	140 (41.2) (4.9)	25 (7.3) (2.3)	72 (21.2) (2.0)	67 (19.7) (1.9)	36 (10.6) (0.9)	340 (100) (2.2)
All Sizes	2,863 (18.8) (100)	1,097 (7.2) (100)	3,612 (23.7) (100)	3,599 (23.6) (100)	4,075 (26.7) (100)	15,246 (100) (100)

Sample: PHY2

Table A 3.7 Parking provision by tenure

thousands/% dwellings

	Owner Occupied	Private Rented	Local Authority/ New Town	Housing Association	Vacant	All Tenures
Integral Garage	1,064 (91.4) (9.0)	19 (1.6) (1.5)	58 (5.0) (1.2)	2 (0.2) (0.5)	21 (1.8) (2.6)	1,164 (100) (6.2)
Garage on Plot	5,176 (88.6) (43.8)	205 (3.5) (16.5)	332 (5.7) (7.4)	19 (0.3) (4.1)	112 (1.9) (13.7)	5,844 (100) (31.0)
Space on Plot	1,655 (55.9) (14.0)	250 (8.5) (20.1)	750 (25.3) (16.7)	142 (4.8) (30.1)	163 (5.5) (20.0)	2,960 (100) (15.7)
Garage/Space Elsewhere	674 (42.8) (5.7)	78 (4.9) (6.3)	688 (43.7) (15.3)	78 (4.9) (16.3)	58 (3.7) (7.2)	1,576 (100) (8.4)
Adequate Street Parking	2,116 (44.0) (17.9)	396 (8.2) (31.8)	1,886 (39.2) (42.0)	156 (3.2) (33.0)	258 (5.4) (31.8)	4,812 (100) (25.6)
Inadequate Street Parking	1,005 (46.6) (8.5)	224 (10.4) (18.0)	700 (32.4) (15.6)	69 (3.2) (14.5)	159 (7.4) (19.6)	2,157 (100) (11.4)
No Parking Provision	130 (39.9) (1.1)	72 (22.0) (5.8)	76 (23.3) (1.7)	7 (2.2) (1.5)	41 (12.6) (5.1)	326 (100) (1.7)
All Dwellings	11,820 (62.7) (100)	1,244 (6.7) (100)	4,490 (23.8) (100)	473 (2.5) (100)	812 (4.3) (100)	18,839 (100) (100)

Sample: PHY1

84

Table A 3.8   Tenure: type of dwelling by construction date

	Pre-1919	1919–1944	1945–1964	Post-1964	All Ages
Owner Occupied					
Houses	2,935 (27.1) (87.0)	2,531 (23.3) (95.7)	2,231 (20.6) (94.7)	3,148 (29.0) (91.3)	10,845 (100) (91.7)
Purpose-built Flats	65 (11.9) (1.9)	84 (15.4) (3.2)	108 (19.9) (4.6)	286 (52.8) (8.3)	543 (100) (4.6)
Converted Flats & Dwellings with Non-residential	374 (86.6) (11.1)	30 (6.9) (1.1)	17 (3.9) (0.7)	11 (2.6) (0.4)	432 (100) (3.7)
All Types	3,374 (28.5)	2,645 (22.4)	2,356 (19.9)	3,445 (29.2)	11,820
Private Rented					
Houses	577 (67.7) (67.0)	131 (15.4) (70.4)	100 (11.7) (70.4)	44 (5.2) (80.0)	852 (100) (68.5)
Purpose-built Flats	28 (28.9) (3.3)	30 (30.9) (16.1)	30 (30.9) (21.1)	9 (9.3) (16.4)	97 (100) (7.8)
Converted Flats & Dwellings with Non-residential	256 (86.8) (29.7)	35 (8.5) (13.5)	12 (4.1) (8.5)	2 (0.6) (3.6)	295 (100) (23.7)
All types	861 (69.2)	186 (15.0)	142 (11.4)	55 (4.4)	1,244
Local Authority/New Town					
Houses	103 (3.6) (62.0)	831 (29.0) (86.9)	1,203 (42.0) (64.5)	724 (25.4) (48.2)	2,861 (100) (63.7)
Purpose-built Flats	34 (2.2) (20.5)	113 (7.2) (11.8)	648 (41.5) (34.8)	767 (49.1) (51.0)	1,562 (100) (34.8)
Converted Flats & Dwellings with Non-residential	29 (43.3) (17.5)	12 (17.9) (1.3)	13 (19.4) (0.7)	13 (19.4) (0.8)	67 (100) (1.5)
All Types	166 (3.7)	956 (21.3)	1,864 (41.5)	1,504 (33.5)	4,490
Housing Association					
Houses	69 (42.1) (41.6)	16 (9.8) (33.3)	3 (1.8) (60.0)	76 (46.3) (29.9)	164 (100) (34.7)
Purpose-built Flats	21 (9.2) (12.6)	31 (13.5) (64.6)	2 (0.9) (40.0)	175 (76.4) (68.1)	229 (100) (48.4)
Converted Flats & Dwellings with Non-residential	76 (95.0) (45.8)	1 (1.2) (2.1)	—	3 (3.8) (1.2)	80 (100) (16.9)
All Types	166 (35.1)	48 (10.1)	5 (1.1)	254 (53.7)	473
Vacant Dwellings					
Houses	276 (52.7) (64.3)	103 (19.7) (80.5)	62 (11.8) (56.9)	83 (15.8) (56.8)	524 (100) (64.5)
Purpose-built Flats	21 (15.8) (4.9)	18 (13.5) (14.0)	34 (25.6) (31.2)	60 (45.1) (41.1)	133 (100) (16.4)
Converted Flats & Dwellings with Non-residential	132 (85.2) (30.8)	7 (4.5) (5.5)	13 (8.4) (11.9)	3 (1.9) (2.1)	155 (100) (19.1)
All Types	429 (52.8)	128 (15.8)	109 (13.4)	146 (18.0)	812
All Tenures					
Houses	3,960 (26.0) (79.2)	3,612 (23.7) (91.1)	3,599 (23.6) (80.5)	4,075 (26.7) (75.4)	15,246 (100) (80.9)
Purpose-built Flats	169 (6.6) (3.4)	276 (10.8) (7.0)	822 (32.0) (18.3)	1,297 (50.6) (24.0)	2,564 (100) (13.6)
Converted Flats & Dwellings with Non-residential	867 (84.4) (17.4)	75 (7.3) (1.9)	55 (5.3) (1.2)	32 (3.0) (0.6)	1,029 (100) (5.5)
All Types	4,996 (26.5)	3,863 (21.0)	4,476 (23.8)	5,404 (28.7)	18,839

Sample: PHY1

85

Table A 3.9   Tenure by type of dwelling

thousands/% dwellings

	Owner Occupied	Private Rented	Local Authority/ New Town	Housing Association	Vacant	All Tenures
Terraced Houses	3,325 (58.2) (28.1)	405 (7.1) (32.6)	1,578 (27.6) (35.2)	135 (2.4) (28.6)	271 (4.7) (33.4)	5,714 (100) (30.3)
Semi-detached Houses	4,135 (71.1) (35.0)	259 (4.5) (20.8)	1,232 (21.2) (27.4)	29 (0.5) (6.1)	158 (2.7) (19.5)	5,813 (100) (30.9)
Detached Houses	3,333 (91.1) (28.2)	184 (5.0) (14.8)	46 (1.3) (1.0)	—	95 (2.6) (11.7)	3,658 (100) (19.4)
Temporary Dwellings	52 (85.2) (0.4)	4 (6.6) (0.3)	5 (8.2) (0.1)	—	—	61 (100) (0.3)
Purpose-built Flats	543 (21.2) (4.6)	97 (3.8) (7.8)	1,562 (60.9) (34.8)	229 (8.9) (48.4)	133 (5.2) (16.3)	2,564 (100) (13.6)
Converted Flats	339 (44.0) (2.9)	213 (27.7) (17.1)	51 (6.6) (1.1)	80 (10.4) (16.9)	87 (11.3) (10.7)	770 (100) (4.1)
Non-residential with Dwellings	93 (35.9) (0.8)	82 (31.7) (6.6)	16 (6.1) (0.4)	—	68 (26.3) (8.4)	259 (100) (1.4)
All Dwellings	11,820 (62.7) (100)	1,244 (6.7) (100)	4,490 (23.8) (100)	473 (2.5) (100)	812 (4.3) (100)	18,839 (100) (100)

Sample: PHY1

Table A 3.10   Occupied post-1944 purpose built flats: tenure and construction date by number of storeys

thousands/% dwellings

	Private Sector[1] 1945–1964	Post-1964	Local Authority/New Town 1945–1964	Post-1964
1–5	132 (94.3)	428 (91.0)	544 (84.0)	591 (77.1)
6–11	7 (5.0)	28 (6.0)	72 (11.1)	61 (8.0)
12 or more	1 (0.7)	14 (3.0)	32 (4.9)	115 (14.9)
All Occupied Purpose-built flats	140 (100)	470 (100)	648 (100)	767 (100)

Sample: PHY15

[1] Includes owner occupied, private rented, housing association

86

Table A 3.11   Dwelling size: occupied houses and flats[1] by tenure

thousand dwellings
median internal floor area (sq m)
median number of habitable rooms

	Owner Occupied	Private Rented	Local Authority/ New Town	Housing Association	All Tenures
House	10,793	848	2,856	164	14,661
	82.6	75.9	71.0	76.5	78.4
	6	6	5	5	6
Flat	975	391	1,629	310	3,305
	60.8	56.1	45.6	45.3	50.9
	4	4	4	4	4
All Occupied Dwellings	11,768	1,239	4,485	474	17,966
	81.5	69.7	65.1	56.9	75.1
	6	5	5	4	5

Sample: PHY11
1 Excludes temporary dwellings.

Table A 3.12   Plot size of houses by tenure

thousands/% dwellings

	Owner Occupied	Private Rented	Local Authority/ New Town	Housing Association	Vacant	All Tenures
1–200m²	3,677 (62.9) (33.9)	379 (6.5) (44.5)	1,332 (22.8) (46.6)	142 (2.4) (86.6)	314 (5.4) (60.0)	5,844 (100) (38.3)
200–500m²	5,432 (73.6) (50.1)	356 (4.8) (41.8)	1,407 (19.0) (49.1)	22 (0.3) (13.4)	169 (2.3) (32.3)	7,386 (100) (48.5)
500–700m²	1,178 (85.9) (10.9)	65 (4.7) (7.6)	102 (7.4) (3.6)	—	27 (2.0) (5.1)	1,372 (100) (9.0)
700–1,000m²	262 (86.2) (2.4)	18 (5.9) (2.1)	16 (5.3) (0.6)	—	8 (2.6) (1.5)	304 (100) (2.0)
Over 1,000m²	296 (87.0) (2.7)	34 (10.0) (4.0)	4 (1.2) (0.1)	—	6 (1.8) (1.1)	340 (100) (2.2)
All Houses	10,845 (71.1) (100)	852 (5.6) (100)	2,861 (18.8) (100)	164 (1.1) (100)	524 (3.4) (100)	15,246 (100) (100)

Sample: PHY2

Table A 3.13   Multi-occupancy by construction date

thousands/% dwellings

	Pre-1919	1919–1944	1945–1964	Post-1964	All Ages
Dwellings with 2 Household Spaces[1]	67 (51.5) (51.5)	21 (16.2) (72.4)	23 (17.7) (85.2)	19 (14.6) (76.0)	130 (100) (61.6)
Dwellings with 3–6 Household Spaces	42 (79.3) (32.3)	6 (11.3) (20.7)	—	5 (9.4) (20.0)	53 (100) (25.1)
Dwellings with 7 or More Household Spaces	21 (75.0) (16.2)	2 (7.1) (6.9)	4 (14.3) (14.8)	1 (3.6) (4.0)	28 (100) (13.3)
All Dwellings	130 (61.6) (100)	29 (13.7) (100)	27 (12.8) (100)	25 (11.9) (100)	211 (100) (100)

Sample: PHY12
[1] Household space = vacant and occupied

Table A 3.14 Type of dwelling by construction type

thousands/% dwellings

	Terraced Houses	Semi-detached Houses	Detached Houses	Temporary Dwellings	Purpose-built Flats	Converted Flats	Non-Residential with Dwelling	All Types
Traditional	5,343 (31.2) (93.5)	5,501 (32.0) (94.6)	3,529 (20.6) (96.5)	5 (0.0) (8.2)	1,761 (10.3) (68.7)	766 (4.5) (99.5)	241 (1.4) (93.1)	17,146 (100) (91.0)
Non-Traditional	371 (21.9) (6.5)	312 (18.4) (5.4)	129 (7.6) (3.5)	56 (3.3) (91.8)	803 (47.5) (31.3)	4 (0.2) (0.5)	18 (1.1) (6.9)	1,693 (100) (9.0)
All Dwellings	5,714 (30.3) (100)	5,813 (30.9) (100)	3,658 (19.4) (100)	61 (0.3) (100)	2,564 (13.6) (100)	770 (4.1) (100)	259 (1.4) (100)	18,839 (100) (100)

Sample: PHY1

Table A 3.15 Tenure by construction type

thousands/% dwellings

	Owner Occupied	Private Rented	Local Authority/ New Town	Housing Association	Vacant	Total
Traditional	11,341 (66.1) (96.0)	1,175 (6.9) (94.5)	3,460 (20.2) (77.1)	420 (2.4) (88.8)	749 (4.4) (92.4)	17,146 (100) (91.0)
Non-Traditional	479 (28.3) (4.0)	69 (4.1) (5.5)	1,029 (60.8) (22.9)	53 (3.1) (11.2)	63 (3.7) (7.6)	1,693 (100) (9.0)
All Dwellings	11,820 (100) (100)	1,244 (100) (100)	4,490 (100) (100)	473 (100) (100)	812 (100) (100)	18,839 (100) (100)

Sample: PHY1

Table A 3.16 Mean market value by region and tenure

	Owner Occupied	Private Rented	Local Authority/ New Town	Housing Association	Vacant	All Tenures
Northern	£26,800	£25,300	£16,500	£17,100	£16,600	£22,600
Yorks & Humbs	£27,600	£26,700	£16,200	£17,900	£19,700	£23,100
North West	£34,100	£13,500	£16,400	£20,100	£16,000	£27,800
East Midlands	£36,800	£19,700	£20,600	£20,900	£21,200	£31,200
West Midlands	£32,300	£16,800	£18,700	£19,500	£21,800	£26,500
South West	£55,900	£44,400	£27,200	£40,300	£40,400	£48,700
East Anglia	£47,100	£40,000	£28,700	£21,500	£35,500	£40,800
Inner London	£92,900	£71,400	£48,800	£56,900	£89,700	£72,100
Outer London	£70,800	£60,800	£46,200	£41,300	£53,100	£64,000
Rest of South East	£66,700	£44,200	£41,100	£38,200	£48,400	£59,200
All Regions	£49,500	£36,500	£27,500	£29,900	£36,600	£42,200

Sample: PHY1

Table A 3.17 Mean market value by dwelling type and tenure

	Terraced Houses	Semi-detached Houses	Detached Houses	Temporary Dwellings	Purpose-built Flats	Converted Flats & Dwellings with Non-Residential
Owner Occupied	£36,500	£42,200	£69,600	£12,100	£45,700	£46,300
Private Rented	£36,900	£32,900	£56,800	–	£35,000	£35,700
Local Authority/ New Town	£29,100	£26,200	£37,400	£11,800	£26,300	£37,700
Housing Association	£21,800	£28,300	–	–	£33,700	£47,100
Vacant	£30,900	£35,300	£56,100	–	£35,200	£40,300
All Dwelling Types	£33,600	£38,000	£68,900	£12,100	£29,900	£40,900

Sample: PHY1

Table A 3.18 Multi-occupancy by region

thousands/% dwellings

	Not Multi-occupied	Multi-occupied	All Dwellings
Northern	1,225 (98.5) (6.6)	19 (1.5) (9.0)	1,244 (100) (6.6)
Yorkshire and Humberside	1,928 (99.1) (10.3)	17 (0.9) (8.1)	1,945 (100) (10.3)
North West	2,505 (99.1) (13.4)	22 (0.9) (10.4)	2,527 (100) (13.4)
East Midlands	1,533 (99.3) (8.2)	11 (0.7) (5.2)	1,544 (100) (8.2)
West Midlands	1,987 (98.9) (10.7)	22 (1.1) (10.4)	2,009 (100) (10.7)
South West	1,841 (99.4) (9.9)	11 (0.6) (5.2)	1,852 (100) (9.8)
East Anglia	802 (99.0) (4.3)	8 (1.0) (3.8)	810 (100) (4.3)
Inner London	1,113 (97.9) (6.0)	24 (2.1) (11.4)	1,137 (100) (6.0)
Outer London	1,649 (98.4) (8.9)	26 (1.6) (12.3)	1,675 (100) (8.9)
Rest of South East	4,045 (98.8) (21.7)	51 (1.2) (24.2)	4,096 (100) (21.8)
All Regions	18,628 (98.9) (100)	211 (1.1) (100)	18,839 (100) (100)

Sample: PHY1

Table A 3.19   Vacancy by region

thousands/% dwellings

	Occupied	Vacant	All Dwellings
Northern	1,200 (96.5) (6.7)	44 (3.5) (5.4)	1,244 (100) (6.6)
Yorkshire and Humberside	1,856 (95.4) (10.3)	89 (4.6) (10.9)	1,945 (100) (10.3)
North West	2,395 (94.8) (13.3)	132 (5.2) (16.2)	2,527 (100) (13.2)
East Midlands	1,487 (96.3) (8.2)	57 (3.7) (7.0)	1,544 (100) (8.2)
West Midlands	1,925 (95.8) (10.7)	84 (4.2) (10.3)	2,009 (100) (10.7)
South West	1,760 (95.0) (9.8)	92 (5.0) (11.3)	1,852 (100) (9.8)
East Anglia	770 (95.1) (4.3)	40 (4.9) (4.9)	810 (100) (4.3)
Inner London	1,051 (92.4) (5.8)	86 (7.6) (10.6)	1,137 (100) (6.0)
Outer London	1,615 (96.4) (9.0)	60 (3.6) (7.4)	1,675 (100) (8.9)
Rest of South East	3,968 (96.9) (21.9)	128 (3.1) (16.0)	4,096 (100) (21.8)
All Regions	18,027 (95.7) (100)	812 (4.3) (100)	18,839 (100) (100)

Sample: PHY1

Table A 4.1 Basic amenities by tenure

thousands/% dwellings

	Owner Occupied	Private Rented	Local Authority/New Town	Housing Association	Vacant	All Tenures
All Amenities Present	11,676 (63.5) (98.8)	1,142 (6.2) (91.8)	4,418 (24.1) (98.4)	468 (2.5) (98.9)	672 (3.7) (82.8)	18,376 (100) (97.5)
Lacking One or More Amenities	144 (31.1) (1.2)	102 (22.0) (8.2)	72 (15.6) (1.6)	5 (1.1) (1.1)	140 (30.2) (17.2)	463 (100) (2.5)
Lacking Sink	24 (0.2)	11 (0.9)	—	—	40 (4.9)	75 (0.4)
Lacking Indoor WC	36 (0.3)	44 (3.5)	22 (0.5)	—	37 (4.6)	139 (0.7)
Lacking Bath/Shower	52 (0.4)	44 (3.5)	23 (0.5)	2 (0.4)	49 (6.0)	170 (0.9)
Lacking Wash Hand Basin	47 (0.4)	59 (4.7)	23 (0.5)	2 (0.4)	75 (9.2)	206 (1.1)
Lacking H&C Water at 3 Points	106 (0.9)	86 (6.9)	45 (1.0)	5 (1.1)	44 (5.4)	286 (1.5)
All Dwellings	11,820	1,244	4,490	473	812	18,839

Sample: PHY1

Table A 4.2 Type of hot water systems by condition

thousands/% dwellings

	In Good Order	Repair/Replace	No System	All Dwellings
Central Hot Water System	18,255 (99.0) (98.9)	188 (1.0) (83.2)	—	18,443 (100) (97.9)
Individual Heaters	207 (84.5) (1.1)	38 (15.5) (16.8)	—	245 (100) (1.3)
No System	—	—	151 (100) (100)	151 (100) (0.8)
All Dwellings	18,462 (98.0) (100)	266 (1.2) (100)	151 (0.8) (100)	18,839 (100) (100)

Sample: PHY1

Table A 4.3 Adequacy of space in the kitchen/bathroom by tenure

thousands/% dwellings

	Owner Occupied		Private Rented		Local Authority/New Town		Housing Association		Vacant		All Tenures	
	Kitchen	Bathroom	Kitchen	Bathroom	Kitchen	Bathroom	Kitchen	Bathroom	Kitchen	Bathroom	Kitchen	Bathroom
Adequate Space	11,633 (98.4)	11,568 (97.9)	1,172 (94.2)	1,163 (93.5)	4,395 (97.9)	4,354 (97.0)	462 (97.7)	451 (95.4)	804 (99.0)	759 (93.5)	18,466 (98.0)	18,295 (97.1)
Inadequate Space	187 (1.6)	200 (11.7)	72 (5.8)	37 (3.0)	95 (2.1)	113 (2.5)	11 (2.3)	20 (4.2)	8 (1.0)	4 (0.5)	373 (2.0)	374 (2.0)
No Bathroom		52 (0.4)		44 (3.5)		23 (0.5)		2 (0.4)		49 (6.0)		170 (0.9)
All Dwellings	11,820 (100)	11,820 (100)	1,244 (100)	1,244 (100)	4,490 (100)	4,490 (100)	473 (100)	473 (100)	812 (100)	812 (100)	18,839 (100)	18,839 (100)

Sample: PHY1

Table A 4.4 Type of drainage by area and tenure

	Rural Areas					All Urban Dwellings	All Rural Dwellings	All Areas
	Owner Occupied	Private Rented	Local Authority/ New Town	Housing Association	Vacant			
Mains Drainage	1,327 (71.6) (77.7)	172 (9.3) (53.1)	277 (14.9) (95.2)	5 (0.3) (100)	73 (3.9) (63.5)	16,346 (89.8) (99.7)	1,854 (10.2) (75.9)	18,200 (96.6)
Other Drainage	382 (64.7) (22.3)	152 (25.8) (46.9)	14 (2.4) (4.8)	—	42 (7.1) (36.5)	49 (7.7) (0.3)	590 (92.3) (24.1)	639 (3.4)
All Types	1,709 (69.9) (100)	324 (13.3) (100)	291 (11.9) (100)	5 (0.2) (100)	115 (4.7) (100)	16,395 (87.0) (100)	2,444 (13.0) (100)	18,839 (100)

Sample: PHY1

Table A 4.5 Heating systems: type and adequacy

System	Adequate	Inadequate	All Systems
Central Heating >60%	10,830 (99.8) (63.3)	27 (0.2) (1.6)	10,857 (100) (57.7)
Central Heating ≤60%	2,674 (93.4) (15.6)	188 (6.6) (10.8)	2,862 (100) (15.2)
Other Fixed Heating Only	3,503 (72.0) (20.5)	1,364 (28.0) (78.5)	4,867 (100) (25.8)
No Fixed Heating	95 (37.5) (0.6)	158 (62.5) (9.1)	253 (100) (1.3)
All Types of Heating	17,102 (90.8) (100)	1,737 (9.2) (100)	18,839 (100) (100)

Sample: PHY1

Table A 4.6   Type of central heating

System	Fuel type						All Fuels
	Mains Gas	Electricity	Fuel Oil	Solid Fuel	Communal	Bottle Gas or Other	
Waterborne Single Purpose Boiler	6,929 (87.3) (68.0)	36 (0.4) (2.7)	499 (6.3) (92.8)	292 (3.7) (21.8)	151 (1.9) (59.7)	31 (0.4) (41.9)	7,938 (100) (57.9)
Waterborne Back Boiler	2,420 (69.1) (23.8)	—	25 (0.7) (4.6)	1,030 (29.4) (76.9)	—	25 (0.7) (33.8)	3,500 (100) (25.5)
Ducted Air	668 (78.7) (6.6)	129 (15.2) (9.7)	14 (1.6) (2.6)	—	38 (4.5) (15.0)	—	849 (100) (6.2)
Under Floor	—	160 (96.4) (12.0)	—	—	6 (3.6) (2.4)	—	166 (100) (1.2)
Ceiling Heating	97 (59.1) (0.9)	67 (40.9) (5.0)	—	—	—	—	164 (100) (1.2)
Storage Heaters	—	924 (100) (69.5)	—	—	—	—	924 (100) (6.7)
Other	70 (39.3) (0.7)	15 (8.4) (1.1)	—	17 (9.6) (1.3)	58 (32.6) (22.9)	18 (10.1) (24.3)	178 (100) (1.3)
All Systems	10,184 (74.2) (100)	1,331 (9.7) (100)	538 (3.9) (100)	1,339 (9.8) (100)	253 (1.9) (100)	74 (0.5) (100)	13,719 (100) (100)

Sample: PHY19

Table A 4.7   Type of heating (where no central heating)

System	Fuel Type					All Fuels
	Mains Gas	Electricity	Solid Fuel	Bottle Gas, Fuel Oil or Paraffin	None	
Convectors	804 (89.8) (24.2)	91 (10.2) (15.2)	—	—	—	895 (100) (17.5)
Stove/Range	13 (6.6) (0.4)	—	173 (88.3) (16.1)	10 (5.1) (15.2)	—	196 (100) (3.8)
Radiant/Open Fire	2,454 (66.8) (73.9)	304 (8.3) (50.7)	902 (24.5) (83.9)	16 (0.4) (24.2)	—	3,676 (100) (71.8)
Oil Radiator	—	17 (100) (2.8)	—	—	—	17 (100) (0.3)
Other Fixed	49 (59.0) (1.5)	34 (41.0) (5.7)	—	—	—	83 (100) (1.6)
Portable Only	—	154 (79.4) (25.7)	—	40 (20.6) (60.6)	—	194 (100) (3.8)
No Heating Seen	—	—	—	—	59 (100) (100)	59 (100) (1.2)
All Systems	3,320 (64.8) (100)	600 (11.7) (100)	1,075 (21.0) (100)	66 (1.3) (100)	59 (1.2) (100)	5,120 (100)

Sample: PHY18

Table A 4.8 Dwellings with defective services by construction date and tenure

thousands/% dwellings defective

	Cold Water Supply	Hot Water Supply	Cooking and Waste	Drainage/ Sanitary Conveniences	Heating	Electrical System — All Defects	Electrical System — Rewiring	All Dwellings
Construction Date								
Pre-1900	50 (1.4)	166 (4.5)	446 (12.1)	234 (6.3)	509 (13.8)	699 (18.9)	365 (9.9)	3,694
1900–1919	12 (0.9)	54 (4.1)	150 (11.5)	62 (4.8)	156 (12.0)	227 (17.4)	98 (7.5)	1,302
1919–1944	6 (0.2)	61 (1.5)	349 (8.8)	120 (3.0)	384 (9.7)	506 (12.8)	208 (5.2)	3,963
1945–1964	3 (0.1)	51 (1.1)	344 (7.7)	62 (1.4)	511 (11.4)	585 (13.1)	286 (6.4)	4,476
Post-1964	9 (0.2)	45 (0.8)	71 (1.3)	25 (0.5)	191 (3.5)	130 (2.4)	23 (0.4)	5,404
Tenure								
Owner Occupied	25 (0.2)	99 (0.8)	507 (4.3)	177 (1.5)	584 (4.9)	1,143 (9.7)	497 (4.2)	11,820
Private Rented	13 (1.1)	57 (4.6)	248 (19.9)	99 (8.0)	293 (23.6)	358 (28.8)	196 (15.8)	1,244
Local Authority/ New Town	7 (0.2)	48 (1.1)	451 (10.0)	118 (2.6)	726 (16.2)	507 (11.3)	244 (5.4)	4,490
Housing Association	2 (0.4)	14 (3.0)	13 (2.8)	10 (2.1)	46 (9.7)	24 (5.1)	2 (0.4)	473
Vacant	33 (4.1)	159 (19.6)	141 (17.4)	99 (12.2)	101 (12.4)	113 (13.9)	41 (5.1)	812
All Defective Dwellings	80 (0.4)	377 (2.0)	1,360 (7.2)	503 (2.7)	1,750 (9.3)	2,145 (11.4)	980 (5.2)	18,839

Sample: PHY1

Table A 4.9 Provision of insulation and double glazing by construction date

thousands/% households

	Pre-1900	1900–1919	1919–1944	1945–1964	Post-1964	All Ages
Loft Insulation						
Not Applicable (No Loft)	438 (20.3) (13.9)	120 (5.6) (9.6)	155 (7.2) (3.9)	509 (23.6) (11.5)	931 (43.3) (16.9)	2,153 (11.8)
Insulation	1,767 (13.8) (55.9)	824 (6.4) (66.2)	3,048 (23.7) (77.4)	3,336 (26.0) (75.6)	3,861 (30.1) (70.0)	12,836 (70.2)
No Insulation	734 (37.0) (23.2)	158 (8.0) (12.7)	532 (26.8) (13.5)	321 (16.2) (7.3)	239 (12) (4.3)	1,984 (10.9)
Don't Know	221 (17.0) (7.0)	144 (11.1) (11.5)	205 (15.7) (5.2)	245 (18.8) (5.6)	488 (37.4) (8.8)	1,303 (7.1)
Wall Insulation						
Insulation	193 (7.5) (6.1)	82 (3.2) (6.6)	340 (13.2) (8.6)	541 (20.9) (12.3)	1,427 (55.2) (25.9)	2,583 (14.2)
No Insulation	2,714 (19.9) (85.9)	999 (7.3) (80.2)	3,306 (24.3) (83.9)	3,433 (25.2) (77.8)	3,175 (23.3) (57.5)	13,627 (74.5)
Don't Know	253 (12.2) (8.0)	165 (8.0) (13.2)	294 (14.2) (7.5)	437 (21.2) (9.9)	917 (44.4) (16.6)	2,066 (11.2)
Double Glazing						
No Double Glazing	2,223 (18.8) (70.4)	853 (7.2) (68.5)	2,361 (20.0) (59.9)	2,996 (25.4) (67.9)	3,378 (28.6) (61.2)	11,811 (64.6)
Less Than Whole Dwelling Double Glazed	639 (16.3) (20.2)	318 (8.1) (25.5)	1,023 (26.1) (26.0)	932 (23.8) (21.1)	1,010 (25.7) (18.3)	3,922 (21.5)
Whole Dwelling Double Glazed	298 (11.7) (9.4)	75 (2.9) (6.0)	556 (21.9) (14.1)	483 (19.0) (11.0)	1,131 (44.5) (20.5)	2,543 (13.9)
All Households	3,160 (17.3)	1,246 (6.8)	3,940 (21.6)	4,411 (24.1)	5,519 (30.2)	18,276

Sample: I1

Table A 4.10   Cost of repair by construction date

£/dwelling

% Dwellings	Pre-1900	1900–1918	1919–1944	1945–1964	Post-1964	All Ages
2	10,600	7,500	4,800	3,250	1,720	5,900
5	7,500	5,400	3,400	2,200	990	3,900
10	5,400	4,000	2,500	1,530	580	2,600
25	3,100	2,400	1,420	540	200	1,200
50	1,370	1,140	610	300	20	350
75	430	400	165	30	0	10

Sample: PHY1

Table A 4.11   Cost of repair by tenure

£/dwelling

% Dwellings	Owner Occupied	Local Authority	Private Rented	Housing Association	Vacant	All Tenures
2	5,800	3,600	9,700	4,300	12,500	5,900
5	3,800	2,500	6,800	2,400	8,100	3,900
10	2,550	1,750	4,900	1,270	5,500	2,600
25	1,100	850	2,750	380	2,700	1,200
50	315	285	1,200	55	800	350
75	0	40	320	0	75	10

Sample: PHY1

Table A 4.12 Dwellings requiring some repair to the main building elements by date of construction

thousands/% dwellings

	Pre-1900	1900–1918	1919–1944	1945–1964	Post-1964	All Ages
(External)						
Chimneys	1,815 (49.1)	660 (50.7)	1,524 (38.5)	1,147 (25.6)	232 (4.3)	5,378 (28.5)
Roof Structure	953 (25.8)	225 (17.3)	328 (8.3)	174 (3.9)	116 (2.1)	1,796 (9.5)
Roof Covering	1,826 (49.4)	600 (46.1)	1,298 (32.8)	650 (14.5)	258 (4.8)	4,632 (24.6)
Wall Structure	735 (19.9)	195 (15.0)	428 (10.8)	329 (7.4)	149 (2.8)	1,836 (9.7)
Wall Surface	1,890 (51.2)	637 (48.9)	1,592 (40.2)	1,053 (23.5)	598 (11.1)	5,770 (30.6)
Windows	1,727 (46.8)	570 (43.8)	1,486 (37.5)	1,223 (27.3)	761 (14.1)	5,767 (30.6)
External Doors	919 (24.9)	295 (22.7)	821 (20.7)	693 (15.5)	544 (10.1)	3,272 (17.4)
DPC	269 (7.3)	107 (8.2)	174 (4.4)	84 (1.9)	34 (0.6)	668 (3.5)
Drainage	1,554 (42.1)	527 (40.5)	1,062 (26.8)	907 (20.3)	420 (7.8)	4,470 (23.7)
(Internal)						
Floors	1,557 (42.1)	498 (13.5)	1,056 (26.6)	744 (16.6)	496 (9.2)	4,351 (23.1)
Internal Walls	1,826 (49.4)	550 (42.2)	1,217 (30.7)	884 (19.7)	596 (11.0)	5,073 (26.9)
Ceilings	1,773 (48.0)	588 (45.2)	1,487 (37.5)	1,433 (32.0)	703 (13.0)	5,984 (31.8)
Total Dwellings Requiring Some Repairs to at Least One Element	4,396 (88.0)		3,250 (82.0)	3,133 (70.0)	2,270 (42.0)	13,049 (69.3)
All Dwellings	4,996		3,963	4,476	5,404	18,839

Sample: PHY1

Table A 4.13 Defects in dwellings of non-traditional construction

thousands/% defective dwellings

	No Defects	Defects			All Dwellings
		Urgent and Widespread	All Urgent	All Defects	
Dwellings with Private Balconies	729 (93.5)	9 (1.2)	29 (3.7)	51 (6.5)	780
Dwellings with Concrete in their Construction — Frame Spalling	1,069 (93.0)	16 (1.4)	45 (3.9)	81 (7.0)	1,150
Dwellings with Concrete Panels — Panel Spalling	855 (92.9)	14 (1.5)	33 (3.6)	65 (7.1)	920
Dwellings with the Jointed Panels — Panel Disjointing	461 (94.1)	18 (3.7)	15 (3.1)	29 (5.9)	490

Sample: PHY21

96

Table A 4.14 Cost of repair by construction date and distribution of cost between building elements

	Pre-1870	1870–1899	1900–1918	1919–1944	1945–1964	Post-1964	All Ages
Mean Repair Cost (£)	2,940	1,960	1,710	1,010	600	210	969
							(% of mean repair cost)
External Structure	70	72	73	74	66	61	71
Internal Structure	26	24	22	20	22	30	23
Amenities/Services	4	4	5	6	12	9	6
External							
Chimneys	9	12	14	14	13	6	12
Roofs	21	21	21	17	9	13	18
Walls	19	17	17	19	19	14	18
Windows/Doors	11	13	13	18	20	23	16
Damp Proof Course	8	7	6	3	1	3	5
Internal							
Internal Floors	8	5	4	3	2	2	4
Walls/Ceilings	14	16	15	13	14	20	15

Sample: PHY1

Table A 4.15 Cost of repair by construction date and distribution of cost between building elements, for post-1944 dwellings

	Houses				Flats			
	1944–64		1964 +		1944–64		1964 +	
	Trad	Non-Trad	Trad	Non-Trad	Trad	Non-Trad	Trad	Non-Trad
Mean Repair Cost (£)	588	1,077	197	412	439	521	167	360
								(% of mean repair cost)
External Structure	67	67	63	74	49	49	49	44
Internal Structure	23	22	30	22	23	21	26	35
Amenities/Services	10	11	7	4	23	21	20	15
Common Parts	0	0	—	—	5	9	5	6
External								
Chimneys	16	6	9	2	5	2	2	0
Roofs	11	5	15	13	7	4	9	5
Walls	15	33	10	17	15	26	17	24
Windows/Doors	20	18	26	24	20	17	21	15
Internal								
Walls/Ceilings	15	14	20	16	18	14	20	25

Sample: PHY1

Table A 4.16   Matters defective: construction date by type of defect

	Pre–1900	1900–1918	1919–1944	1945–1964	Post–1964	All Ages
Repair	1,079 (29.2)	352 (27.0)	635 (16.0)	464 (10.4)	204 (3.8)	2,734 (14.5)
Stability	345 (9.3)	87 (6.7)	133 (3.4)	92 (2.1)	27 (0.5)	684 (3.6)
Freedom from Damp	696 (18.8)	209 (16.0)	215 (5.4)	99 (2.2)	52 (1.0)	1,271 (6.7)
Drainage and Sanitary Conveniences	272 (7.4)	75 (5.8)	128 (3.2)	70 (1.6)	27 (0.5)	572 (3.0)
Internal Arrangement	652 (17.6)	203 (15.6)	202 (5.1)	69 (1.5)	36 (0.7)	1,162 (6.2)
Natural Lighting	395 (10.7)	89 (6.8)	61 (1.5)	56 (1.3)	41 (0.8)	642 (3.4)
Ventilation	269 (7.3)	71 (5.5)	108 (2.7)	56 (1.3)	31 (0.6)	536 (2.8)
Cold Water Supply	50 (1.4)	12 (0.9)	7 (0.2)	3 (0.1)	9 (0.2)	81 (0.4)
Preparation of Cooking/Waste Disposal	476 (12.9)	158 (12.1)	350 (8.8)	328 (7.3)	69 (1.3)	1,381 (7.3)

Sample: PHY1

Table A 4.17   Matters defective: tenure by type of defect

thousands/% dwellings defective

	Owner Occupied	Private Rented	Local Authority/ New Town	Housing Association	Vacant	All Tenures
Repair	1,365 (11.5)	387 (31.1)	608 (13.5)	49 (10.4)	334 (41.1)	2,734 (14.5)
Stability	354 (3.0)	106 (8.5)	120 (2.7)	8 (1.7)	96 (11.8)	684 (3.6)
Freedom from Damp	692 (5.9)	70 (5.6)	302 (6.7)	37 (7.8)	170 (20.9)	1,271 (6.7)
Drainage/Sanitary Conveniences	194 (1.6)	94 (7.6)	114 (2.5)	12 (2.5)	158 (19.5)	572 (3.0)
Internal Arrangement	668 (5.7)	225 (18.1)	140 (3.1)	23 (4.9)	106 (13.1)	1,162 (6.2)
Natural Lighting	353 (3.0)	136 (10.9)	74 (1.6)	20 (4.2)	59 (7.3)	642 (3.4)
Ventilation	303 (2.6)	96 (7.7)	84 (1.9)	7 (1.5)	46 (5.7)	535 (2.8)
Cold Water Supply	17 (0.1)	10 (0.8)	7 (0.2)	1 (0.2)	46 (5.7)	81 (0.4)
Preparation of Cooking/Waste Disposal	476 (4.0)	207 (16.6)	414 (9.2)	15 (3.2)	269 (33.1)	1,381 (7.3)

Sample: PHY1

98

Table A 4.18   Regional distribution of dwellings in poor environments

thousands/% dwellings

	Poor Environments	Not Poor Environments	All Environments
North	121 (9.7) (6.0)	1,123 (90.3) (6.7)	1,244 (100) (6.6)
Yorkshire and Humberside	252 (13.0) (12.6)	1,693 (87.0) (10.1)	1,945 (100) (10.3)
North West	390 (15.4) (19.5)	2,137 (84.6) (12.6)	2,527 (100) (13.2)
East Midlands	116 (7.5) (5.8)	1,428 (92.5) (8.5)	1,544 (100) (8.2)
West Midlands	157 (7.8) (7.8)	1,852 (92.2) (11.0)	2,009 (100) (10.7)
South West	143 (7.7) (7.1)	1,709 (92.3) (10.2)	1,852 (100) (9.8)
East Anglia	25 (3.1) (1.2)	785 (96.9) (4.7)	810 (100) (4.3)
Inner London	298 (26.2) (14.9)	839 (73.8) (5.0)	1,137 (100) (6.0)
Outer London	222 (13.3) (11.1)	1,453 (86.7) (8.6)	1,675 (100) (8.9)
Rest of South East	281 (6.9) (14.0)	3,815 (93.1) (22.6)	4,096 (100) (21.8)
All Regions	2,005 (10.6) (100)	16,834 (89.4) (100)	18,839 (100) (100)

Sample: PHY1

99

Table A 5.1 Condition by construction date

thousands/% dwellings

	Pre-1870	1870–1899	1900–1918	1919–1944	1945–1964	Post-1964	All Dwellings
Lacking Basic Amenities	69 (5.4)	165 (6.8)	69 (5.3)	94 (2.4)	22 (0.5)	44 (0.8)	463 (2.5)
Unfit	186 (14.6)	367 (15.1)	139 (10.7)	135 (3.4)	55 (1.2)	27 (0.5)	909 (4.8)
In Poor Repair	463 (36.4)	688 (28.4)	358 (27.5)	517 (13.1)	309 (6.9)	95 (1.8)	2,430 (12.9)
Failing on Three	48 (3.8)	92 (3.8)	35 (2.7)	21 (0.5)	3 (0.1)	5 (0.1)	204 (1.1)
Failing on Two	103 (8.1)	216 (8.9)	89 (65.8)	79 (2.0)	24 (0.5)	15 (0.3)	526 (2.8)
Failing on One	369 (29.0)	509 (21.0)	283 (21.7)	527 (13.3)	329 (7.4)	121 (2.2)	2,138 (11.4)
Failing on None	757 (59.1)	1,616 (66.5)	895 (68.7)	3,336 (84.2)	4,120 (92.0)	5,264 (97.4)	15,971 (84.8)
All Dwellings	1,271 (100)	2,433 (100)	1,302 (100)	3,961 (100)	4,468 (100)	5,354 (100)	18,839 (100)

Sample: PHY1

Table A 5.2 Improvements to dwellings since construction by construction date

thousands/% dwellings

	As Built	Modifications	Conversions	All Dwellings
Pre-1870	114 (9.0)	928 (73.0)	229 (18.0)	1,271 (100)
1870–1900	436 (18.0)	1,526 (63.0)	461 (19.0)	2,423 (100)
1901–1918	338 (26.0)	834 (64.0)	130 (10.0)	1,302 (100)
All pre-1919	888 (17.8)	3,288 (65.8)	820 (16.4)	4,996 (100)

Sample: PHY4

Table A 5.3 Unfit dwellings, dwellings lacking basic amenities and dwellings in poor repair by construction date and improvements since construction

thousands/% dwellings

	Pre-1870			1870–1899			1900–1918		
	As Built	Modifi-cations	Conver-sions	As Built	Modifi-cations	Conver-sions	As Built	Modifi-cations	Conver-sions
Lacking Basic Amenities	31 (27.2)	32 (3.4)	8 (3.5)	85 (19.5)	56 (3.7)	19 (4.1)	28 (8.3)	34 (4.1)	8 (6.2)
Unfit	45 (39.5)	129 (13.9)	25 (10.9)	117 (26.8)	183 (12.0)	56 (12.1)	43 (12.7)	84 (10.1)	14 (10.8)
In Poor Repair	62 (54.4)	403 (43.4)	49 (21.4)	159 (36.5)	436 (28.6)	85 (18.4)	99 (29.3)	227 (27.2)	34 (26.2)
Failing on None	45 (39.5)	493 (53.1)	165 (72.1)	244 (56.0)	1,025 (67.2)	348 (75.5)	23 (6.8)	577 (69.2)	90 (69.2)
All Dwellings	114	928	229	436	1,526	461	338	834	130

Sample: PHY4

Table A 5.4 Housing in poor condition in urban and rural areas by construction date

thousands/% dwellings

	Urban			Rural			All Dwellings
	Poor Condition	Good Condition	All Urban	Poor Condition	Good Condition	All Rural	
Pre-1919	1,342 (33.3) (58.1)	2,682 (66.7) (19.2)	4,024 (100) (24.7)	403 (41.4) (72.0)	569 (58.6) (29.0)	972 (100) (38.5)	4,996 (100) (26.5)
1919–1944	555 (15.3) (24.1)	3,072 (84.7) (21.9)	3,627 (100) (22.2)	71 (21.1) (12.7)	265 (78.9) (13.5)	336 (100) (13.3)	3,963 (100) (21.0)
1945–1964	299 (7.6) (12.9)	3,650 (92.4) (26.0)	3,949 (100) (24.2)	57 (10.8) (10.2)	470 (89.2) (23.9)	527 (100) (20.9)	4,476 (100) (23.8)
Post-1964	113 (2.4) (4.9)	4,601 (97.6) (32.9)	4,714 (100) (28.9)	28 (4.1) (5.0)	662 (95.9) (33.6)	690 (100) (27.3)	5,404 (100) (28.7)
All Ages	2,309 (14.2) (100)	14,005 (85.5) (100)	16,314 (100) (100)	559 (22.1) (100)	1,966 (77.9) (100)	2,525 (100) (100)	18,839 (100) (100)

Sample: PHY1

Table A 5.5   Housing in poor condition in urban and rural areas by tenure

thousands/% dwellings

	Urban			Rural			All Dwellings
	Poor Condition	Good Condition	All Urban	Poor Condition	Good Condition	All Rural	
Owner Occupied	1,215 (12.0) (52.6)	8,864 (88.0) (63.3)	10,079 (61.8)	301 (17.3) (53.8)	1,440 (82.7) (73.3)	1,741 (100) (69.0)	11,820 (100) (62.7)
Private Rented	380 (40.1) (16.4)	567 (59.9) (4.1)	947 (100) (5.8)	143 (48.1) (25.6)	154 (51.9) (7.8)	297 (100) (11.8)	1,244 (100) (6.7)
Local Authority/New Town	443 (10.5) (19.2)	3,759 (89.5) (26.8)	4,202 (100) (25.8)	32 (11.1) (5.7)	256 (88.9) (13.0)	288 (100) (11.4)	4,490 (100) (23.8)
Housing Association	29 (6.8) (1.3)	398 (93.2) (2.8)	427 (100) (2.6)	2 (4.3) (0.4)	44 (95.7) (2.2)	46 (100) (1.8)	473 (100) (2.5)
Vacant	242 (36.7) (10.5)	417 (63.3) (3.0)	659 (100) (4.0)	81 (52.9) (14.5)	72 (47.1) (3.7)	153 (100) (6.0)	812 (100) (4.3)
All Tenures	2,309 (14.2) (100)	14,005 (85.8) (100)	16,314 (100) (100)	559 (22.1) (100)	1,966 (77.9) (100)	2,525 (100) (100)	18,839 (100) (100)

Sample: PHY1

Table A 5.6   Dwellings in poor condition by poor environments

thousands/% dwellings

	All Amenities Present	Lacking Basic Amenities	Fit	Unfit	Good Repair	Poor Repair	All Dwellings
Poor Environments	1,872 (93.4) (10.2)	133 (6.6) (28.7)	1,721 (85.8) (9.6)	284 (14.2) (31.2)	1,494 (74.5) (9.1)	511 (25.5) (21.0)	2,005 (100) (10.6)
Not Poor Environments	16,504 (98.0) (89.8)	330 (2.0) (71.3)	16,209 (96.3) (90.4)	625 (3.7) (68.8)	14,915 (88.6) (90.9)	1,919 (11.4) (79.0)	16,834 (100) (89.4)
All Environments	18,376 (97.5) (100)	463 (2.5) (100)	17,930 (95.2) (100)	909 (4.8) (100)	16,409 (87.1) (100)	2,430 (12.9) (100)	18,839 (100) (100)

Sample: PHY1

Table A 6.1   Age of head of household by construction date

thousands/% households

	Pre-1919	1919–1944	1944–1964	Post-1964	All Households
Aged 17–39	1,691 (28.1) (38.4)	1,130 (18.7) (28.7)	1,212 (20.1) (27.5)	1,993 (33.1) (36.2)	6,026 (100) (33.0)
Aged 40–59	1,379 (22.6) (31.3)	1,423 (23.3) (36.1)	1,283 (21.1) (29.1)	2,015 (33.0) (36.4)	6,100 (100) (33.4)
Aged 60–74	914 (21.2) (20.7)	998 (23.2) (25.3)	1,458 (33.9) (33.0)	933 (21.7) (16.9)	4,303 (100) (23.5)
Aged 75 and Over	422 (22.8) (9.6)	389 (21.1) (9.9)	458 (24.8) (10.4)	578 (31.3) (10.5)	1,847 (100) (10.1)
All Ages	4,406 (24.1) (100)	3,940 (21.6) (100)	4,411 (24.1) (100)	5,519 (30.2) (100)	18,276 (100) (100)

Sample: I1

Table A 6.2   Age of head of household by tenure[1]

thousands/% households

	Owner Occupied	Private Rented	Local Authority/ New Town	Housing Association	All Tenures
Aged 17–39	3,858 (64.0) (33.4)	591 (9.8) (46.0)	1,343 (22.3) (27.2)	234 (3.9) (47.5)	6,026 (100) (33.0)
Aged 40–59	4,526 (74.1) (39.2)	290 (4.8) (22.5)	1,212 (19.9) (24.5)	72 (1.2) (14.6)	6,100 (100) (33.4)
Aged 60–74	2,506 (58.2) (21.7)	256 (6.0) (19.9)	1,463 (34.0) (29.6)	78 (1.8) (15.8)	4,303 (100) (23.5)
Aged 75 and Over	665 (36.0) (5.7)	149 (8.1) (11.6)	924 (50.0) (18.7)	109 (5.9) (22.1)	1,847 (100) (10.1)
All Ages	11,555 (63.3) (100)	1,286 (7.0) (100)	4,942 (27.0) (100)	493 (2.7) (100)	18,276 (100) (100)

Sample: I1

[1] Totals for households in each tenure group differ from those for occupied dwellings. This is in part due to some dwellings containing more than one household. However, much of the difference is due to the effect of the grossing procedures for each separate sample (see Appendix C). The calculation of the number of households who share a single dwelling cannot be derived from subtracting the number of occupied dwellings from the number of households.

Table A 6.3   Age of head of household by households in dwellings which lacked basic amenities, were unfit or were in poor repair

thousands/% dwellings

	Amenities[1]		Fitness		Poor Repair		All Households
	All Amenities Present	Lacking Basic Amenities	Fit	Unfit	Under £1,000	Over £1,000	
Aged 17–39	5,952 (98.8) (33.2)	74 (1.2) (20.6)	5,778 (95.9) (32.9)	248 (4.1) (34.8)	5,271 (87.5) (33.1)	755 (12.5) (31.9)	6,026 (33.0)
Aged 40–59	6,037 (99.0) (33.7)	63 (1.0) (17.5)	5,913 (96.9) (33.7)	187 (3.1) (25.9)	5,317 (87.2) (33.4)	783 (12.8) (33.1)	6,100 (33.4)
Aged 60–74	4,193 (97.4) (23.4)	110 (2.6) (30.7)	4.136 (96.1) (23.5)	167 (3.9) (23.3)	3,753 (87.1) (23.6)	550 (12.9) (23.4)	4,303 (23.5)
Aged 75 and Over	1,735 (93.9) (9.7)	112 (6.1) (31.2)	1,731 (93.7) (9.9)	116 (6.3) (16.0)	1,572 (85.1) (9.9)	275 (14.9) (11.6)	1,847 (10.1)
All Ages	17,917 (98.0) (100)	359 (2.0) (100)	17,558 (96.1) (100)	718 (3.9) (100)	15,913 (87.1) (100)	2,363 (12.9) (100)	18,276 (100)

Sample: I1

[1] Five basic amenities — bath, sink, WC inside dwellings, wash hand basin, hot and cold water at 3 points

Table A 6.4   Households living in dwellings in poor condition by household type

thousands/% households

	Poor Condition	Good Condition	All Households
Single Person	278 (22.6) (10.2)	953 (77.4) (6.1)	1,231 (100) (6.7)
Small Adult	367 (11.5) (13.5)	2,829 (88.5) (18.2)	3,196 (100) (17.5)
Single Parent	48 (12.6) (1.7)	333 (87.4) (2.1)	381 (100) (2.1)
Small Family	421 (12.4) (15.4)	2,979 (87.6) (19.2)	3,400 (100) (18.6)
Large Family	371 (15.9) (13.7)	1,969 (84.1) (12.7)	2,340 (100) (12.8)
Large Adult	420 (15.7) (15.4)	2,251 (84.3) (14.5)	2,671 (100) (14.6)
Older Smaller	383 (14.2) (14.1)	2,321 (85.8) (14.9)	2,704 (100) (14.8)
Single OAP	436 (18.6) (16.0)	1,917 (81.4) (12.3)	2,353 (100) (12.9)
All Households	2,724 (14.9) (100)	15,552 (85.1) (100)	18,276 (100) (100)

Sample: I1

Table A 6.5   Age of head of household by length of residence

	Length of Residence					
	0–2 Years	2–5 Years	5–10 Years	10–20 Years	20 Years or More	All Households
Aged 17–39	2,125 (35.3) (61.6)	2,143 (35.6) (51.6)	1,088 (18.1) (32.5)	643 (10.6) (17.2)	27 (0.4) (0.7)	6,026 (100) (33.0)
Aged 40–59	911 (14.9) (26.4)	1,274 (20.9) (30.7)	1,186 (19.5) (35.5)	1,755 (28.7) (46.9)	974 (16.0) (27.2)	6,100 (100) (33.4)
Aged 60–74	342 (7.9) (9.9)	482 (11.2) (11.6)	696 (16.2) (20.8)	897 (20.9) (23.9)	1,886 (43.8) (52.6)	4,303 (100) (23.5)
Aged 75 and Over	71 (3.8) (2.1)	253 (13.7) (6.1)	374 (20.3) (11.2)	450 (24.4) (12.0)	699 (37.8) (19.5)	1,847 (100) (10.1)
All Ages	3,449 (18.9) (100)	4,152 (22.7) (100)	3,344 (18.3) (100)	3,745 (20.5) (100)	3,586 (19.6) (100)	18,276 (100) (100)

Sample: I1

Table A 6.6   Household income[1] by households living in dwellings which lacked basic amenities, were unfit or were in poor repair

	Amenities		Fitness		Poor Repair		All Households
	All Amenities Present	Lacking Basic Amenities	Fit	Unfit	Under £1,000	Over £1,000	
£0–£2,999	4,263 (95.9) (23.8)	180 (4.1) (50.1)	4,174 (93.9) (23.8)	269 (6.1) (37.5)	3,799 (85.6) (23.8)	644 (14.4) (27.2)	4,443 (100) (24.3)
£3,000–£5,999	4,272 (97.7) (23.8)	99 (2.3) (27.4)	4,146 (94.9) (23.6)	255 (5.1) (31.3)	3,726 (85.2) (23.4)	645 (14.8) (27.3)	4,371 (100) (23.9)
£6,000–£8,999	3,957 (98.9) (22.1)	45 (1.1) (12.6)	3,880 (97.0) (22.1)	122 (3.0) (17.0)	3,526 (88.1) (22.2)	476 (11.9) (20.2)	4,002 (100) (21.9)
£9,000–£11,999	2,697 (99.0) (15.1)	27 (1.0) (7.6)	2,652 (97.4) (15.1)	72 (2.6) (10.0)	2,411 (88.5) (15.2)	313 (11.5) (13.2)	2,724 (100) (14.9)
£12,000–£14,999	1,650 (99.8) (9.2)	4 (0.2) (1.2)	1,637 (99.0) (9.3)	17 (1.0) (2.4)	1,468 (88.8) (9.2)	186 (11.2) (7.9)	1,654 (100) (9.1)
£15,000 and Over	1,078 (99.6) (6.0)	4 (0.4) (1.1)	1,069 (98.8) (6.1)	13 (1.2) (1.8)	983 (90.9) (6.2)	99 (9.1) (4.2)	1,082 (100) (5.9)
All Households	17,917 (98.0) (100)	359 (2.0) (100)	17,558 (96.1) (100)	718 (3.9) (100)	15,913 (87.1) (100)	2,363 (12.9) (100)	18,276 (100) (100)

[1] Household income refers to net income of head of household and spouse.

Sample: I1

Table A 6.7 Income of households occupying dwellings in poor condition by tenure

thousands/% households in dwellings in poor condition
* thousands/% households

	Owner Occupied	Private Rented	Local Authority/ New Town	Housing Association	All Households in Poor Condition Dwellings	* All Tenures
£0–£2,999	335 (41.1) (21.5)	267 (32.8) (41.7)	201 (24.7) (41.2)	12 (1.4) (36.4)	815 (100) (29.9)	4,443 (100) (24.3)
£3,000–£5,999	366 (49.8) (23.4)	174 (23.8) (27.1)	175 (2.3) (35.6)	20 (2.7) (60.6)	735 (100) (27.0)	4,371 (100) (23.9)
£6,000–£8,999	342 (66.4) (22.0)	99 (19.2) (15.4)	74 (14.4) (15.2)	—	515 (100) (18.9)	4,002 (100) (21.9)
£9,000–£11,999	252 (70.2) (16.1)	70 (19.5) (11.0)	36 (10.0) (7.3)	1 (0.3) (3.0)	359 (100) (13.2)	2,724 (100) (14.9)
£12,000–£14,999	171 (88.9) (10.9)	18 (9.4) (2.8)	3 (1.7) (0.7)	—	192 (100) (7.0)	1,654 (100) (9.1)
£15,000 and Over	95 (88.0) (6.1)	13 (12.0) (2.0)	—	—	108 (100) (4.0)	1,082 (100) (5.9)
All households	1,561 (57.3) (100)	641 (23.5) (100)	489 (18.0) (100)	33 (1.2) (100)	2,724 (100) (100)	18,276 (100) (100)

Sample: I1

Table A 6.8 Household income by region

thousands/% households

	North	Rest of England	South East	All Areas
£0–£2,999	1,478 (33.3) (27.3)	1,402 (31.6) (22.4)	1,563 (35.1) (23.7)	4,443 (100) (24.4)
£3,000–£5,999	1,415 (32.4) (26.2)	1,592 (36.4) (25.4)	1,364 (31.2) (20.6)	4,371 (100) (23.9)
£6,000–£8,999	1,294 (32.3) (23.9)	1,289 (32.2) (20.5)	1,419 (35.5) (21.5)	4,002 (100) (21.9)
£9,000–£11,999	599 (22.0) (11.1)	979 (35.9) (15.6)	1,146 (42.1) (17.4)	2,724 (100) (14.9)
£12,000–£14,999	354 (21.4) (6.6)	631 (38.2) (10.1)	669 (40.4) (10.1)	1,654 (100) (9.1)
£15,000 and Over	263 (24.3) (4.9)	377 (34.8) (6.0)	442 (40.9) (6.7)	1,082 (100) (5.9)
All Households	5,403 (29.6) (100)	6,270 (34.3) (100)	6,603 (36.1) (100)	18,276 (100) (100)

Sample: I1

Table A 6.9   Tenure by region

thousands/% households

	North	Rest of England	South East	All Areas
Owner Occupied	3,216 (27.8) (59.5)	4,026 (34.9) (64.2)	4,313 (37.3) (65.3)	11,555 (100) (63.3)
Private Rented	381 (31.3) (8.3)	470 (35.5) (7.5)	435 (33.2) (7.2)	1,286 (100) (7.0)
Local Authority/ New Town	1,581 (32.0) (29.3)	1,645 (33.3) (26.2)	1,716 (34.7) (26.0)	4,942 (100) (27.0)
Housing Association	225 (45.6) (2.9)	129 (26.1) (2.1)	139 (28.3) (1.5)	493 (100) (2.7)
All Tenures	5,403 (29.6) (100)	6,270 (34.3) (100)	6,603 (36.1) (100)	18,276 (100) (100)

Sample: I1

Table A 6.10   Length of residence by region

thousands/% households

	North	Rest of England	South East	All Areas
0–2 Years	847 (24.6) (15.7)	1,339 (38.8) (21.4)	1,263 (36.6) (19.1)	3,449 (100) (18.9)
2–5 Years	1,034 (24.9) (19.1)	1,408 (33.9) (22.4)	1,710 (41.2) (26.0)	4,152 (100) (22.7)
5–10 Years	1,182 (35.4) (21.9)	996 (29.8) (15.9)	1,166 (34.8) (17.7)	3,344 (100) (18.3)
10–20 Years	1,174 (31.3) (21.7)	1,408 (37.6) (22.5)	1,163 (31.1) (17.6)	3,745 (100) (20.5)
20 Years and over	1,166 (32.5) (21.6)	1,119 (31.2) (17.8)	1,301 (36.3) (19.7)	3,586 (100) (19.6)
All Households	5,403 (29.6) (100)	6,270 (34.3) (100)	6,603 (36.1) (100)	18,276 (100) (100)

Sample: I1

Table A 6.11   Age of head of household by region

thousands/% households

	North	Rest of England	South East	All Areas
Aged 17–39	1,619 (26.9) (30.0)	2,015 (33.4) (32.1)	2,392 (39.7) (36.2)	6,026 (100) (33.0)
Aged 40–59	1,917 (31.4) (35.5)	2,152 (35.3) (34.3)	2,031 (33.3) (30.8)	6,100 (100) (33.4)
Aged 60–74	1,341 (31.2) (24.8)	1,416 (32.9) (22.6)	1,546 (35.9) (23.4)	4,303 (100) (23.5)
Aged 75 and Over	526 (28.5) (9.7)	687 (37.2) (11.0)	634 (34.3) (9.6)	1,847 (100) (10.1)
All Ages	5,403 (29.6) (100)	6,270 (34.3) (100)	6,603 (36.1) (100)	18,276 (100) (100)

Sample: I1

Table A 6.12   Employment status by region

	North	Rest of England	South East	All Areas
Working	2,900 (27.4) (53.7)	3,681 (34.8) (58.7)	3,988 (37.8) (60.3)	10,569 (100) (57.8)
Unemployed	456 (34.3) (8.4)	505 (38.0) (8.1)	369 (27.7) (5.6)	1,330 (100) (7.3)
Retired	1,431 (29.6) (26.5)	1,637 (33.8) (26.1)	1,773 (36.6) (26.9)	4,841 (100) (26.5)
Other	616 (40.1) (11.4)	447 (29.1) (7.1)	473 (30.8) (7.2)	1,536 (100) (8.4)
All Households	5,403 (29.6) (100)	6,270 (34.3) (100)	6,603 (36.1) (100)	18,276 (100) (100)

Sample: I1

Table A 6.13 Households in dwellings in poor condition by age of head of household by region

thousands/% dwellings

	North			Rest of England			South East			All Regions		
	Good Condition	Poor Condition	All Dwellings	Good Condition	Poor Condition	All Dwellings	Good Condition	Poor Condition	All Dwellings	Good Condition	Poor Condition	All Dwellings
Aged 17–39	1,344 (83.0) (30.0)	275 (17.0) (30.0)	1,619 (30.0)	1,700 (84.4) (32.2)	315 (15.6) (32.0)	2,015 (32.1)	2,136 (89.3) (36.9)	256 (10.7) (31.2)	2,392 (36.2)	5,180 (86.0) (33.3)	846 (14.0) (31.0)	6,026 (33.0)
Aged 40–59	1,637 (85.4) (36.5)	280 (14.6) (30.3)	1,917 (35.5)	1,835 (85.3) (34.6)	317 (14.7) (32.3)	2,152 (34.3)	1,763 (86.8) (30.6)	268 (13.2) (32.7)	2,031 (30.8)	5,235 (85.8) (33.6)	865 (14.2) (31.8)	6,100 (33.4)
Aged 60–74	1,091 (81.4) (24.3)	250 (18.6) (27.2)	1,341 (24.8)	1,203 (85.0) (22.8)	213 (15.0) (21.6)	1,416 (22.6)	1,356 (87.7) (23.4)	190 (12.3) (23.2)	1,546 (23.4)	3,650 (84.8) (23.5)	653 (15.2) (24.0)	4,303 (23.5)
Aged 75 and Over	411 (78.1) (9.2)	115 (21.9) (12.5)	526 (9.7)	548 (79.8) (10.4)	139 (20.2) (14.1)	687 (11.0)	528 (83.3) (9.1)	106 (16.7) (12.9)	634 (9.6)	1,487 (80.5) (9.6)	360 (19.5) (13.2)	1,847 (10.1)
All Ages	4,483 (83.0) (100)	920 (17.0) (100)	5,403 (100)	5,286 (84.3) (100)	984 (15.7) (100)	6,270 (100)	5,783 (87.6) (100)	820 (12.4) (100)	6,603 (100)	15,552 (85.1) (100)	2,724 (14.9) (100)	18,276 (100)

Sample: I1

109

Table A 6.14 Households in dwellings in poor condition by employment status by region

thousands/% dwellings

	North			Rest of England			South East			All Regions		
	Good Condition	Poor Condition	All Conditions	Good Condition	Poor Condition	All Conditions	Good Condition	Poor Condition	All Conditions	Good Condition	Poor Condition	All Conditions
Working	2,479 (85.5) (55.3)	421 (14.5) (45.7)	2,900 (53.7)	3,185 (86.5) (60.2)	496 (13.5) (50.4)	3,681 (58.7)	3,543 (88.8) (61.3)	445 (11.2) (54.3)	3,988 (60.3)	9,207 (87.1) (59.2)	1,362 (12.9) (50.0)	10,569 (57.8)
Unemployed	331 (72.6) (7.4)	125 (27.4) (13.6)	456 (8.4)	386 (76.4) (7.3)	119 (23.6) (12.1)	505 (8.1)	324 (87.8) (5.6)	45 (12.2) (5.5)	369 (5.6)	1,041 (78.3) (6.7)	289 (21.7) (10.6)	1,330 (7.3)
Retired	1,133 (79.2) (25.3)	298 (20.8) (32.4)	1,431 (26.5)	1,347 (8.3) (25.5)	290 (17.7) (29.5)	1,637 (26.1)	1,509 (85.1) (26.1)	264 (14.9) (32.2)	1,773 (26.9)	3,989 (82.4) (25.6)	852 (17.6) (31.3)	4,841 (26.5)
Other	540 (87.7) (12.0)	76 (12.3) (8.3)	616 (11.4)	368 (82.3) (7.0)	79 (17.7) (8.0)	447 (7.1)	407 (86.0) (7.0)	66 (14.0) (8.0)	473 (7.2)	1,315 (85.6) (8.5)	221 (14.4) (8.1)	1,536 (8.4)
All Households	4,483 (83.0) (100)	920 (17.0) (100)	5,403 (100)	5,286 (84.3) (100)	984 (15.7) (100)	6,270 (100)	5,783 (87.6) (100)	820 (12.4) (100)	6,603 (100)	15,552 (85.1) (100)	2,724 (14.9) (100)	18,276 (100)

Sample: I1

110

Table A 6.15 Households in dwellings in poor condition by household income by region

thousands/% dwellings

	North			Rest of England			South East			All Regions		
	Good Condition	Poor Condition	All Conditions	Good Condition	Poor Condition	All Conditions	Good Condition	Poor Condition	All Conditions	Good Condition	Poor Condition	All Conditions
£0–£2,999	1,154 (78.1) (25.7)	324 (21.9) (35.2)	1,478 (27.4)	1,123 (80.1) (21.2)	279 (19.9) (28.4)	1,402 (22.4)	1,351 (86.4) (23.3)	212 (13.6) (25.9)	1,563 (23.7)	3,628 (81.1) (23.3)	815 (18.3) (29.9)	4,443 (24.3)
£3,000–£5,999	1,178 (83.3) (26.4)	237 (16.7) (25.8)	1,415 (26.2)	1,296 (81.4) (24.5)	296 (18.6) (30.1)	1,592 (25.4)	1,162 (85.2) (20.1)	202 (14.8) (24.6)	1,364 (20.7)	3,636 (83.2) (23.4)	735 (16.8) (27.0)	4,371 (23.9)
£6,000–£8,999	1,091 (84.3) (24.3)	203 (15.7) (22.1)	1,294 (23.9)	1,113 (86.3) (21.1)	176 (13.7) (17.9)	1,289 (20.5)	1,283 (90.4) (22.2)	136 (9.6) (16.6)	1,419 (21.5)	3,487 (87.1) (22.4)	515 (12.9) (18.9)	4,002 (21.9)
£9,000–£11,999	494 (82.5) (11.0)	105 (17.5) (11.4)	599 (11.1)	872 (89.1) (16.5)	107 (10.9) (10.8)	979 (15.6)	999 (87.2) (17.3)	147 (12.8) (17.9)	1,146 (17.4)	2,365 (86.8) (15.2)	359 (13.2) (13.2)	2,724 (14.9)
£12,000–£14,999	315 (89.0) (7.0)	39 (11.0) (4.2)	354 (6.6)	538 (85.3) (10.2)	93 (14.7) (9.4)	631 (10.1)	609 (91.0) (10.5)	60 (9.0) (7.3)	669 (10.1)	1,462 (88.4) (9.4)	192 (11.6) (7.0)	1,654 (9.1)
£15,000 and over	251 (95.4) (5.6)	12 (4.6) (1.3)	263 (4.9)	344 (91.2) (6.5)	33 (8.8) (3.4)	377 (6.0)	379 (85.7) (6.6)	63 (14.3) (7.7)	442 (6.7)	974 (90.0) (6.3)	108 (10.0) (4.0)	1,082 (5.9)
All Households	4,483 (83.0)	920 (17.0)	5,403	5,286 (84.3)	984 (15.7)	6,270	5,783 (87.6)	820 (12.4)	6,603	15,552 (85.1)	2,724 (14.9)	18,276

Sample: I1

111

Table A 6.16 Owner occupiers' attitude to repair and maintenance by age and income

thousands/% owner occupiers

	Age of Head of Household				Income						All Owner Occupiers
	17–39	40–59	60–74	75 and Over	£0–£2,999	£3,000 – £5,999	£6,000 – £8,999	£9,000 – £11,999	£12,000 – £14,999	£15,000 and Over	
Constantly Repairing Home	1,135 (40.7) (29.4)	1,245 (44.8) (27.6)	368 (13.2) (14.7)	36 (1.3) (5.4)	143 (5.1) (8.6)	401 (14.4) (18.1)	617 (22.1) (22.2)	672 (24.2) (29.1)	511 (18.3) (32.9)	443 (15.9) (42.6)	2,787 (100) (24.1)
Prompt Maintenance to Home	1,164 (25.8) (30.2)	1,846 (41.1) (40.8)	1,172 (26.1) (46.7)	313 (7.0) (47.1)	746 (16.6) (45.2)	1,062 (23.7) (48.1)	1,003 (22.3) (36.1)	707 (15.7) (30.6)	589 (13.1) (38.0)	388 (8.6) (37.2)	4,495 (100) (38.8)
Essential Maintenance to Home	1,244 (34.7) (32.2)	1,206 (33.6) (26.6)	859 (23.9) (34.3)	281 (7.8) (42.3)	684 (19.1) (41.4)	634 (17.7) (28.6)	970 (27.0) (34.9)	781 (21.7) (33.8)	356 (9.9) (22.9)	165 (4.6) (15.8)	3,590 (100) (31.1)
Tend To Get Behind With Maintenance	291 (47.3) (7.5)	206 (33.7) (4.6)	100 (16.4) (4.0)	16 (2.6) (2.4)	58 (9.5) (3.5)	100 (16.3) (4.5)	179 (29.2) (6.4)	135 (22.0) (5.8)	95 (15.5) (6.1)	46 (7.5) (4.4)	613 (100) (5.3)
Do Not Bother About House Although Is My Responsibilty	22 (41.5) (0.6)	9 (18.9) (0.2)	5 (9.4) (0.2)	16 (30.2) (2.4)	14 (26.9) (0.8)	12 (23.1) (0.5)	7 (13.5) (0.3)	17 (32.7) (0.7)	2 (3.8) (0.1)	—	52 (100) (0.4)
Do Not Regard House As My Responsibility	2 (11.8) (0.1)	11 (58.8) (0.2)	2 (11.8) (0.1)	3 (17.6) (0.4)	9 (50.0) (0.5)	5 (27.8) (0.2)	4 (22.2) (0.1)	—	—	—	18 (100) (0.1)
All Owner Occupiers	3,852 (33.3) (100)	4,519 (39.2) (100)	2,504 (21.7) (100)	670 (5.8) (100)	1,654 (14.3) (100)	2,214 (19.2) (100)	2,780 (24.1) (100)	2,312 (20.0) (100)	1,553 (13.4) (100)	1,042 (9.0) (100)	11,555 (100) (100)

Sample: I2

Table A 6.17   Occupiers' attitude to repair and maintenance by tenure and dwelling condition

thousands/% households

	Owner Occupiers		Local Authority/ New Town		Private Rented		Housing Association	
	Good Condition	Poor Condition	Good Condition	Poor Condition	Good Condition	Poor Condition	Good Condition	Poor Condition
Constantly Repairing Home	2,347 (23.5)	440 (28.2)	367 (8.2)	59 (12.1)	31 (4.8)	45 (7.0)	13 (2.8)	4 (12.1)
Prompt Maintenance to Home	4,074 (40.8)	421 (27.0)	1,090 (24.5)	74 (15.1)	147 (22.8)	125 (19.5)	54 (11.7)	4 (12.1)
Essential Maintenance to Home	3,103 (31.0)	487 (31.2)	1,671 (37.5)	127 (25.9)	188 (29.2)	171 (26.7)	223 (48.6)	4 (12.1)
Tend To Get Behind With Maintenance	451 (4.5)	162 (10.3)	120 (2.7)	19 (3.9)	25 (3.9)	35 (5.5)	23 (5.0)	1 (3.0)
Do Not Bother About House Although Is My Responsibility	10 (0.1)	42 (2.7)	156 (3.5)	16 (3.3)	5 (0.8)	6 (0.9)	6 (1.2)	1 (3.0)
Do Not Regard House As My Responsibility	9 (0.1)	9 (0.6)	1,049 (23.6)	194 (39.7)	249 (38.5)	259 (40.4)	141 (30.7)	19 (57.7)
All Households	9,994 (100)	1,561 (100)	4,453 (100)	489 (100)	645 (100)	641 (100)	460 (100)	33 (100)

Sample: I1

Table A 6.18   Local Authority/New Town tenants' attitude to repair and maintenance by age and income

thousands/% local authority tenants

	Age of Head of Household				Income						All Local Authority/ New Town Tenants
	17–39 years	40–59 years	60–74 years	75 years and over	£0–£2,999	£3,000–£5,999	£6,000–£8,999	£9,000–£11,999	£12,000–£14,999	£15,000 and over	
Constantly Repairing Home	186 (43.7) (13.9)	122 (28.6) (10.0)	76 (17.8) (5.2)	42 (9.9) (4.5)	129 (30.2) (5.7)	165 (38.7) (10.2)	92 (21.7) (11.6)	34 (8.0) (12.5)	5 (1.2) (23.9)	1 (0.2) (4.2)	426 (100) (8.6)
Prompt Maintenance to Home	314 (27.9) (23.3)	289 (25.1) (24.0)	454 (39.9) (31.0)	107 (9.2) (11.5)	285 (24.5) (12.8)	403 (34.6) (25.1)	329 (28.3) (41.5)	140 (12.0) (51.5)	7 (0.6) (33.3)	—	1,164 (100) (23.6)
Essential Maintenance to Home	514 (28.6) (38.2)	507 (28.2) (41.8)	529 (29.4) (36.2)	248 (13.8) (26.8)	916 (51.0) (41.2)	554 (30.9) (34.7)	224 (12.4) (28.2)	74 (4.1) (27.2)	8 (0.4) (38.1)	22 (1.2) (91.6)	1,798 (100) (36.3)
Tend To Get Behind With Maintenance	63 (45.3) (4.7)	15 (10.8) (1.2)	24 (17.3) (1.6)	37 (26.6) (4.0)	71 (51.1) (3.2)	49 (35.5) (3.2)	16 (11.3) (2.0)	2 (1.4) (0.7)	—	1 (0.7) (4.2)	139 (100) (2.8)
Do Not Bother About House Although Is My Responsibility	38 (22.2) (2.8)	25 (14.5) (2.1)	41 (23.8) (2.8)	68 (39.5) (7.4)	94 (54.7) (4.2)	61 (35.4) (3.8)	16 (9.3) (2.0)	1 (0.6) (0.4)	—	—	172 (100) (3.5)
Do Not Regard House As My Responsibility	228 (18.3) (17.0)	254 (20.4) (21.0)	339 (27.3) (23.2)	422 (34.0) (45.8)	734 (59.0) (32.9)	370 (29.8) (23.0)	117 (9.4) (14.7)	21 (1.7) (7.7)	1 (0.1) (4.7)	—	1,243 (100) (25.2)
All Local Authority/New Town Tenants	1,343 (27.2) (100)	1,212 (24.7) (100)	1,463 (29.6) (100)	924 (18.6) (100)	2,229 (45.1) (100)	1,602 (32.4) (100)	794 (16.1) (100)	272 (5.5) (100)	21 (0.4) (100)	24 (0.3) (100)	4,942 (100) (100)

Sample: I3

114

Table A 6.19 Private-rented sector tenants'[1] attitudes to repair and maintenance by age and income

thousands/% private rented sector tenants

	Age of Head of Household				Income						All Private Rented Sector Tenants
	17–39 years	40–59 years	60–74 years	75 years and over	£0–£2,999	£3,000–£5,999	£6,000–£8,999	£9,000–£11,999	£12,000–£14,999	£15,000 and over	
Constantly Repairing Home	38 (50.0) (6.4)	14 (18.4) (4.9)	19 (25.0) (7.6)	5 (6.6) (3.3)	12 (16.0) (3.2)	17 (22.0) (4.8)	40 (52.0) (10.9)	2 (2.7) (1.8)	— —	5 (6.6) (31.2)	76 (100) (5.9)
Prompt Maintenance to Home	72 (26.5) (12.0)	127 (46.7) (44.7)	52 (19.1) (20.7)	21 (7.7) (13.7)	51 (18.8) (13.4)	48 (17.7) (13.6)	134 (49.1) (37.0)	14 (5.2) (12.7)	20 (7.4) (29.0)	5 (1.8) (31.2)	272 (100) (21.2)
Essential Maintenance to Home	147 (40.9) (24.6)	62 (17.3) (21.8)	98 (27.3) (39.0)	52 (14.5) (34.0)	124 (34.4) (32.6)	129 (35.8) (36.6)	57 (16.1) (16.2)	47 (13.1) (42.7)	2 (0.6) (2.9)	— —	359 (100) (27.9)
Tend To Get Behind With Maintenance	41 (68.3) (6.9)	5 (8.3) (1.8)	10 (16.7) (4.0)	4 (6.7) (2.6)	13 (22.0) (3.4)	19 (32.2) (5.3)	20 (32.2) (5.3)	8 (13.6) (7.3)	— —	— —	60 (100) (4.7)
Do Not Bother About House Although Is My Responsibility	—	—	9 (81.8) (3.6)	2 (18.2) (1.8)	11 (100) (3.2)	—	—	—	—	—	11 (100) (0.9)
Do Not Regard House As My Responsibility	300 (59.2) (50.1)	76 (15.0) (26.8)	63 (12.4) (25.1)	69 (13.6) (45.1)	169 (33.0) (44.2)	139 (27.3) (39.6)	108 (21.6) (30.6)	39 (7.7) (35.5)	47 (9.2) (68.1)	6 (1.2) (37.6)	508 (100) (39.4)
All Private Rented Sector Tenants	591 (46.5) (100)	290 (22.1) (100)	256 (19.5) (100)	149 (11.9) (100)	380 (29.5) (100)	352 (27.4) (100)	359 (28.0) (100)	110 (8.5) (100)	69 (5.4) (100)	16 (1.2) (100)	1,286 (100) (100)

Sample: I4

[1] Excludes Housing Association tenants because of small sample

Table A 6.20 Occupants' view of condition and change in state of repair by tenure[1]

thousands/% households

	Owner Occupiers			Private Rented			Local Authority/New Town		
	Worse	Better	Same	Worse	Better	Same	Worse	Better	Same
Dwelling Thought to be in Good Condition	552 (5.0) (71.3)	6,996 (63.0) (98.6)	3,542 (32.0) (96.1)	250 (22.5) (88.5)	483 (43.3) (94.9)	379 (34.1) (76.5)	315 (8.1) (43.6)	1,159 (29.9) (85.0)	2,408 (62.0) (84.3)
Dwelling Thought to be in Poor Condition	222 (47.7) (28.7)	99 (21.3) (1.4)	144 (31.0) (3.9)	32 (18.4) (11.5)	26 (14.9) (5.1)	116 (66.7) (23.5)	407 (38.4) (55.2)	205 (19.3) (15.0)	448 (42.3) (15.7)
All Households	774 (6.7)	7,095 (61.4)	3,686 (31.9)	282 (21.9)	509 (39.6)	495 (38.5)	722 (14.6)	1,364 (27.6)	2,856 (57.8)

Sample: I5

[1] Excludes Housing Association tenants because of small sample size.

115

Table A 6.21 Attitude to repair and maintenance by tenure[1] and view of change in condition over the last 5 years

thousands/% households

	Owner Occupied			Private Rented			Local Authority/New Town		
	Worse	Better	Same	Worse	Better	Same	Worse	Better	Same
Constantly Repairing Home	84 (10.9)	2,361 (33.3)	342 (9.3)	7 (2.4)	62 (12.2)	7 (1.4)	81 (11.2)	164 (12.0)	181 (6.3)
Prompt Maintenance to Home	128 (16.5)	2,790 (39.4)	1,577 (42.8)	12 (4.2)	192 (37.7)	68 (13.7)	129 (17.9)	382 (28.0)	653 (22.9)
Essential Maintenance to Home	431 (55.6)	1,684 (23.7)	1,475 (40.0)	47 (16.7)	15 (21.4)	15 (41.1)	179 (24.8)	501 (36.7)	1,118 (39.2)
Tend to get Behind with Maintenance	92 (11.9)	249 (3.5)	272 (7.4)	30 (10.6)	15 (2.9)	15 (3.0)	51 (7.1)	32 (2.3)	56 (2.0)
Don't Bother About House Although is my Responsibility	30 (3.9)	8 (0.1)	14 (0.4)	5 (1.8)	5 (1.0)	1 (0.2)	27 (3.7)	18 (1.3)	127 (4.4)
Do not Regard House as my Responsibility	9 (1.2)	3 (0.0)	6 (0.1)	181 (64.3)	126 (24.8)	201 (40.6)	255 (35.3)	267 (19.6)	721 (25.2)
All Households	774 (6.7)	7,095 (61.4)	3,686 (31.9)	282 (21.9)	509 (39.6)	495 (38.5)	722 (14.6)	1,364 (27.6)	2,856 (57.8)

Sample: I5

[1] Excludes Housing Association tenants because of small sample size.

Table A 6.22 Reasons why households who thought the condition of their home had deteriorated had not carried out any work, by tenure

thousands/% households who considered dwelling to have deteriorated

	Owner Occupied	Private Rented	Local Authority/New Town	Housing Association
Waiting for Council to do it	12 (1.6)	2 (0.7)	424 (58.7)	1 (2.2)
Can't Afford to	442 (57.1)	40 (14.2)	146 (20.2)	24 (53.3)
Not Bothered About it	13 (1.7)	18 (6.4)	8 (1.1)	—
Waiting for Grant/Approval	24 (3.1)	—	—	—
Doing Something Now	165 (21.3)	2 (0.7)	1 (0.1)	—
Not my Responsibility	13 (1.7)	155 (55.0)	79 (10.9)	16 (35.6)
Other	167 (21.6)	46 (16.3)	107 (14.8)	10 (22.2)
All Households who Considered Dwelling to Have Deteriorated	774 (66.7)	282 (21.9)	722 (14.6)	45 (9.1)

Percentages do not total 100% as respondents can give more than one reason.

Sample: I7

Table A 7.1 Work undertaken during 1986: construction date by tenure

thousands/% households

	Occupants								Landlords[1]					
	Owner Occupied		Private Rented		Local Authority/ New Town		Housing Association		Private Rented		Local Authority/ New Town		Housing Association	
	Work Done	No Work Done	Work Done	No Work Done	Work Done	No Work Done	Work Done	No Work Done	Work Done	No Work Done	Work Done	No Work Done	Work Done	No Work Done
Pre-1919	2,472 (75.4) (27.8)	808 (24.6) (30.1)	285 (37.0) (71.1)	485 (63.0) (54.8)	79 (39.7) (4.1)	120 (60.3) (4.0)	83 (52.9) (30.6)	74 (47.1) (33.2)	382 (49.6) (67.3)	387 (50.4) (54.3)	115 (57.5) (4.8)	85 (42.5) (3.5)	106 (67.5) (31.4)	51 (32.5) (34.2)
1919–1944	2,171 (81.3) (24.5)	500 (18.7) (18.7)	50 (26.6) (12.5)	138 (73.4) (15.6)	440 (43.1) (23.0)	580 (56.9) (19.1)	32 (52.5) (11.9)	29 (47.5) (13.0)	61 (32.4) (11.2)	128 (67.6) (18.2)	530 (52.1) (22.1)	488 (47.9) (20.3)	50 (80.6) (16.9)	12 (19.4) (9.3)
1945–1964	1,543 (74.8) (17.4)	520 (25.2) (19.4)	59 (33.2) (14.7)	119 (66.8) (13.5)	921 (42.5) (48.1)	1,244 (57.5) (41.1)	3 (66.7) (1.1)	2 (33.3) (0.7)	97 (54.5) (17.1)	81 (45.5) (11.3)	1,019 (47.1) (41.4)	1,146 (52.9) (46.3)	2 (33.3) (0.4)	3 (66.7) (1.9)
Post-1964	2,689 (75.9) (30.3)	852 (24.1) (31.8)	7 (4.7) (7.7)	143 (95.3) (16.1)	473 (30.4) (24.8)	1,085 (69.6) (35.8)	152 (56.3) (56.4)	118 (43.7) (52.9)	29 (19.3) (4.4)	121 (80.7) (16.2)	798 (51.2) (31.7)	761 (48.8) (29.9)	182 (67.7) (51.3)	87 (32.3) (54.6)
All Dwellings	8,875 (76.8) (100)	2,680 (23.2) (100)	401 (31.2) (100)	885 (68.8) (100)	1,913 (38.7) (100)	3,029 (61.3) (100)	270 (54.8) (100)	223 (45.2) (100)	569 (44.2) (100)	717 (55.8) (100)	2,462 (49.8) (100)	2,480 (50.2) (100)	340 (69.1) (100)	153 (30.9) (100)

Sample: I1

[1] Work undertaken by landlords is based on tenants' reports.

Table A 7.2 Major works undertaken during 1986: construction date by tenure

thousands/% households

	Occupants								Landlords[1]					
	Owner Occupied		Private Rented		Local Authority/ New Town		Housing Association		Private Rented		Local Authority/ New Town		Housing Association	
	Major Work Done	No Major Work Done	Major Work Done	No Major Work Done	Major Work Done	No Major Work Done	Major Work Done	No Major Work Done	Major Work Done	No Major Work Done	Major Work Done	No Major Work Done	Major Work Done	No Major Work Done
Pre-1919	809 (24.7) (33.8)	2,471 (75.3) (27.0)	33 (4.3) (59.0)	737 (95.7) (59.8)	5 (2.5) (3.9)	194 (97.5) (4.0)	2 (1.3) (50.0)	155 (98.7) (31.7)	130 (16.9) (60.2)	639 (83.1) (59.7)	27 (13.5) (4.5)	173 (86.5) (4.0)	17 (10.8) (28.3)	140 (89.2) (32.3)
1919–1944	596 (22.3) (25.0)	2,075 (77.7) (22.6)	5 (2.7) (9.8)	183 (97.3) (14.9)	41 (4.0) (32.0)	979 (96.0) (20.3)	2 (3.3) (50.0)	59 (96.7) (12.1)	20 (10.6) (9.3)	169 (89.4) (15.8)	112 (11.0) (18.8)	906 (89.0) (20.8)	10 (16.1) (16.7)	52 (83.9) (12.0)
1945–1964	363 (17.6) (15.2)	1,700 (82.4) (18.5)	17 (9.5) (31.2)	161 (90.5) (13.1)	42 (1.9) (32.8)	2,123 (98.1) (44.1)	—	5 (100) (1.0)	43 (24.2) (19.9)	135 (75.8) (12.6)	262 (12.1) (44.0)	1,903 (87.9) (43.8)	—	5 (100) (1.2)
Post-1964	620 (17.5) (26.0)	2,921 (82.5) (31.9)	—	150 (100) (12.2)	40 (2.6) (31.3)	1,518 (97.4) (31.0)	—	270 (100) (55.2)	23 (15.6) (9.8)	127 (84.4) (11.1)	195 (12.5) (31.8)	1,364 (87.5) (30.6)	33 (12.3) (54.7)	236 (87.3) (51.9)
All Dwellings	2,388 (20.7) (100)	9,167 (79.3) (100)	55 (4.3) (100)	1,231 (95.7) (100)	128 (2.6) (100)	4,814 (97.4) (100)	4 (0.6) (100)	489 (99.4) (100)	216 (16.8) (100)	1,070 (83.2) (100)	596 (12.1) (100)	4,346 (87.9) (100)	60 (12.0) (100)	433 (87.8) (100)

Sample: I1

(1) Work undertaken by landlords is based on tenants' reports.

Table A 7.3 Type of work carried out, in 1986, when major jobs were undertaken by occupants and landlords

% of occasions reported (1−5 most frequent jobs)

	Occupants			Landlords[1]	
	Owner Occupiers	Private Rented	Local Authority/ New Town	Private Rented	Local Authority/ New Town
Extensions	8	—	—	1	1
Roof Covering	10	2	—	21 (2)	7
Roof Timbers	1	11	—	4	1
Chimney Stacks	7	—	—	10	1
Gutters/Downpipes	6	—	—	24 (1)	6
Building External Walls	3	—	2	1	1
Pointing External Walls	4	—	—	1	3
Rendering External Walls	4	—	—	1	1
Damp Proof Course	4	—	—	3	1
Windows	16 (4)	22 (5)	6	9	28 (1)
Double Glazing	14	—	6	2	2
Outside Decoration/Paint	8	—	—	20 (3)	8
Outside Doors	8	—	2	1	9 (5)
Floor Joists	1	6	—	2	1
Floor Covering	7	6	—	3	2
Stairs	1	—	—	—	1
Timber Treatment	2	—	—	2	1
Rebuild Internal Walls	10	5	19 (3)	1	3
Plasterwork	9	13	26 (2)	2	5
Ceiling	6	3	15	1	4
Inside Doors	4	—	16 (5)	1	2
Internal Decoration	33 (1)	61 (1)	35 (1)	—	3
Electrical Supply	14	25 (3)	13	13 (4)	14 (3)
Gas Supply	2	3	—	10	1
Hot/Cold Water Pipes	6	2	8	3	3
Foundations	1	5	—	—	—
Drains	2	—	—	6	3
Bathroom Fitments	16 (4)	25 (3)	18 (4)	8	5
Kitchen Units	20 (2)	27 (2)	16	9	4
Central Heating	17 (3)	2	2	13 (4)	22 (2)
Other Heating	6	3	11	3	6
Wall Insulation	1	—	—	—	14 (3)
Loft/Roof Insulation	2	—	—	1	4
Draughtproofing	1	—	—	—	1
Other Work	10	33	30	6	4

Sample: I8

[1] Work undertaken by local authorities and private landlords is based on tenants' reports.

Table A 7.4 Type of work carried out, in 1986, when major jobs were undertaken by owner occupiers or landlords by construction date

% of occasions reported (1–5 most frequent jobs)

	Owner Occupiers[1]				Private Landlords				Local Authority Landlords			
	Pre-1919	1919–1944	1945–1964	Post-1964	Pre-1919	1919–1944	1945–1964	Post-1964	Pre-1919	1919–1944	1945–1964	Post-1964
Extensions	8	11	9	4	2	—	—	2	—	2	—	1
Roof Covering	20 (3)	6	7	2	41 (1)	—	—	—	17 (3)	13	5	4
Roof Timbers	3	1	1	—	8	—	—	—	7	3	11 (4)	—
Chimney Stacks	10	4	1	9	21 (3)	—	—	—	—	2	1	1
Gutters/Downpipes	12	4	5	—	29 (2)	—	10 (3)	55 (1)	10	23 (2)	3	—
Building External Walls	4	3	2	2	1	—	—	—	—	4	1	—
Pointing External Walls	8	4	3	1	2	—	—	—	10	15 (5)	—	1
Rendering External Walls	5	6	2	1	1	—	—	—	13	3	1	—
Damp Proof Course	9	1	1	—	6	—	—	—	—	1	1	—
Windows	29 (1)	10	9	9	13	21 (2)	5 (4)	—	17 (3)	40 (1)	30 (1)	19 (3)
Double Glazing	16	18 (3)	20 (3)	6	4	—	—	—	7	2	2	1
Outside Decoration/Paint	9	10	2	6	20 (4)	21 (2)	—	55 (1)	13	10	6	7 (4)
Outside Doors	6	9	4	12 (5)	1	—	—	—	10	23 (2)	6	4
Floor Joists	2	1	—	—	4	—	—	—	—	1	1	—
Floor Covering	10	10	2	1	7	—	—	—	3	5	1	1
Stairs	2	1	—	—	—	—	—	—	—	2	—	—
Timber Treatment	3	1	1	6	4	—	—	—	—	1	—	—
Rebuild Internal Walls	10	12	10	6	2	4	—	—	3	3	2	5
Plasterwork	11	13 (5)	5	6	5	—	—	—	13	7	7	—
Ceilings	8	8	3	2	2	—	—	—	17 (3)	3	2	5
Inside Doors	6	6	3	1	2	—	—	—	3	7	1	—
Internal Decoration	22 (2)	33 (1)	32 (1)	19 (1)	—	—	—	—	10	3	3	3
Electrical Supply	14	13 (5)	18 (4)	13 (3)	11	58 (1)	—	—	23 (2)	3	26 (2)	1
Gas Supply	3	2	1	1	20 (4)	—	—	—	—	1	1	—
Hot/Cold Water Pipes	8	7	9	1	7	4	—	—	7	5	4	1
Foundations	1	1	1	—	—	—	—	—	—	—	—	—
Drains	3	2	1	1	—	—	—	39 (3)	—	1	5	—
Bathroom Fitments	17 (5)	13 (5)	29 (2)	8	15	4	—	5 (4)	3	7	6	5
Kitchen Units	17 (5)	30 (2)	17	—	2	5	50 (1)	—	3	3	1	7 (4)
Central Heating	18 (4)	16 (4)	18 (4)	16 (2)	15	8 (5)	33 (2)	—	7	23 (2)	21 (3)	26 (2)
Other Heating	4	2	2	13 (3)	7	—	—	—	27 (1)	7	8 (5)	1
Wall Insulation	1	1	1	1	—	—	—	—	13	4	7	29 (1)
Loft/Roof Insulation	4	2	2	—	1	—	5 (4)	—	7	3	5	2
Draughtproofing	4	—	—	—	—	—	—	—	—	—	—	2
Other	11	11	11	8	4	9 (4)	—	—	10	2	3	5

Sample: I8

[1] Breakdown of work by tenants is not provided as the sample size is too small.

Table A 7.5 Owner occupiers undertaking work in 1986: person responsible for undertaking work (contractor/DIY) by income[1] and age of head of household

% jobs done

	Work Done by Contractor	Work Done by DIY	Work Done by DIY/Contractor	Work Done by Other	All Work Done
£0−£2,999	80.3	15.6	0.3	3.8	100.4
	10.6	6.9	0.7	11.1	9.4
£3,000−£5,999	79.8	15.1	2.8	2.3	100.0
	18.6	11.8	10.6	12.1	16.6
£6,000−£8,999	69.9	22.3	3.1	4.7	100.0
	23.9	25.8	17.5	36.1	24.7
£9,000−£11,999	60.7	30.7	5.6	3.0	100.0
	20.1	34.2	30.4	21.9	23.7
£12,000−£14,999	75.6	17.0	4.9	2.5	100.0
	16.1	12.2	17.1	11.7	15.2
£15,000 and Over	70.6	17.7	9.6	2.1	100.0
	10.7	9.0	23.7	7.1	10.8
17−39 Years	62.3	31.2	4.6	1.9	100.0
	33.2	55.8	39.9	22.6	37.8
40−59 Years	72.0	17.8	5.9	4.3	100.0
	39.4	32.8	53.4	53.2	39.1
60−74 Years	84.0	11.5	1.4	3.1	100.0
	24.1	11.1	6.7	19.9	20.5
75 Years and Over	92.1	2.5	−	5.4	100.0
	3.3	0.3		4.3	2.6
All Households	71.3	21.1	4.4	3.2	100.0
	100.0	100.0	100.0	100.0	100.0

Sample: I19

[1] Net income of head of household and spouse.

Table A 7.6 Owner occupiers undertaking work in 1986: income and age of household by reason for undertaking work

% jobs done

	Economy	Comfort/ Appearance	Repair to Remedy Defect	To Increase Value of Property	Required by Bank/Building Society	All Reasons
£0−£2,999	1.2	47.7	45.3	5.1	0.7	100.0
£3,000−£5,999	4.1	55.7	29.6	9.3	1.3	100.0
£6,000−£8,999	5.8	46.6	35.0	11.6	1.0	100.0
£9,000−£11,999	3.8	48.5	34.5	11.6	1.6	100.0
£12,000−£14,999	4.4	51.9	30.2	12.2	1.3	100.0
£15,000 and Over	4.2	47.3	31.6	14.4	2.5	100.0
17−39 Years	4.1	43.8	34.8	14.7	2.6	100.0
40−59 Years	5.3	51.2	31.8	10.8	0.9	100.0
60−74 Years	3.3	57.5	33.6	5.4	0.2	100.0
75 Years and Over	0.0	54.8	41.3	3.5	0.3	100.0
All Households	4.3	49.5	33.6	11.2	1.4	100.0

Sample: I19

121

Table A 7.7   Owner occupiers undertaking work in 1986: type of work undertaken by source of finance

% jobs done

	Relatives	Bank/Building Society	Mortgage	Savings Only	Savings and Other	All Funding
Repair	7.0	5.8	11.0	72.5	3.7	100.0
Services	8.1	7.6	9.5	71.5	3.3	100.0
External Decoration	7.7	4.1	6.6	77.1	4.5	100.0
Internal Decoration	6.4	4.8	9.3	76.6	2.9	100.0
Enhancement	8.3	6.9	15.6	65.8	3.4	100.0
All Types of Work	7.4	6.2	12.7	70.6	3.1	100.0

Sample: 119

Table A 7.8   Tenants undertaking work in 1986: work undertaken by age of head of household and income

% jobs done

	Tenants Undertaking Work	Mean Value of Work Undertaken £	All Tenants
£0−£2,999	22.8	214	41.4
£3,000−£5,999	33.0	268	32.2
£6,000−£8,999	33.8	753	18.2
£9,000−£11,999	8.6	396	6.1
£12,000−£14,999	*	*	1.5
£15,000 and Over	*	*	0.6
17−39 Years	46.0	463	32.9
40−59 Years	25.8	390	33.5
60−74 Years	26.0	185	23.5
75 Years and Over	2.2	213	10.1

Sample: 110
* Sample too small to produce meaningful results.

Table A 7.9   Tenants undertaking work in 1986: reason for undertaking work by length of residence

% jobs done

	Economy	Comfort/Appearance	Repair to Remedy Defect	Other
0−2 Years	—	47.8	55.2	—
2−5 Years	0.8	73.2	25.2	0.8
5−10 Years	4.9	54.8	38.9	1.4
10−20 Years	0.4	80.7	17.3	1.6
20 Years or More	1.5	86.4	11.1	1.0
All Tenants	1.5	72.5	24.9	1.1

Sample: 110

Table A 7.10   Tenants whose landlords undertook work in 1986: difficulty experienced in getting landlord to carry out work

% jobs done by landlord

	Private Rented		Local Authority		Housing Association	
	Work Requested	Work Not Requested	Work Requested	Work Not Requested	Work Requested	Work Not Requested
Initiation of Work	42.0	58.0	30.0	70.0	20.0	80.0
Difficulty in Getting Landlord to do Work						
Difficult	15.6		51.7		16.0	
Not Difficult	84.4		48.3		84.0	

Sample: 116

Table A 8.1   Private sector: grants[1] given between 1981 and 1986 by tenure

thousands/% grants

	Owner Occupiers	Landlords	Tenants	All Grants
Improvement Grants	245 (77.0)	58 (18.2)	15 (4.7)	318
Intermediate Grants	67 (82.7)	11 (13.6)	3 (3.7)	81
Repair Grants	328 (96.5)	9 (2.6)	3 (0.9)	340
Special Grants	10 (19.2)	42 (80.8)	—	52
All Home Improvement Grants	650 (82.1)	120 (15.2)	21 (2.7)	791
Home Insulation Grants	1,550 (98.0)	—	32 (2.0)	1,582
Other Grants	39 (72.2)	—	15 (27.8)	54

Sample: POS 9

[1] Figures used are a combination of information collected by the EHCS and statistics from local authority returns.

Table A 8.2   Private sector: grants[1] given between 1981 and 1986 by construction date

thousands/% grants

	Pre-1919	1919–1944	1945–1964	Post-1964	All Grants
Improvement Grants	275 (86.5)	36 (11.3)	7 (2.2)	—	318
Intermediate Grants	59 (72.8)	20 (24.7)	2 (2.5)	—	81
Repair Grants	331 (97.4)	9 (2.6)	—	—	340
Special Grants	36 (69.2)	—	—	16 (30.8)	52
All Home Improvement Grants	701 (88.6)	65 (8.2)	9 (1.2)	16 (2.0)	791
Home Insulation Grants	396 (25.0)	659 (41.7)	345 (21.8)	182 (11.5)	1,582
Other Grants	33 (61.1)	2 (3.7)	18 (33.3)	1 (1.9)	54

Sample: POS 9

[1] Figures used are a combination of information collected by the EHCS and statistics from local authority returns.

Table A 8.3   Owner-occupiers: Home Improvement Grants given between 1981 and 1986 by household income[1]

thousands/% households

	£0–£2,999	£3,000–£5,999	£6,000–£8,999	£9,000–£11,999	£12,000–£14,999	Over £15,000	All Households
No Grant	1,569 (14.2) (95.0)	2,179 (19.8) (94.2)	2,615 (23.7) (92.1)	2,152 (19.5) (95.1)	1,486 (13.5) (95.5)	1,014 (9.3) (97.0)	11,015 (100) (94.4)
Grant	82 (12.6) (5.0)	134 (20.6) (5.8)	223 (34.3) (7.9)	110 (16.9) (4.9)	70 (10.8) (4.5)	31 (4.8) (3.0)	650 (100) (5.6)
All Households	1,651 (14.2) (100)	2,313 (19.8) (100)	2,838 (24.3) (100)	2,262 (19.4) (100)	1,556 (13.3) (100)	1,045 (9.0) (100)	11,665[2] (100) (100)

Sample: POS 6

[1] Refers to net income of head of household and spouse.

[2] Household totals differ slightly to those produced in chapters 6 and 7 because these figures are grossed on the basis of the postal survey. Each different sub-sample of the survey gives marginally different grossed totals (Appendix C).

Table A 8.4 Owner-occupiers: Home Improvement Grants given between 1981 and 1986 by age of head of household

thousands/% households

	17−39 Years	40−59 Years	60−74 Years	75 Years & Above	All Households
No Grant	3,560 (32.3) (92.2)	4,369 (39.7) (95.7)	2,408 (21.8) (94.6)	678 (6.2) (97.4)	11,015 (100) (94.4)
Grant	301 (46.3) (7.8)	194 (29.8) (4.3)	137 (21.1) (5.4)	18 (2.8) (2.6)	650 (100) (5.6)
All Households	3,861 (33.1) (100)	4,563 (39.1) (100)	2,545 (21.8) (100)	696 (6.0) (100)	11,665 (100) (100)

Sample: POS 6

Table A 8.5 Owner-occupiers: Home Improvement Grants given between 1981 and 1986 by length of residence

thousands/% households

	0−2 Years	2−5 Years	5−10 Years	10−20 Years	20 Years & Above	All Households
No Grant	2,002 (18.2) (96.3)	2,733 (24.8) (94.2)	2,054 (18.6) (92.6)	2,269 (20.6) (95.7)	1,957 (17.8) (93.4)	11,015 (100) (94.4)
Grant	77 (11.8) (3.7)	169 (26.0) (5.8)	163 (25.1) (7.4)	102 (15.7) (4.3)	139 (21.4) (6.6)	650 (100) (5.6)
All Households	2,079 (17.8) (100)	2,902 (24.9) (100)	2,217 (19.0) (100)	2,371 (20.3) (100)	2,096 (18.0) (100)	11,665 (100) (100)

Sample: POS 6

Table A 8.6 Private sector: grants given between 1981 and 1986 by condition of stock in 1981

thousands/% grants
* thousands/% dwellings

	Satisfactory	All Un-Satisfactory	Dwellings in Worst Condition[1]	All Grants
Improvement Grants	101 (31.8) (1.0)	217 (68.2) (5.7)	61 (19.2) (11.6)	318 (100) (2.3)
Intermediate Grants	−	81 (100) (2.1)	20 (24.7) (3.8)	81 (100) (0.6)
Repairs Grants	107 (31.5) (1.1)	233 (68.5) (6.2)	20 (5.9) (3.8)	340 (100) (2.4)
Special Grants	22 (42.3) (0.2)	30 (57.7) (0.8)	7 (13.5) (1.3)	52 (100) (0.4)
All Home Improvement Grants	230 (29.1) (2.3)	561 (70.9) (14.9)	108 (13.7) (20.5)	791 (100) (5.7)
Home Insulation Grants	1,146 (72.4) (11.3)	436 (27.6) (11.5)	75 (4.7) (14.2)	1,582 (100) (11.4)
Other Grants	14 (31.8) (0.1)	30 (68.2) (0.8)	16 (36.4) (3.0)	44 (100) (0.3)
* All Dwellings	10,127 (72.8) (100)	3,777 (27.2) (100)	527 (3.8) (100)	13,904 (100) (100)

Sample: POS 7
[1] Unfit and in serious disrepair.

Table A 8.7 Private sector: Home Improvement Grants given between 1981 and 1986 to unsatisfactory dwellings, in 1981, by region

thousands/% grants

	North	Rest of England	South East	All Grants
Grants to All Unsatisfactory Dwellings	180 (32.1) (15.3)	153 (27.3) (12.9)	228 (40.6) (16.1)	561 (100) (14.9)
Grants to Dwellings in the Worst Condition	39 (36.1) (3.3)	22 (20.4) (1.9)	47 (43.5) (3.3)	108 (100) (2.9)
No Grant	995 (30.9) (84.7)	1,034 (32.2) (87.1)	1,187 (36.9) (83.9)	3,216 (100) (85.1)
All Unsatisfactory Dwellings	1,175 (31.1)	1,187 (31.4)	1,415 (37.5)	3,777 (100)

Sample: POS 10

Table A 8.8 Private sector: powers used on individual dwellings between 1981 and 1986 by construction date

thousands/% dwellings where powers used

	Pre-1919	1919–1944	1944–1964	Post-1964	All Ages
Clearance or Closure	31 (73.8) (16.5)	4 (9.5) (20.0)	7 (16.7) (33.3)	—	42 (18.3)
Compulsory Renovation	77 (100.0) (40.9)	—	—	—	77 (33.6)
Compulsory Acquisition	2 (100.0) (1.1)	—	—	—	2 (0.9)
Other Powers	58 (70.7) (30.9)	16 (19.5) (80.0)	8 (9.8) (38.1)	—	82 (35.8)
Non-statutory Action	20 (76.9) (10.6)	—	6 (23.1) (28.6)	—	26 (11.4)
All Powers	188 (82.1)	20 (8.7)	21 (9.2)		229

Sample: POS 7

Table A 8.9   Private sector: powers used on individual dwellings between 1981 and 1986 by condition of the stock in 1981

thousands/% dwellings

	Satisfactory	All Unsatisfactory	Dwellings in Worst Condition	All Dwellings
Clearance or Closure	4 (9.5) (0.0)	38 (90.5) (1.0)	14 (33.3) (2.7)	42 (100) (0.3)
Compulsory Renovation	3 (3.9) (0.0)	74 (96.1) (2.0)	14 (18.2) (2.7)	77 (100) (0.6)
Compulsory Acquisition	—	2 (100) (0.1)	2 (100) (0.4)	2 (100) (0.0)
Other Powers	20 (24.3) (0.2)	62 (75.7) (1.6)	11 (13.4) (2.1)	82 (100) (0.6)
Non-statutory Action	4 (15.4) (0.0)	22 (84.6) (0.6)	10 (38.5) (1.9)	26 (100) (0.2)
All Powers	31 (13.5) (0.3)	198 (86.5) (5.2)	51 (22.3) (9.7)	229 (100) (1.6)
All Dwellings	10,127 (72.8) (100)	3,777 (27.2) (100)	527 (3.8) (100)	13,904 (100) (100)

Sample: POS 1

Table A 8.10   Private sector: powers used on dwellings between 1981 and 1986 by region

thousands/% dwellings where powers used

	North	Rest of England	South East	All Areas
Clearance or Closure	27 (64.3) (39.6)	10 (23.8) (18.2)	5 (11.9) (4.7)	42 (100) (18.3)
Compulsory Renovation	5 (6.5) (7.4)	19 (24.7) (34.5)	53 (68.8) (50.0)	77 (100) (33.6)
Compulsory Acquisition	—	—	2 (100.0) (1.9)	2 (100) (0.9)
Other Powers	22 (26.8) (32.4)	20 (24.4) (36.4)	40 (48.8) (37.7)	82 (100) (35.8)
Non-statutory Action	14 (53.8) (20.6)	6 (23.1) (10.9)	6 (23.1) (5.7)	26 (100) (11.4)
All Powers	68 (29.7) (100)	55 (24.0) (100)	106 (46.3) (100)	229 (100) (100)

Sample: POS 7

Table A 8.11   Private sector: dwelling in block or group repair schemes undertaken between 1981 and 1986, by condition of stock in 1981

thousands/% dwellings

	Satisfactory	All Unsatisfactory	Dwellings in Worst Condition	All Dwellings
Dwellings in Block/ Group Schemes	48 (31.6) (0.5)	104 (68.4) (2.8)	27 (17.8) (5.1)	152 (100) (1.1)
All Dwellings	10,127 (72.8) (100)	3,777 (27.2) (100)	527 (3.8) (100)	13,904 (100) (100)

Sample: POS 1

Table A 8.12   Private sector: dwellings in block or group repair schemes, undertaken between 1981 and 1986 by region

thousands/% dwellings in block or group repair schemes

	North	Rest of England	South East	All Areas
DOE Enveloping Schemes	2 (20.0) (4.2)	7 (70.0) (11.1)	1 (10.0) (2.4)	10 (100) (6.6)
Other Enveloping Schemes	—	6 (75.0) (9.5)	2 (25.0) (4.9)	8 (100) (5.3)
Block Repair or Improvement Schemes	28 (30.4) (58.3)	44 (47.8) (69.8)	19 (20.7) (46.3)	9 (100) (59.8)
Other Schemes	18 (41.9) (37.5)	6 (14.0) (9.5)	19 (44.2) (46.3)	43 (100) (28.3)
All Schemes	48 (31.6) (100)	63 (41.4) (100)	41 (27.0) (100)	152 (100) (100)

Sample: POS 4

Table A 8.13   Private sector: dwellings in area-based programmes between 1981 and 1986 by construction date

thousands/% dwellings in action area

	Pre-1919	1919– 1944	1945– 1964	Post-1964	All Ages
Housing Action Areas	185 (95.8) (21.7)	4 (2.1) (10.8)	4 (2.1) (50.0)	—	193 (100) (21.5)
General Improvement Areas	539 (94.7) (63.3)	28 (4.9) (75.7)	2 (0.4) (25.0)	—	569 (100) (63.4)
Other Areas	128 (94.8) (15.0)	5 (3.7) (13.5)	2 (1.5) (25.0)	—	135 (100) (15.1)
All Area-based programmes	852 (95.0) (100)	37 (4.1) (100)	8 (0.9) (100)	—	897 (100) (100)

Sample: POS 8

Table A 8.14 Private sector: dwellings in area-based programmes between 1981 and 1986 by size of programme

thousands/% dwellings in area-based programmes

	Up to 149 Dwellings	150–300 Dwellings	300 and over Dwellings	All Dwellings
Housing Action Areas	23 (11.9) (21.9)	56 (29.0) (25.6)	114 (59.1) (19.9)	193 (100) (21.5)
General Improvement Areas	71 (12.5) (67.6)	135 (23.7) (61.6)	363 (63.8) (63.3)	569 (100) (63.4)
Other Areas	11 (8.1) (10.5)	28 (20.8) (12.8)	96 (71.1) (16.8)	135 (100) (15.1)
All Area-based Programmes	105 (11.7) (100)	219 (24.4) (100)	573 (63.9) (100)	897(100) (100)

Sample: POS 8

Table A 8.15 Private sector: households in area-based programmes between 1981 and 1986 by length of residence

% households

	0–2 Years	2–5 Years	5–10 Years	10–20 Years	20 Years or More	All Households
Housing Action Area	38.0	17.5	8.8	7.3	28.4	100
General Improvement Area	33.3	14.6	15.2	14.6	22.3	100
Other Areas	39.3	12.6	10.4	10.4	27.3	100
All Area-based Programmes	34.5	15.1	13.4	12.9	24.1	100

Sample: POS 8

Table A 8.16 Private sector: households in area-based programmes between 1981 and 1986 by income of household

% households

	£0– £2,999	£3,000– £5,999	£6,000– £8,999	£9,000– £11,999	£12,000– £14,999	£15,000– and Over	All Households
Housing Action Area	8.0	16.8	37.2	13.9	24.1	—	100
General Improvement Area	25.7	35.2	25.2	8.6	1.7	3.6	100
Other	18.4	34.5	20.6	16.2	4.4	5.9	100
All Area-based Programmes	21.4	31.9	26.5	10.8	6.0	3.4	100

Sample: POS 8

Table A 8.17 Private sector: dwellings in area-based programmes between 1981 and 1986 by action taken

% dwellings

	No Specific Action on Dwellings	Specific Action on Dwellings	
Housing Action Areas	45.8	54.2	(100)
General Improvement Areas	66.2	33.8	(100)
Other Areas	64.5	35.5	(100)
All Area-based programmes	61.9	38.1	(100)

Sample: POS 8

Table A 8.18 Private sector: type of action on individual dwellings in area-based programmes between 1981 and 1986

% dwellings with specific action

	Dwellings in Block Schemes	Compulsory Action on the Dwelling	Home Improvement Grants	Total with Action on Individual Dwellings
Housing Action Areas	29.8	18.3	32.7	54.2
General Improvement Areas	11.1	2.9	26.7	33.8
Other Areas	3.1	17.6	22.9	35.5
All Area-based programmes	12.8	9.3	27.0	37.1

Sample: POS 8

Table A 8.19 Private sector: dwellings in area-based programmes between 1981 and 1986 by condition of the stock in 1981

thousands/% dwellings

	Satisfactory	All Unsatisfactory	Dwellings in Worst Condition	All Dwellings
Housing Action Areas	65 (33.7) (0.6)	128 (66.3) (3.4)	31 (16.1) (5.9)	193 (100) (1.4)
General Improvement Area	308 (54.1) (3.0)	261 (45.9) (6.9)	57 (10.0) (10.8)	569 (100) (4.1)
Other Areas	59 (43.7) (0.6)	76 (56.3) (2.0)	3 (2.2) (0.6)	135 (100) (1.0)
All Area-based Programmes	432 (48.2) (4.3)	465 (51.8) (12.3)	91 (10.1) (17.3)	897 (100) (6.5)
All Dwellings	10,127 (72.8) (100)	3,777 (27.2) (100)	527 (3.8) (100)	13,904 (100) (100)

Sample: POS 1

130

Table A 8.20 Private sector: unsatisfactory dwellings in 1981, in area-based programmes between 1981 and 1986 by region

thousands/% dwellings

	North	Rest of England	South East	All Dwellings
All Unsatisfactory Dwellings in Area-based Programmes	220 (47.3) (18.7)	154 (33.1) (13.0)	91 (19.6) (6.4)	465 (100) (12.3)
Dwellings in Worst Condition in Area-based Programmes	61 (67.0) (5.2)	22 (24.2) (1.9)	8 (8.8) (0.6)	91 (100) (2.4)
No Area-based Programmes	955 (28.8) (81.3)	1,033 (31.2) (87.0)	1,324 (40.0) (93.6)	3,312 (100) (87.7)
All Unsatisfactory Dwellings	1,175 (31.1) (100)	1,187 (31.4) (100)	1,415 (37.5) (100)	3,777 (100) (100)

Sample: POS 10

Table A 8.21 Private sector: dwellings in area-based programmes between 1981 and 1986 by surveyors' recommendations in 1981

thousands/% dwellings

	No Action	Surveyors' Recommendation		
		Potential G.I.A.	Potential H.A.A.	All Areas
Housing Action Area	56 (29.0) (0.5)	86 (44.6) (6.2)	51 (26.4) (12.5)	193 (100) (1.4)
General Improvement Area	241 (42.4) (2.0)	192 (33.7) (13.9)	136 (23.9) (33.4)	569 (100) (4.1)
Other/Non-statutory Action	59 (43.9) (0.5)	70 (51.9) (5.1)	6 (4.4) (1.5)	135 (100) (1.0)
All Area-based Programmes	356 (39.7) (2.9)	348 (38.8) (25.3)	193 (21.5) (47.4)	897 (100) (6.5)
No Action	11,764 (90.4) (97.1)	1,029 (7.9) (74.7)	214 (1.6) (52.6)	13,007 (100) (93.5)
All Dwellings	12,120 (87.2) (100)	1,377 (9.9) (100)	407 (2.9) (100)	13,904 (100) (100)

Sample: POS 1

Table A 8.22 Public sector[1]: block renovation between 1981 and 1986 by size of programme

thousands/% dwellings in block schemes

	10 Dwellings or Less	11−49 Dwellings	50−149 Dwellings	150−300 Dwellings	300 and over Dwellings	All Programmes
Block Renovation	15 (2.2)	121 (17.6)	145 (21.1)	113 (16.5)	292 (42.6)	686 (100)

Sample: POS 5

[1] Local authority and new town dwellings

Table A 8.23 Public sector: block renovation between 1981 and 1986 by condition in 1981

thousands/% dwellings

	Satisfactory	All Unsatisfactory	Dwellings in Worst Conditions	All Dwellings
Block Renovation	493 (71.9) (12.0)	193 (28.1) (23.4)	3 (0.4) (15.0)	686 (100) (13.9)
All Dwellings	4,111 (83.3) (100)	824 (16.7) (100)	20 (0.4) (100)	4,935 (100) (100)

Sample: POS 2

Table A 8.24 Public sector: dwellings in estate programmes between 1981 and 1986 by construction date and type of dwelling

thousands/% dwellings in action area

	Pre-1944	1945–1964	Post-1964	Total in Estate Programmes	All Dwellings
Houses	177 (5.6) (14.7)	193 (6.1) (9.1)	45 (1.4) (3.1)	415 (13.0) (8.4)	3,181 (100) (64.5)
Flats	25 (1.4) (2.1)	122 (7.0) (5.7)	137 (7.8) (9.4)	284 (16.2) (5.8)	1,754 (100) (35.5)
Total in Estate Programmes	202 (4.1) (16.8)	315 (6.4) (14.8)	182 (3.7) (12.5)	699 (14.2) (14.2)	—
All Dwellings	1,202 (24.4)	2,125 (43.1)	1,453 (29.4)		4,935 (100)

Sample: POS 3

Table A 8.25 Public sector: dwellings in estate programmes between 1981 and 1986 by region

thousands/% dwellings

	North	Rest of England	South East	All Regions
Estate Programmes	279 (40.0) (17.8)	166 (23.7) (10.2)	254 (36.3) (14.6)	699 (100) (14.2)
All Dwellings	1,571 (31.8)	1,620 (32.8)	1,744 (35.4)	4,935 (100)

Sample: POS 3

Table A 8.26 Public sector: dwellings in estate programmes between 1981 and 1986 by size of programme

thousands/% dwellings in estate programme

	Up to 49 Dwellings	50–149 Dwellings	150–300 Dwellings	300 and over Dwellings	All Sizes
Estate Programmes	129 (18.5) (15.6)	119 (17.0) (13.2)	104 (14.9) (13.5)	347 (49.6) (14.2)	699 (100) (14.2)
No Action	697 (16.5) (84.4)	782 (18.5) (86.8)	668 (15.7) (86.5)	2,089 (49.3) (85.8)	4,236 (100) (85.8)
	826 (16.7) (100)	901 (18.3) (100)	772 (15.6) (100)	2,436 (49.4) (100)	4,935 (100) (100)

Sample: POS 3

Table A 8.27 Public sector: estate programmes between 1981 and 1986 by condition in 1981

thousands/% dwellings

	Satisfactory	All Unsatisfactory	Dwellings in Worst Conditions	All Dwellings
Estate Programmes	447 (63.9) (10.9)	252 (36.1) (30.6)	–	699 (100) (14.2)
All Dwellings	4,111 (83.3)	824 (16.7)	20 (0.4)	4,935 (100)

Sample: POS 2

Table A 8.28 Private sector: completed action between 1981 and 1986 by condition in 1986

% dwellings subject to action

Completed Action 1981–1986	Good Condition	Poor Condition	Total
Area Action	80.5	19.5	100
Dwelling Action	72.8	27.2	100
Area and Dwelling Action	80.0	20.0	100
All Action	74.7	25.3	100

Sample: POS 11

133

Table A 8.29 Public sector: completed action between 1981 and 1986 by condition in 1986

thousands/% dwellings subject to action

Completed Action 1981–1986	Good Condition	Poor Condition	All Dwellings
Estate Action	136 (87.7) (18.3)	19 (12.3) (13.4)	155 (100) (17.5)
Action on Dwelling	307 (77.5) (41.3)	89 (22.5) (62.7)	396 (100) (44.7)
Action on Dwelling and Estate	301 (89.9) (40.4)	34 (10.1) (23.9)	335 (100) (37.8)
All Action	744 (84.0) (100)	142 (16.0) (100)	886 (100) (100)

Sample: POS 12

134

Table A 9.1 Change in number of dwellings lacking amenities, unfit, in 'serious' disrepair 1981–86 and the number of each condition category which were demolished or were no longer used as dwellings

thousand dwellings

	Lacking amenities			Unfit			'Serious' disrepair		
	Number	Demolished/ No Longer Used	% Demolished NLU	Number	Demolitions/ No Longer Used	% Demolished/ NLU	Number	Demolitions/ No Longer Used	% Demolished/ NLU
Pre-1919	−276	68	24.6	− 99	75	75.0	−102	83	83.0
North	−130	28	21.5	− 45	42	93.3	− 7	34	100.0
Rest of England	− 76	19	25.0	+ 96	15	—	+ 74	23	—
South East	−108	21	19.4	−114	20	17.5	−132	19	13.3

Sample: L.3, L.5, L.6

Table A 9.2 Age of head of households by condition in 1981 and 1986

% households

	1981				1986			
	Lacking Amenity	Unfit	Serious Disrepair	All House-holds	Lacking Amenity	Unfit	Serious Disrepair	All House-holds
17–19 Years	2.4	4.5	4.9		1.7	5.0	4.7	
	17.3	25.9	23.4	29.3	24.7	34.5	22.5	28.0
40–59 Years	2.4	3.7	5.5		0.9	3.0	5.9	
	19.7	24.8	30.8	34.0	16.0	25.3	34.8	33.6
60–70 Years	5.6	5.6	6.5		2.7	3.5	6.0	
	36.9	29.4	28.7	27.0	34.5	22.3	26.7	25.7
75 Years and Over	11.0	10.5	10.9		3.9	5.7	7.3	
	26.1	19.9	17.1	9.7	24.8	17.9	16.0	12.7
All Ages	4.1	5.1	6.2		2.0	4.1	5.8	
	(100)	(100)	(100)	(100)	(100)	(100)	(100)	(100)

Sample: L.2, L.4

135

Table A 9.3 Household type[1] by condition in 1981 and 1986

	1981				1986			
	Lacking Amenity	Unfit	Serious Disrepair	All Households	Lacking Amenity	Unfit	Serious Disrepair	All Households
Single	5.4	8.6	6.4		3.3	5.9	6.9	
Person	8.4	10.4	7.9	6.4	11.2	9.9	8.1	6.8
Small	2.1	3.8	3.7		1.7	4.4	4.3	
Adult	8.3	11.3	11.0	15.7	13.8	17.0	12.0	15.9
Single	0.9	2.8	3.4		–	8.4	6.8	
Parent	0.5	1.0	1.3	1.9		2.6	1.5	1.3
Small	2.4	3.1	3.1		1.8	6.2	7.3	
Family	11.3	11.4	12.2	19.3	11.8	20.2	16.8	13.3
Large	1.5	4.0	6.2		1.2	3.7	5.3	
Family	4.8	9.4	13.4	12.1	6.0	8.8	8.8	9.8
Large	2.9	4.1	5.4		0.7	1.2	5.9	
Adult	9.6	10.6	14.5	13.2	0.8	5.3	19.4	18.6
Older	5.9	6.9	5.5		1.5	2.6	4.7	
Smaller	24.8	20.8	18.6	16.6	14.6	12.9	16.2	19.8
Single	8.7	8.9	7.0		4.9	6.6	7.0	
OAP	32.3	25.1	21.1	14.8	35.8	23.3	17.2	14.5
All	4.1	5.1	6.2		2.0	4.1	5.8	
Households	(100)	(100)	(100)	(100)	(100)	(100)	(100)	(100)

[1] Household Type

Single Person:	Single person (not pensioners)
Small Adult:	Two adults (not pensioners) no children
Single Parent:	One adult (not pensioners) one or more children
Single Family:	Two adults (not pensioners) and one or two children; one adult and one or more children and one or more pensioners; one or more children and one or more pensioners
Large Family:	Two adults (not pensioners) three or more children; two adults (not pensioners) and one or more children and one or more pensioners; three or more adults or one or more children
Large Adult:	One adult and two pensioners; two adults and one or more pensioners; three or more adults (not pensioners); three or more pensioners
Older Smaller:	One adult and one pensioner; two pensioners
Single Pensioner:	One pensioner

Sample: L.2, L.4

Table A 9.4 Length of residence by condition in 1981 and 1986

% households

	1981				1986			
	Lacking Amenity	Unfit	Serious Disrepair	All House-holds	Lacking Amenity	Unfit	Serious Disrepair	All House-holds
Up to 1 Year	3.8	4.5	5.4		0.8	3.7	2.6	
	7.3	7.1	6.9	8.2	4.4	10.0	5.6	11.1
1–2 Years	1.9	3.0	4.1		1.9	2.5	4.4	
	2.5	3.4	3.8	6.0	7.2	4.5	5.0	7.2
2–5 Years	2.4	4.1	4.9		0.7	2.8	2.8	
	9.3	12.5	13.0	16.1	6.2	12.3	8.0	18.0
5–10 Years	2.0	3.0	3.5		1.8	5.2	8.3	
	8.3	10.4	10.7	18.1	15.5	21.9	25.0	17.1
10–20 Years	3.4	4.0	5.4		1.3	2.5	2.8	
	17.7	17.5	20.5	22.6	15.6	13.9	12.0	23.0
20 Years or More	8.0	8.7	9.8		4.3	6.5	11.2	
	54.9	49.1	45.1	29.0	51.1	37.4	45.0	23.6
All Households	4.1	5.1	6.2		2.0	4.1	5.8	
	(100)	(100)	(100)	(100)	(100)	(100)	(100)	(100)

Sample: L.2, L.4

Table A 9.5 Income[1] by condition in 1981 and 1986

% households

	1981				1986			
	Lacking Amenities	Unfit	Serious Disrepair	All House-holds	Lacking Amenities	Unfit	Serious Disrepair	All House-holds
Lowest Income Group	8.2	8.1	9.0		3.1	4.5	6.3	
	55.1	43.4	40.0	27.5	47.2	35.5	33.0	29.3
Second Income Group	5.0	6.5	7.2		2.4	4.5	6.3	
	24.1	24.5	22.6	19.6	32.2	28.8	29.0	26.4
Third Income Group	2.3	4.5	4.7		0.9	3.5	4.6	
	15.2	23.7	21.2	27.7	9.3	17.8	17.0	20.9
Highest Income Group	0.9	1.7	3.9		1.0	3.1	5.1	
	5.6	8.4	16.2	25.2	11.3	17.9	21.0	23.4
All Incomes	4.1	5.1	6.2		2.0	4.1	5.8	
	(100)	(100)	(100)	(100)	(100)	(100)	(100)	(100)

[1]Income is divided into 4 groups each of which approximate a quarter of the population

Sample: L.2, L.4

Table A 9.6   Employment status by condition in 1981 and 1986

% households

	1981				1986			
	Lacking Amenity	Unfit	Serious Disrepair	All House-holds	Lacking Amenity	Unfit	Serious Disrepair	All House-holds
Working	2.2	3.3	5.0		1.3	4.0	5.4	
	33.9	45.6	50.4	62.4	35.2	51.9	48.5	53.1
Unemployed	5.0	7.8	8.8		2.8	4.3	4.5	
	4.8	5.9	5.6	3.9	8.0	5.9	4.3	5.6
Retired	8.0	7.4	8.2		3.3	4.6	6.9	
	46.1	33.7	31.4	23.5	54.4	37.2	39.0	32.7
Other	6.0	7.4	7.5		0.5	2.3	5.4	
	15.2	14.8	12.6	10.2	2.4	5.0	8.2	8.6
All Households	4.1	5.1	6.2		2.0	4.1	5.8	
	(100)	(100)	(100)	(100)	(100)	(100)	(100)	(100)

Sample: L.2, L.4

Appendix A

A.1 Main physical survey: two forms were used, one designed for houses, the other for flats. These forms are largely identical, that for flats having additional pages 5, 6, 9, 10. The form for flats is reproduced here.

A.2 Longitudinal physical survey:

A.3 Interview survey:

A.4 Postal survey:

A.5 Market values survey:

Address ▢▢▢▢ ▢   Local Authority ▢▢▢▢▢   Surveyor ▢▢▢▢▢

Address [   ]

Local Authority [   ]

Surveyor [   ]

1. Survey record

	Date		Start time		Finish time		Internal inspection			External inspection		
	Day	Mth	Hrs	Mins	Hrs	Mins	Full	Partial	None	Full	Partial	None
	▢	▢	▢	▢	▢	▢	1	2	3	1	2	3
	▢	▢	▢	▢	▢	▢	1	2	3	1	2	3
	▢	▢	▢	▢	▢	▢	1	2	3	1	2	3
			Inspection outcome				1	2	3	1	2	3

Survey outcome

Data collected	Address untraceable	Dwelling demolished	No longer usable as dwelling	Refused opportunity	Other reason
1	2	3	4	5	6
			Please specify:		

Survey summary

Unfit	Amenities absent	Items defective	Non-traditional	Modification
Y N	Y N	specify no: ___	Y N	Y N

Check dimensions have been completed

Photographs taken

1	2	3	4	5	6	None 7

Form type

						2

2. Dwelling Identification

Number of dwellings at the address

One dwelling only 01	More than one dwelling specify no: ___ ___	Address part of one dwelling 66	Unobtainable 99

Number of addresses associated with the dwelling

One address only 01	More than one dwelling at address 66	More than one address specify no: ___ ___	Unobtainable 99

Type of dwelling

End terrace	Mid terrace	Semi-detached	Detached house	Temporary dwelling	Dwelling in converted building	Purpose built flats	Non residential with flats
1	2	3	4	5	6	7	8
Change to Form 1					**Identify module now**		

Whether occupied

Occupied	Vacant awaiting sale	Vacant awaiting demolition	Vacant being modernised	Vacant short term	Vacant long term	No longer used as dwelling	Unknown
1	2	3	4	5	6	7	9

Turn to page 2 to complete Interior section. If access is not possible go to page 4 section 5

3. Interior

Rooms	1	2	3	4	Kitchen	Bath	Hall/landing/stairwell	5	6	7	8	9	Balcony	Number of habitable rooms
Does room exist	Y N	Y N	Y N	Y N	Y N	Y N	Y N	Y N	Y N	Y N	Y N	Y N	Y N	Specify no: __ __
Was room located	Y N	Y N	Y N	Y N	Y N	Y N	Y N	Y N	Y N	Y N	Y N	Y N	Y N	
Level (B,G,1,2,3,etc)														
Additional part	Y N	Y N	Y N	Y N	Y N	Y N	Y N	Y N	Y N	Y N	Y N	Y N	Y N	
Front/back position(F,B,T,C)														
Left/right position(L,R,T,C)														
Room inspected	Y N	Y N	Y N	Y N	Y N	Y N	Y N							

Floors *(answer in tenths)*

	1	2	3	4	Kitchen	Bath	Hall/landing/stairwell
Solid Floors	Y N	Y N	Y N	Y N	Y N	Y N	Y N
Faults	Y N	Y N	Y N	Y N	Y N	Y N	Y N
Replace structure							
Replace only boards or screed							
Refix boards, repair screed							
Leave							

Walls *(answer in tenths)*

	1	2	3	4	Kitchen	Bath	Hall/landing/stairwell
Faults	Y N	Y N	Y N	Y N	Y N	Y N	Y N
Rebuild partition wall							
Hack -off replaster							
Isolated repair, fill cracks							
Leave							

Ceilings *(answer in tenths)*

	1	2	3	4	Kitchen	Bath	Hall/landing/stairwell
Faults	Y N	Y N	Y N	Y N	Y N	Y N	Y N
Take down and renew							
Isolated, repair fill cracks							
Leave							

Doors/Frames *(answer in numbers)*

	1	2	3	4	Kitchen	Bath	Hall/landing/stairwell
Faults	Y N	Y N	Y N	Y N	Y N	Y N	Y N
Renew							
Repair, rehang							
Leave							

Windows/Frames

	1	2	3	4	Kitchen	Bath	Hall/landing/stairwell
Faults	Y N	Y N	Y N	Y N	Y N	Y N	Y N

Heating

	1	2	3	4	Kitchen	Bath	Hall/landing/stairwell
Fixed CH	Y N	Y N	Y N	Y N	Y N	Y N	Y N
Fixed other	Y N	Y N	Y N	Y N	Y N	Y N	Y N

Defects

	1	2	3	4	Kitchen	Bath	Hall/landing/stairwell
Sloping floors/cracks distortion	1	1	1	1	1	1	1
Rising damp	2	2	2	2	2	2	2
Penetrating damp	3	3	3	3	3	3	3
Slight mould growth	4	4	4	4	4	4	4
Serious mould growth	5	5	5	5	5	5	5
Unsafe staircase	6	6	6	6	6	6	6
Trip steps/low headroom	7	7	7	7	7	7	7
Interconnecting rooms	8	8	8	8	8	8	
Inadequate space					9	9	
Natural lighting	10	10	10	10	10	10	10
Ventilation	11	11	11	11	11	11	11
Electrical safety	12	12	12	12	12	12	12
Excessive draughts	13	13	13	13	13	13	13

Stairs

Present	Y N

Location	Hall 12	Specify room no. __ __	Kitchen 10

Type	Transverse 1	Parallel 2	Square 3	Circular 4

Action	None 1	Minor repair 2	Major repair 3	Replace 4

Reliability of internal assessment	Reasonably reliable 1	Doubtful 2	Very doubtful 3

Ceiling Heights

	Level (B,G,1,2 etc)	Main part	Additional part
Principal floor	☐☐	☐ • ☐☐ m	☐ • ☐☐ m
Next principal floor	☐☐	☐ • ☐☐ m	☐ • ☐☐ m

Summary of internal defects

Whether defective

seriously defective	defective	just acceptable	satisfactory	not known	
1	2	3	4	9	Internal repair
1	2	3	4	9	Heating
1	2	3	4	9	Stability
1	2	3	4	9	Freedom from damp
1	2	3	4	9	Internal arrangement
1	2	3	4	9	Natural lighting
1	2	3	4	9	Ventilation
1	2	3	4	9	Power & lighting

Please turn over the page and finish kitchen & bathroom questions

Interior (continued)

Amenities

Action

Summary of internal defects cont'd

Whether defective

Kitchen

	Present	Working order	None	Repair	Replace	Install	Hot water	Cold water	Shared	Elsewhere inside	Elsewhere outside		seriously defective	just defective acceptable	satisfactory	not known	
Cold water supply	Y N	Y N	1	2	3	4			Y N	Y N	Y N		1	2	3	4	9	Cold water supply
Sink	Y N	Y N	1	2	3	4	Y N	Y N	Y N	Y N	Y N							
Cupboards/worktop	Y N	Y N	1	2	3	4			Y N									
Cooking provision	Y N	Y N	1	2	3	4			Y N	Y N	Y N		1	2	3	4	9	Preparation of cooking Waste disposal

Bathroom

WC	Y N	Y N	1	2	3	4			Y N	Y N	Y N							
Bath/shower	Y N	Y N	1	2	3	4	Y N	Y N	Y N	Y N	Y N							
Wash hand basin	Y N	Y N	1	2	3	4	Y N	Y N	Y N	Y N	Y N		1	2	3	4	9	Drainage/ Sanitary Conveniences

Services

	Present					n/a
Central heating	Y N	1	2	3		8
Central hot water system	Y N	1	2	3	4	8
Individual hot water system	Y N	1	2	3	4	8
Electrical system	Y N	1	2	3	4	
Hot & cold water at 3 points	Y N					

Heating

Central heating	Single purpose unit 01	Water borne Back boiler to other heater 02	Ducted air 03	Under floor 04	Ceiling heating 05	Storage heaters 06	Other 07	None 77
Main fuel to CH	Balanced flue 01	Mains Gas Other 02	Bottle gas(LPG) 03	Electricity Normal 04	Off-peak 05	Fuel oil 06	Solid fuel 07	Communal/ district heating 08	Other 09	None 77

Other main heating	Supplementary storage heaters 1	Convectors 2	Enclosed stove/ range 3	Radiant/open fire 4	Oil filled radiator 5	Other fixed 6	Portable only 7	No heating seen 8
Main fuel to other heating	Balanced flue 01	Mains Gas Other 02	Bottle gas(LPG) 03	Electricity Normal 04	Off-peak 05	Fuel oil 06	Solid fuel 07	Paraffin 08	Other 09	None 77

4. Occupancy

Tenure of dwelling	Owner occupied 1	Private furnished 2	Private unfurnished 3	Local authority/ New town 4	Housing association 5	Other 6	Unknown 9

Number of household spaces occupied in dwelling	None 77	One 01	More than one, specify no: ___ ___	Unknown 99

Number of household spaces vacant in dwelling	None 77	One 01	More than one, specify no: ___ ___	Unknown 99

5. Dwelling Shape

Plan type	Simple plan 1	Simple with additional part 2	Complex plan 3	Unknown 9

specify:

```
                    B
        1   2   3
    L   4   5   6   R
        7   8   9
                    F
```

Additional part	Front elevation			Back elevation			Left elevation			Right elevation				
	Left 1	Centre 2	Right 3	Left 4	Centre 5	Right 6	Front 7	Centre 8	Back 9	Front 10	Centre 11	Back 12	None 77	Unknown 99

Attic/basement in dwelling	Attic only 1	Basement only 2	Attic and basement 3	Neither 4	Unknown 9

Entry floor to dwelling(B,G,1,2,etc)	Specify: ___ ___	Unknown 99

6. External Dimensions of Dwelling

	No of floors	Level (B,G, 1,2,etc)	Width (metres)	Depth (metres)	Whether measured
Main structure	☐☐	☐☐	☐☐.☐	☐☐.☐	Y N
		☐☐	☐☐.☐	☐☐.☐	
		☐☐	☐☐.☐	☐☐.☐	
Additional part	☐☐	☐☐	☐☐.☐	☐☐.☐	Y N
		☐☐	☐☐.☐	☐☐.☐	
		☐☐	☐☐.☐	☐☐.☐	

7. Access - shared facilities

External to dwelling within/attached to module

	Accessway on typical/upper level		Main entrance to module	Lifts (include separate lobby)		Other areas on typical/upper level	
	Main horizontal	Stairway		In module	Other on level	2nd horizontal	2nd stairway
Does access/area exist?	Y N	Y N	Y N	Y N	Y N	Y N	Y N
Balcony/Deck/Corridor/ Lobby/Other		▓		▓			
Spacious/Average/Tight							
Enclosed	Y N	Y N	Y N	▓			
Additional part	Y N	Y N	Y N	Y N			
Front/Back/Centre/Thru							
Left//Right/Centre/Thru							
External to module	Y N	Y N	Y N	Y N			
Number of lifts							

Number in module

Dwellings accessed from typical/upper level	Specify no. — —	Unknown 99

Number of upper access levels	None 77	Specify — —	Unknown 99

Dwellings on lowest dwelling level	Specify no. — —	Unknown 99

Total dwellings in module	Specify no. — — —	Unknown 999

Floor/treads *(answer in m²)*

Faults	Y N	Y N	Y N
Modify structure			
Renew surface			
Repair surface			

Walls *(answer in m²)*

Faults	Y N	Y N	Y N
Modify structure			
Renew surface			
Repair surface			

Ceiling/soffits *(answer in m²)*

Faults	Y N	Y N	Y N
Modify structure			
Renew surface			
Repair surface			

Accessway doors/screens *(answer in numbers)*

Faults	Y N	Y N	Y N
Replace			
Repair/rehang			

Accessway windows/louvres

Faults	Y N	Y N	Y N

Balustrades *(answer in meter lengths)*

Faults	Y N	Y N	Y N
Replace			
Repair			

Defects

Structural faults	1	1	1
Penetrating damp	2	2	2
Mould growth	3	3	3
Bad arrangement	4	4	4
Ventilation	5	5	5
Electical safety	6	6	6
Artificial lighting	7	7	7

Access to lowest dwelling level

Level (B,G,1,2 etc) —	Direct from plot 1	As typical/ upper level 2	Other, 3
			Specify (B,D,C,L,S,O) —

Lowest storey of module

Level (B,G) —	Dwelling only 1	Dwelling & other 2	Services for dwgs 3	Commercial 4	Void 5

Shared facilities

	Exists?	Non func./ unaccept.	Functions but defects	Just acceptable	good order
Lifts	Y N	1	2	3	4
Refuse disposal	Y N	1	2	3	4
Storage facilities	Y N	1	2	3	4
Garaging	Y N	1	2	3	4

Ill treatment

	Extensive	Moderate	Minor	None
Vandalism	1	2	3	4
Soiled surfaces	1	2	3	4
Grafitti	1	2	3	4
Litter/rubbish	1	2	3	4

Security of module

Multiple access 1	Single access 2	Restricted entry 3

8. Module Shape

Plan type	Simple plan 1	Simple with additional part 2	Complex plan 3		Unknown 9

specify:

```
                    B
              1   2   3
          L   4   5   6   R
              7   8   9
                    F
```

Additional part	Front elevation			Back elevation			Left elevation			Right elevation			None	Unknown
	Left 01	Centre 02	Right 03	Left 04	Centre 05	Right 06	Front 07	Centre 08	Back 09	Front 10	Centre 11	Back 12	77	99

Attic/basement in module	Attic only 1	Basement only 2	Attic and basement 3	Neither 4	Unknown 9

Entry floor to module (B,G,1,2,etc)	Specify: __ __	Unknown 99

9. External Dimensions of Module

	No of floors	Same as dwelling	Width (metres)	Depth (metres)	Whether measured?
Main part	☐☐	Y N	☐☐ • ☐	☐☐ • ☐	Y N
Additional part	☐☐	Y N	☐☐ • ☐	☐☐ • ☐	Y N

Upper floor size in relation to floor measured	About the same size 1	Bigger 2		Smaller 3
Does the elevation contain	Indentations 1	Projections 2	Both 3	Neither 4

10. Dimensions of Plot

Width of plot	Same width as module 55	Specify (metres) __ __	Over 20 metres 66	Public plot 77	Unknown 99
Depth of front garden	No front garden 55	Specify (metres) __ __	Over 20 metres 66	Public plot 77	Unknown 99
Depth of back garden	No back garden 55	Specify (metres) __ __	Over 50 metres 66	Public plot 77	Unknown 99

11. Exterior

Attachment of module to other buildings (in tenths of area)

	Front	Back	Left	Right
Main part	☐	☐	☐	☐
Additional part	☐	☐	☐	☐

11. Exterior (continued)

View system selected

	2 views	4 views
	1	2

Front

Seen		Not seen		
1		2		
Front only	With left	With right	Left only	Right only
1	2	3	4	5

Back

Seen		Not seen		Does not exist
1		2		8
Back only	With left	With right	Left only	Right only
1	2	3	4	5

Chimney Stacks

Masonry (Front) / Masonry (Back)

- Number
- Faults (Y N / Y N)
- Rebuild
- Part rebuild
- Repoint/flashings/refix
- Leave
- Urgency (U F B)
- Replacement period

Roof Structure

Pitched	Mansard	Flat	Mono	Chalet	Unknown

- Tenths of area
- Faults (Y N / Y N / Y N / Y N / Y N)
- Replace
- Strengthen
- Leave
- Urgency (U F B)
- Replacement period

Roof Covering

Slate	Plain tile	Single lap tile	Felt	Metal	Concrete screed	Unknown

- Tenths of area
- Faults (Y N)
- Renew
- Isolated repairs
- Leave
- Urgency (U F B)
- Replacement period

Walls

Windows doors	Void	Wall

- Tenths of area

Wall structure

Masonry cavity	Masonry solid <9"	Masonry solid = 9"	Masonry solid >9"	In-situ concrete	Pre-fab concrete	Timber

- Net tenths of area
- Faults (Y N)
- Rebuild
- Repair
- Leave
- Urgency (U F B)
- Replacement period

Wall Surface

Brick face	Stone face	Rend-ered	Timber	Tile hung	Con-crete panel	Metal/ plastic

- Net tenths of area
- Faults (Y N)
- Renew/repoint
- Isolated Repairs
- Surface finish
- Leave
- Urgency (U F B)
- Replacement period

7

11. Exterior (continued)

Front   **Back**

Windows/Frames

	Wood casement	Wood sash	Steel	Wood double glazed	Metal UVPC db glzd			Wood casement	Wood sash	Steel	Wood double glazed	Metal UVPC db glzd
Number							Number					
Faults	Y N	Y N	Y N	Y N	Y N	Y N	Faults	Y N	Y N	Y N	Y N	Y N	Y N
Replace							Replace					
Repair/replace sash or member												
Ease sashes etc reglaze												
Repaint							Repaint					
Leave							Leave					
Urgency (U F B)							Urgency (U F B)					
Replacement period							Replacement period					

Doors/Frames

	Mainly wood	Mainly metal				Mainly wood	Mainly metal	
Number				Number			
Faults	Y N	Y N	Y N	Faults	Y N	Y N	Y N
Replace				Replace			
Repair member				Repair member			
Ease/reglaze/adjust ironmongery							
Repaint				Repaint			
Leave				Leave			
Urgency (U F B)				Urgency (U F B)			
Replacement period				Replacement period			

Damp Proof Course

	Existing DPC	None	Not obtained			Existing DPC	None	Not obtained
Tenths of length				Tenths of length			
Faults	Y N			Faults	Y N		
Replace				Replace			
Leave				Leave			
Urgency (U F B)				Urgency (U F B)			
Replacement period				Replacement period			

Drainage System
(in tenths of lengths)

	Soil drainage	Surface drainage			Soil drainage	Surface drainage
Faults	Y N	Y N	Faults	Y N	Y N
Replace/relay			Replace/relay		
Repair			Repair		
Leave			Leave		
Urgency (U F B)			Urgency (U F B)		
Replacement period			Replacement period		

Features

Roof features	Y N		Elevation features	Y N		Roof features	
Full gables	___	__ __	Bays	__ __		Full gables	___
Half gables	___	__ __	Porches	__ __		Half gables	___
Dormers	__ __	__ __	Balconies	__ __		Dormers	__ __
Slopes		Y N	Ornamentation	Y N		Slopes	___
Other, specify	Y N	Y N	Parapets	Y N		Other, specify	Y N
		Y N	Turrets	Y N			
		Y N	Steps	Y N			
		Y N	Lift towers	Y N			
		Y N	Stairwells	Y N			
		Y N	Fins/ext, frames	Y N			
		Y N	Other, specify	Y N			

8

11. Exterior (continued)

Left

Seen 1	Not seen 2	Already completed 3	Does not exist 4

Right

Seen 1	Not seen 2	Already completed 3	Does not exist 4

Chimney Stacks

Masonry (Left) | | Masonry (Right)

Left						Right	
		Number					
Y	N	Y	N	Faults	Y	N	Y	N
		Rebuild			
		Part rebuild			
		Repoint/flashings/refix			
		Leave			
		Urgency (U F B)			
		Replacement period			

Roof Structure

Left: Pitched	Mansard	Flat	Mono	Chalet	Unknown		Right: Pitched	Mansard	Flat	Mono	Chalet	Unknown
						Tenths of area						
Y N	Y N	Y N	Y N	Y N	Y N	Faults	Y N	Y N	Y N	Y N	Y N	Y N
						Replace						
						Strengthen						
						Leave						
						Urgency (U F B)						
						Replacement period						

Roof Covering

Left: Slate	Plain tile	Single lap tile	Felt	Metal	Concrete screed	Unknown		Right: Slate	Plain tile	Single lap tile	Felt	Metal	Concrete screed	Unknown
							Tenths of area							
Y N	Y N	Y N	Y N	Y N	Y N	Y N	Faults	Y N	Y N	Y N	Y N	Y N	Y N	Y N
							Renew							
							Isolated repairs							
							Leave							
							Urgency (U F B)							
							Replacement period							

Walls

Left: Windows doors	Void	Wall		Right: Windows doors	Void	Wall
			Tenths of area			

Wall structure

Left: Masonry cavity	Masonry solid<9	Masonry solid = 9	Masonry solid>9	In-situ concrete	Pre-fab concrete	Timber		Right: Masonry cavity	Masonry solid<9	Masonry solid = 9	Masonry solid>9	In-situ concrete	Pre-fab concrete	Timber
							Net tenths of area							
Y N	Y N	Y N	Y N	Y N	Y N	Y N	Faults	Y N	Y N	Y N	Y N	Y N	Y N	Y N
							Rebuild							
							Repair							
							Leave							
							Urgency (U F B)							
							Replacement period							

Wall Surface

Left: Brick face	Stone face	Rend-ered	Timber	Tile hung	Concrete panel	Metal/ plastic		Right: Brick face	Stone face	Rend-ered	Timber	Tile hung	Concrete panel	Metal/ plastic
							Net tenths of area							
Y N	Y N	Y N	Y N	Y N	Y N	Y N	Faults	Y N	Y N	Y N	Y N	Y N	Y N	Y N
							Renew/repoint							
							Isolated Repairs							
							Surface finish							
							Leave							
							Urgency (U F B)							
							Replacement period							

11. Exterior (continued)

Left   **Right**

Windows/Frames

Left	Wood casement	Wood sash	Steel	Wood double glazed	Metal UVPC db glzd		Right	Wood casement	Wood sash	Steel	Wood double glazed	Metal UVPC db glzd
Number							Number					
Faults	Y N	Y N	Y N	Y N	Y N		Faults	Y N	Y N	Y N	Y N	Y N
Replace							Replace					
Repair/replace sash or member							Repair/replace sash or member					
Ease sashes etc reglaze							Ease sashes etc reglaze					
Repaint							Repaint					
Leave							Leave					
Urgency (U F B)							Urgency (U F B)					
Replacement period							Replacement period					

Doors/Frames

Left	Mainly wood	Mainly metal			Right	Mainly wood	Mainly metal	
Number					Number			
Faults	Y N	Y N	Y N		Faults	Y N	Y N	Y N
Replace					Replace			
Repair member					Repair member			
Ease/reglaze/adjust ironmongery					Ease/reglaze/adjust ironmongery			
Repaint					Repaint			
Leave					Leave			
Urgency (U F B)					Urgency (U F B)			
Replacement period					Replacement period			

Damp Proof Course

Left	Existing DPC	None	Not obtained		Right	Existing DPC	None	Not obtained
Tenths of length					Tenths of length			
Faults	Y N				Faults	Y N		
Replace					Replace			
Leave					Leave			
Urgency (U F B)					Urgency (U F B)			
Replacement period					Replacement period			

Drainage System
(in tenths of lengths)

Left	Soil drainage	Surface drainage		Right	Soil drainage	Surface drainage
Faults	Y N	Y N		Faults	Y N	Y N
Replace/relay				Replace/relay		
Repair				Repair		
Leave				Leave		
Urgency (U F B)				Urgency (U F B)		
Replacement period				Replacement period		

Features

Roof features (Left)		Elevation features		Roof features (Right)	
	Y N	Elevation features	Y N		
Full gables	___	Bays	___	Full gables	___
Half gables	___	Porches	___	Half gables	___
Dormers	___ ___	Balconies	___ ___	Dormers	___ ___
Slopes	___	Ornamentation	Y N	Slopes	___
Other, specify	Y N	Parapets	Y N	Other, specify	Y N
	Y N	Turrets	Y N		
	Y N	Steps	Y N		
	Y N	Lift towers	Y N		
	Y N	Stairwells	Y N		
	Y N	Fins/ext, frames	Y N		
	Y N	Other, specify	Y N		

12. Structural Faults

Any faults present   [Y | N]   **Notes**

	None	Non-urgent	Urgent local	Urgent widespread
Chimney distortion	1	2	3	4
Roof: spreading	1	2	3	4
distortion	1	2	3	4
Wall: distortion	1	2	3	4
severe cracks	1	2	3	4
main part, settlement	1	2	3	4
additional part, settlement	1	2	3	4
Crosswall separated	1	2	3	4
Wall tie failure	1	2	3	4
Frame spalling	1	2	3	4
Panel spalling/cracked	1	2	3	4
Panels disjointed	1	2	3	4
Severe systematic cracks in render	1	2	3	4
Private balcony defects	1	2	3	4
Other, specify: [_____]	1	2	3	4

13. Construction

Building method	Traditional 1		Probably traditional 2		Probably non-traditional 3		Non-traditional 4	
Predominant structural component	n/a 8	Boxwall 1	Crosswall 2	Frame 3	Large panel 4	Small panel 5	Other 6	Unknown 9
Material of structural component	n/a 88	In situ concrete 01 / No fines concrete 02	Pre-cast concrete 03	Masonry 04	Timber 05	Metal 06	Other, specify: 07 _____	Unknown 99
Proprietary name/description	n/a 8	Specify 1 _____						Unknown 9

Date of construction of module	pre 1870 1	1870-1899 2	1900-1918 3	1919-1944 4	1945-1964 5	post 1964 6

Modifications done	Essentially as built 1	Minor modification 2	Major modification			Conversion 6
			Within structure only 3	Extension 4	Both 5	

Type of modification	Not applicable 8	Amenities only 1	Fabric only 2	Both 3

Date of modification	Not applicable 8	Earlier 1	Recently completed 2	Underway 3

Drainage system	Mains 1	Other 2	Unknown 9

14. Summary of whole dwelling

	Whether defective					Whether remediable			
	Seriously defective	Defective	Just acceptable	Satisfactory	Unknown	No	Yes	n/a	
Repair	1	2	3	4	9	1	2	8	refer internal and external works
Stability	1	2	3	4	9	1	2	8	
Freedom from damp	1	2	3	4	9	1	2	8	
Drainage/sanitary conveniences	1	2	3	4	9	1	2	8	
Internal arrangement	1	2	3	4	9	1	2	8	transferred from page 2 and 3
Natural lighting	1	2	3	4	9	1	2	8	
Ventilation	1	2	3	4	9	1	2	8	
Cold water supply	1	2	3	4	9	1	2	8	
Preparation/cooking/waste disposal	1	2	3	4	9	1	2	8	

If any internal or external matters are defective or amenities are missing what should be done to remedy these?

_____

_____

Fitness

Is dwelling___

Fit	Unfit
1	2

?

Borderline decision?

No	Yes
1	2

If borderline give reasons for your decision: _____

_____

What action should be taken under the 1985 Housing Act whether unfit or not

Fit no action	Fit section 190 notice	Fit single Part IX clearance area added	Unfit single Part VI repairs notice	Unfit single Part IX closing or demolition order	Unfit part IX clearance area	
					Large	Small
1	2	3	4	5	6	7

15. Block

Is the plot of the module typical of its neighbours

Yes	No, smaller than	No, larger than	Isolated
1	2	3	4

Parking provision

Integral garage	Garage on plot	Parking space on plot	Garage/space elsewhere	Adequate street parking	Inadequate street parking	None
1	2	3	4	5	6	7

Number of modules in block

One only	Specify	More than 50	Unknown
01	___ ___	55	99

Attachment of module's in block

One module only	Two modules only	Middle of row	End of row
1	2	3	4

Is the module condition representative of the block

Module is block	Worse than most	In worst half	Same as most	In best half	Better than most
1	2	3	4	5	6

Action required on block

n/a	No action	Enhance maintenance	Piecemeal action	Enveloping/ block action	Partial demolition	Demolition	Conversion
88	01	02	03	04	05	06	07

Attachment between blocks

Isolated block	Linkages	No linkages
1	2	3

Is the block representative of its neighbours

In type

Isolated block	Similar to most	Similar to some	No unlike
1	2	3	4

In condition

Isolated block	Worst than most	In worst half	Same as most	In best half	Better than most
1	2	3	4	5	6

16. Locality

Nature of locality	Urban 1	Rural 2

Predominant land use of locality	Residential 1	Commercial 2	Mixed Heavy industry 3	Light industry 4	All 5	Non-residential 6	Agricultural 7

No of dwellings in locality	10 or less 1	11-49 2	50-300 3	Over 300 4		Isolated 5	Go to

Predominant age	pre 1870 1	1870-1899 2	1900-1918 3	1919-1944 4	1944-1964 5	post 1964 6	No predominant age 7

Predominant residential building type	Houses Terraced 01	Semi-detached 02	Detached 03	Mixed 04	Low rise flats 05	High rise flats 06	With commercial 07	Temporary 08	Mixed 09
	Mainly converted 1	Mainly single units 2							

Predominant tenure	Local authority built 1	Privately built 2	Mixed 3	Impossible to ascertain 4

Improvement activity in area	None 1	A little 2	Some 3	Extensive 4	With re-development 5	Re-development only 6

Action required to dwellings in locality

		None	Selective	Compre-hesive	
Type	Clearance	1	2	3	– Go to
	Repairs/improvements	1	2	3	
	Enhanced maintenance	1	2	3	

	Improvements to dwelling access	Y	N
	Improvements to block security	Y	N

Reasons	Dwelling design	Y	N
	Dwelling condition	Y	N
	Environmental factors	Y	N
	Vandalism	Y	N

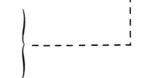 Action required to environment of locality

	Need		Possible	
Enhanced street maintenance	Y	N	Y	N
Action on individual dwellings	Y	N	Y	N
Improvements to street/estate scene	Y	N	Y	N
Improvements to vacant/derelict sites	Y	N	Y	N
Actions to childrens play/public open space	Y	N	Y	N
Action on intrusive industry	Y	N	Y	N
Improvements to traffic & parking provision	Y	N	Y	N
Provision of defensible space	Y	N	Y	N

ENGLISH HOUSE CONDITION SURVEY 1986

ADDRESS						LOCAL AUTHORITY						SURVEYOR						OFFICE USE				
1	2	3	4	5			6	7	8	9	10		11	12	13	14	15	16		17	18	19	20	21

Address of rateable unit   Local authority

Surveyor

Surveyor to code

A   SURVEY RECORD

		Not applicable	Date of visit		Start time	Finish time	
Dates & times of survey:	1 First visit		specify _ _ _ _ _ _ _	specify times on 24hr clock			22-29
	2 Second visit	88888888	specify _ _ _ _ _ _ _	specify times on 24hr clock			30-37
	3 Third visit	88888888	specify _ _ _ _ _ _ _	specify times on 24hr clock			38-45

		Not applicable	Internal inspection			External inspection			
Extent of inspection:	4 First visit		none 3	part 2	full 1	none 3	part 2	full 1	46-47
	5 Second visit	88	none 3	part 2	full 1	none 3	part 2	full 1	48-49
	6 Third visit	88	none 3	part 2	full 1	none 3	part 2	full 1	50-51
	7 Total extent of inspection		none 3	part 2	full 1	none 3	part 2	full 1	52-53

8 Outcome of survey	other reason 6	refused opportunity 5	no longer usable as a dwg 4	dwelling demolished 3	address untraceable 2	data collected 1	54
9 Detailed reason for non-inspection	If 4,5 or 6 specify _ _ _ _ _ _ _ _ _ _ _ _ _ _ _ _ 1			not applicable		8	55
10 Photographs taken	none 7	both 3		rear 2		front 1	56

B   DWELLING IDENTIFICATION

1 Number of dwellings in rateable unit	unobtainable 99	if r.u. is part of one dwelling 66	if more than one dwelling in rateable unit specify no _ _ _ _	one dwg. only 01	57-58
2 Number of rateable units in dwelling	unobtainable 99	if more than one rateable unit in dwelling specify no _ _ _ _ _ _	more than one dwelling in r.u. 66	one rateable unit only 01	59-60
3 Entry floor of dwelling	unobtainable 99	above 2nd specify _ _ _ _	second 02	first floor 01	ground 77	basement 88	61-62

NOW TURN TO PAGE 2 TO COMPLETE INTERIOR SECTIONS C-D

K   SUMMARY OF DWELLING/AREA

1 Where is the dwelling situated	isolated 6	hamlet 5	village 4	provincial town 3	urban conurbation 2	metropolitan conurbation 1	63
2 Does the dwelling/building front on to	unobtainable 9	other 5	classified road 4	mod ped access 3	unmade resd. street 2	made resd. street 1	64
3 Parking provision for dwelling	none 7	inadequate st. parking 6	adequate st. parking 5	garage/space elsewhere 4	parking space on plot 3	garage on plot 2	integral garage 1	65
4 Is the dwelling a (or part of a)	non-residential plus dwelling/s 8	purpose built flats 7	dwelling in converted bldg 6	temporary dwelling 5	detached house 4	semi-detached 3	mid-terrace 2	end terrace 1	66
5 Date of construction of building	post 1964 6	1945-1964 5	1919-1944 4	1900-1918 3	1870-1899 2	pre 1870 1	67
6 Quality assessment	basic 3		better than basic 2		best of its kind 1		68
7 Tenure of dwelling	unobtainable 9	no longer used as dwg. 8	vacant 7	other 6	Housing association 5	Local authority /New town 4	private unfurnished 3	private furnished 2	owner occupied 1	69
8 Is the dwelling in multiple occupation	multi-occupied 4	probably multi-occupied 3	probably not multi-occupied 2	not multi-occupied 1	70
9 Is the dwelling representative of adjacent dwellings	isolated rural 6	isolated urban 5	no-unlike 4	yes-worse than 3	yes-better than 2	yes-same 1	71
10 Would you expect action to be taken under the Housing Act 1985	not applicable 4	potential HAA 3	potential GIA 2	no action 1	72

FINALLY COMPLETE SECTION A : Survey Record — and Check Form

C INTERNAL ELEMENTS

Repairs needed

	Unob.	None/N.A.	Renew 100%	Major 75%	Medium 40%	Minor 15%	Good NIL		Surveyor to code
1 Lower floor	9	8	5	4	3		1		1
2 Lower ceiling	9	8	5	4	3	2	1		2
3 Entry floor	9	8	5	4	3	2	1		3
4 Entry ceiling	9	8	5	4	3	2	1		4
5 Principal fire	9	8	5	4	3	2	1		5
6 Extra for dry rot	9	8	5	4	3	2			6
7 Sound proof party wall	9	8	5			1			7
8 Staircases	9	8	5	4	3	2	1		8
9 First upper floor	9	8	5	4	3	2	1		9
10 First floor ceiling	9	8	5	4	3	2	1		10
11 Second upper floor	9	8	5	4	3	2	1		11
12 Second floor ceiling	9	8	5	4	3	2	1		12
13 Partitions and plaster	9		5	4	3	2	1		13
14 Doors and frames	9		5	4	3	2	1		14
15 Other fires-repairs	9	8	5	4	3	2	1		15
16 Decorations arising	9	8	5	4	3	2	1		16
17 Central heating	9	8	5	4	3	2	1		17
18 Electric power	9	8	5		3	2	1		18
19 Electric light	9	8	5			2	1		19
20 Bad arrangement rooms	9		5	bad arrangement	satisfactory arrangement		1		20

	unob.									
21 Does the dwelling possess central heating	unob. 9	no CH 7	less than half 3	half house CH 2	whole house CH 1					21

22 Principal fuel used for heating	unob. 99	none 77	other 11	com-munal 10	paraffin 09	solid other 08	solid smoke-less 07	fuel oil 06	electricity off peak 05	electricity normal 04	bottle gas (LPG) 03	mains gas other 02	mains gas bal-anced flue 01	22-23

23 Type of principal heating	unob. 99	none 77	other heating portable only 11	other heating oil filled rads. 10	other heating fixed open 09	other heating fixed closed 08	other CH 07	storage heaters 06	ceiling heating 05	under floor CH 04	ducted air CH 03	water-borne CH back boiler 02	water-borne CH single pur-pose 01	24-25

24 Condition of electrical installation	unob. 9	none 7	unsatisfactory 2	satisfactory 1		26

D BASIC AMENITIES

Does the dwelling possess for the exclusive use of the occupants?

1 Sink	unobtainable 9	neither 3	sink elsewhere inside 2	sink in kitchen 1	27
2 H. and C.	unobtainable 9	no points with hot & cold water 3	hot & cold water at less than three points 2	hot & cold water at three points 1	28
3 Bath	unobtainable 9	neither 3	fixed bath elsewhere 2	fixed bath in an inside bathroom 1	29
4 Basin	unobtainable 9	neither 3	w.h.b. elsewhere inside 2	wash hand basin in bathroom 1	30
5 W.C.	unobtainable 9	none 5	W.C. with entrance outside building 4	W.C. with entrance inside building 3	W.C. elsewhere inside dwelling 2	W.C. in/near bathroom 1	31

Repairs needed

	Unob.	None/N.A.	Renew 100%	Major 75%	Medium 40%	Minor 15%	Good NIL		
6 Kitchen sink	9	8	5	4	3	2	1		32
7 Kitchen fittings (PM)	9	8	5	4	3	2	1		33
8 Cold water main	9	8	5	4	3	2	1		34
9 Small kitchen	9	8	YES 5 i.e. less than 1·8m wide		not small 1				35
10 Hot & cold water supply (central)	9	8	5	4	3	2	1		36
11 Bath in bathroom	9	8	5	4	3	2	1		37
12 Wash hand basin	9	8	5	4	3	2	1		38
13 W.C. within dwelling	9	8	5	4	3	2	1		39
14 External or 2nd W.C. inside	9	8	5	4	3	2	1		40
15 Bathroom	9	8	5	bad arrangement	satisfactory arrangement		1		41

E — DWELLING LAYOUT & DIMENSIONS

	Main part Unob.	N.A.	Specify no.		Addition Unob.	N.A.	Specify no.	Surveyor to code
1 Number of floors in dwelling	99		_ _ _ _ flrs	2	99	88	_ _ _ _ flrs	[ ] [ ] 1-2 [ ] 3-4
Number of rooms 3 Lower floor	99	88	_ _ _ _ rms	4	99	88	_ _ _ _ rms	[ ] [ ] 5-6 [ ] 7-8
5 Entry floor	99		_ _ _ _ rms	6	99	88	_ _ _ _ rms	[ ] [ ] 9-10 [ ] 11-12
7 First upper floor	99	88	_ _ _ _ rms	8	99	88	_ _ _ _ rms	[ ] [ ] 13-14 [ ] 15-16
9 Second upper floor	99	88	_ _ _ _ rms	10	99	88	_ _ _ _ rms	[ ] [ ] 17-18 [ ] 19-20
11 Above second floor	99	88	_ _ _ _ rms	12	99	88	_ _ _ _ rms	[ ] [ ] 21-22 [ ] 23-24
13 Whether attic in dwelling	unobtainable 9		no, attic 2		yes, attic 1			[ ] 25

Dwelling dimensions

		Unob.	N.A.			Surveyor to code
Ceiling heights 14 Entry floor	in main part	999		specify ceiling height in metres	H [ ] . [ ] [ ]	26-28
15 "	in addition	999	888	specify ceiling height in metres	H [ ] . [ ] [ ]	29-31
16 Other floor	in main part	999	888	specify ceiling height in metres	H [ ] . [ ] [ ]	32-34
17 "	in addition	999	888	specify ceiling height in metres	H [ ] . [ ] [ ]	35-37
Plan (external) 18 Entry floor	in main part	999999		specify width × depth in metres	W [ ] [ ] . [ ] D [ ] [ ] . [ ]	38-43
19 "	in addition	999999	888888	specify width × depth in metres	W [ ] [ ] . [ ] D [ ] [ ] . [ ]	44-49
20 Other floor	in main part	999999	888888	specify width × depth in metres	W [ ] [ ] . [ ] D [ ] [ ] . [ ]	50-55
21 "	in addition	999999	888888	specify width × depth in metres	W [ ] [ ] . [ ] D [ ] [ ] . [ ]	56-61

22 Plan type of dwelling	unobtainable 9	complex plan 3	simple + addition 2	simple plan 1	[ ] 62

23 Location of addition in relation to main part

unob. 99	n.a. 88	right back 12	right centre 11	right front 10	left back 09	left centre 08	left front 07	back right 06	back centre 05	back left 04	front right 03	front centre 02	front left 01	[ ] [ ] 63-64

F — FLATS & CONVERSIONS

1 Is the dwelling part of a	not a flat/ conversion 8	non-residential +dwellings 6	purpose built block of flats 5	converted house detached 4	converted house semi- detached 3	converted house mid terrace 2	converted house end terrace 1	[ ] 1

Repairs needed

	Unob.	None/ N.A.	Renew 100%	Major 75%	Medium 40%	Minor 15%	Good NIL	
2 Stairs and landings	9	8	5	4	3	2	1	[ ] 2
3 Lifts	9	8	5	4	3	2	1	[ ] 3
4 Access balconies	9	8	5	4	3	2	1	[ ] 4
5 Refuse chute/chamber	9	8	5	4	3	2	1	[ ] 5
6 Service mains	9	8	5	4	3	2	1	[ ] 6

	Main part Unob.	N.A.			Addition Unob.	N.A.		Surveyor to code
7 Number of floors in module	99	88	_ _ _ _ flrs	8	99	88	_ _ _ flrs	[ ] [ ] 7-8 [ ] 9-10
9 Number of dwellings in module	999	not a flat/conversion 888			specify number _ _ _ _ _ _ dwgs.			[ ] [ ] [ ] 11-13
10 Predominant use of lowest storey	9	n.a. 8	void 5	commercial 4	services dwgs. 3	dwgs. + other 2	dwellings only 1	[ ] 14

Module dimensions

Plan (external)		Unob.	N.A.	As dwg.		Surveyor to code
11 Lowest complete dwelling floor	in main part	999999	888888	666666	specify width × depth m W [ ] [ ] . [ ] D [ ] [ ] . [ ]	15-20
12 " " "	in addition	999999	888888	666666	specify width × depth m W [ ] [ ] . [ ] D [ ] [ ] . [ ]	21-26

13 Plan type of module	unob. 9	n.a. 8	complex plan 3	simple + addition 2	simple plan 1	[ ] 27

14 Location of addition in relation to main part

unob. 99	n.a. 88	right back 12	right centre 11	right front 10	left back 09	left centre 08	left front 07	back right 06	back centre 05	back left 04	front right 03	front centre 02	front left 01	[ ] [ ] 28-29

G — PLOT DIMENSIONS

1 Width of plot	unobtainable 99	public plot 77	over 20 metres 66	specify (metres) _ _ _ _ _ _	same width as dwelling 55	[ ] [ ] 30-31
2 Depth front garden	unobtainable 99	public plot 77	over 20 metres 66	specify (metres) _ _ _ _ _ _	no front garden 55	[ ] [ ] 32-33
3 Depth rear garden	unobtainable 99	public plot 77	over 50 metres 66	specify (metres) _ _ _ _ _ _	no rear garden 55	[ ] [ ] 34-35

(H) EXTERNAL ELEMENTS & STRUCTURE

Surveyor
to code

1 Building method	unobtainable 9	non-traditional 4		probably non-traditional 3			probably traditional 2	traditional 1

☐ 1

| **2 Predominent structural component** | unobtainable 9 | other 6 | small panel 5 | large panel 4 | frame 3 | crosswall 2 | boxwall 1 | not applicable 8 |

☐ 2

| **3 Materials of structural component** | unobtainable 99 | other 07 | metal 06 | timber 05 | masonry 04 | pre-cast concrete 03 | no-fines concrete 02 | insitu. concrete 01 | not applicable 88 |

☐☐ 3-4

| **4 Proprietory name/description** | unobtainable 9 | specify . . . . .1 | not applicable 8 |

☐ 5

| **5 Construction of external walls** | unobtainable 9 | other 8 | timber 7 | prefab concrete 6 | insitu. concrete 5 | masonry solid <9" 4 | masonry solid=9" 3 | masonry solid >9" 2 | masonry cavity 1 |

☐ 6

| **6 Type of roof structure** | pitched & flat 3 | flat roof 2 | pitched roof 1 |

☐ 7

| **7 Type of additional structure** | unobtainable 9 | not applic. 8 | Stepped addition: full width 6 / shared 5 / single 4 | Straight addition: full width 3 / shared 2 / single 1 |

☐ 8

Repairs needed

	Unob.	None/ N.A.	Renew 100%	Major 75%	Medium 40%	Minor 15%	Good NIL	
8 Foundations	▨	▨	5	4	3	2	1	. . . . .
9 External & party wall structure	▨	▨	5	4	3	2	1	. . . . .
10 External wall surface	▨	▨	5	4	3	2	1	. . . . .
11 Damp proof course	9	8	5	4	3	2	1	. . . . .
12 External doors & windows	▨	▨	5	4	3	2	1	. . . . .
13 Chimney stacks	9	8	5	4	3	2	1	. . . . .
14 Pitched roof coverings	9	8	5	4	3	2	1	. . . . .
15 Pitched roof timbers	9	8	5	4	3	2	1	. . . . .
16 Flat roofs	9	8	5	4	3	2	1	. . . . .
17 Roof drainage	▨	▨	5	4	3	2	1	. . . . .
18 Soil drainage	9	8	5	4	3	2	1	. . . . .
19 External paint	▨	▨	5	4	3	2	1	. . . . .
20 Yard pavings and walls	9	8	5	4	3	2	1	. . . . .

☐ 9
☐ 10
☐ 11
☐ 12
☐ 13
☐ 14
☐ 15
☐ 16
☐ 17
☐ 18
☐ 19
☐ 20
☐ 21

(I) IMPROVEMENTS

1 Modifications done	conversion 6	major modification: both 5 / extension only 4 / within structure only 3		minor modification 2	essentially as built 1

☐ 22

| **2 Type of modification** | both 3 | fabric only 2 | amenities only 1 | not applicable 8 |

☐ 23

| **3 Date of modification** | underway 3 | recently completed 2 | earlier 1 | not applicable 8 |

☐ 24

| **4 Is the dwelling physically improvable?** | unob. 9 | NO other specify _ _ _ _ _ 5 | NO non-availability of services 4 | NO insufficient space 3 | YES improvable 2 | already has five amenities 1 |

☐ 25

| **5 Where can the bathroom be added?** | unobtainable 9 | not improvable 8 | externally only 7 | outside dwelling but within building 6 | internally with loss only 5 | internally with loss or external 4 | internally without loss of bed space 3 | already has bathroom with limited space 2 | already has bathroom 1 |

☐ 26

(J) FITNESS

| **1 Is the dwelling unfit** | unfit 2 | not unfit 1 |

☐ 27

| **2 Is this a borderline decision** | Yes 2 | No 1 | . . . . . . |

☐ 28

3 If borderline decision give arguments for your decision:-   . . . .

| **4 Would you expect action to be taken under the Housing Act 1985 whether unfit or not?** | unfit Pt IX clearance area: large 7 / small 6 | unfit single Pt IX closing or demolition order 5 | unfit single Pt VI repairs notice 4 | fit single Pt IX clearance area added 3 | fit Sec 190 notice 2 | fit no action 1 |

☐ 29

5 Indicate below those matters which you consider defective whether the dwelling is unfit or not unfit

(a) repair	(b) stability	(c) free from damp	(cc) internal arrangement	(d) natural light	(e) ventilation	(f) water supply	(g) drainage & san. conv.	(h) cooking & waste water
unob. 9	unob. 9	unob. 9	unob. 9	unob. 9	unob. 9	unob. 9	unob. 9	unob. 9
seriously defective 3	seriously defective 3	seriously defective 3	seriously defective 3	seriously defective 3	seriously defective 3	seriously defective 3	seriously defective 3	seriously defective 3
defective 2	defective 2	defective 2	defective 2	defective 2	defective 2	defective 2	defective 2	defective 2
not def. 1	not def. 1	not def. 1	not def. 1	not def. 1	not def. 1	not def. 1	not def. 1	not def. 1
☐ 30	☐ 31	☐ 32	☐ 33	☐ 34	☐ 35	☐ 36	☐ 37	☐ 38

NOW TURN
TO PAGE 1
SECTION K
SUMMARY

NOP 6900

1986 ENGLISH HOUSE CONDITION SURVEY

Serial No: ☐☐☐☐☐☐☐☐☐
(5)(6)(7)(8)(9)(10)(11)(12)(13)

①(14)

RECORD OF CALLS MADE

	Day	Date	Time	Result
1				
2				
3				
4				
5				
6				
7				
8				

FINAL OUTCOME

(15)

Interview - - - - - - - - - - - - - - - - - 1
No trace of address - - - - - - - - - - - 2
Vacant - boarded up/derelict - - - - - 3
         - being converted/modernised - 4
         - other - - - - - - - - - - - - - 5
Demolished - - - - - - - - - - - - - - - 6
Non-residential - - - - - - - - - - - - - 7
No contact after 4+ calls - - - - - - - 8
Respondent ill/deaf - - - - - - - - - - 9
Respondent away/in hospital
(until _____) - - - - - 0
Refused - - - - - - - - - - - - - - - - - X

NOTES ON ADDRESS

Interviewer Name _____

Interviewer Number ☐☐☐☐
(16)(17)(18)(19)

IF TEMPERATURE SUB-SAMPLE FILL IN
THERMOMETER NUMBER

☐☐☐
(20)(21)(22)

TOTAL NUMBER OF CALLS

☐
(23)

CONTACTS ONLY

RESPONDENT   (24)
   Head of Household   1
   Partner   2
   Other (WRITE IN)   3

DATE OF INTERVIEW

DAY ☐☐ / ☐☐ MONTH
    (25)(26)   (27)(28)

DAY OF WEEK

Mon Tues Wed Thurs Fri Sat Sun
 1   2   3   4   5   6   7   (29)

TIME AT START (24HR CLOCK)

☐☐ . ☐☐
(30)(31) (32)(33)

TIME AT END

☐☐ . ☐☐
(34)(35) (36)(37)

Q1 How many people are there in your household including yourself - that is to say people who normally live here and with whom you normally share at least one meal a day or share a living room with?

☐ (38)

(38)

Q2 Are there any other households apart from yours living at _____ (READ OUT EXACT ADDRESS FROM SAMPLE SHEET). IF YES: How many?:

WRITE NUMBER IN BOX THEN OBTAIN LOCATION OR NAMES OF OTHER HOUSEHOLDS AND COMPLETE INTERVIEWS AT EACH HOUSEHOLD (UP TO A MAXIMUM OF 4 - SEE INSTRUCTIONS). IF NONE WRITE '0'.

☐ (39)

(39)

Q3 Does your household share any rooms with any other houshold?
    IF YES: Which rooms?

(40)

```
No  - none shared --------------------- 1
Yes - kitchen ----------------------- 2
      bathroom --------------------- 3
      WC -------------------------- 4
      Other ------------------------ 5
```

(40)

Q4 Do you know when this building was built?

(41)

```
Before 1870 --------------------------- 1
1870 - 1899 --------------------------- 2
1900 - 1918 --------------------------- 3
1919 - 1944 --------------------------- 4
1945 - 1964 --------------------------- 5
1965 or later ------------------------- 6
No idea -------------------------------- 7
```

(41)

Q5 Does your household own or rent this accommodation?

(42)

```
OWN - Buying with a mortgage or
          loan -------------------- 1 GO
    - Own outright ------------- 2 TO
SHARED OWNERSHIP - Part owned, part rented - 3 Q9
RENT OR RENT FREE - furnished or unfurnished- 4 ASK Q 6
```

(42)

IF RENTED

Q6 Does this house/flat go with the present job of anyone in the household?

(43)
```
Yes -------------- 1
No  -------------- 2
```

(43)

Q7 SHOWCARD A Who is the house/flat rented from?

(44)

AN ORGANISATION
- Local authority or council/new town — 1 GO
- Housing Association or Co-operative or housing charitable trust ------- 2 TO
- Property Company ------------------- 3
- Employer ------------------------- 4 Q12
- Other organisation --------------- 5

AN INDIVIDUAL
- A relative of a household member ---- 6
- Employer-------------------------- 7 ASK Q8
- A private landlord who is not a relative or employer -------------- 8

(44)

Q8 Does your landlord live in the building?

(45)

Yes ----------------- 1 NOW GO
No ----------------- 2 TO Q 12

(45)

ASK ALL OWNER OCCUPIERS - RENTERS GO TO Q12

Q9 Is this the first property you have owned?

(46)

Yes ------------- 1
No ------------- 2

(46)

Q10 SHOWCARD B Who did you buy this property from?

(47)

Private owner/developer ------------ 1
Local council - sitting tenant ------- 2
            - moved in ------------ 3
Housing association ----------------- 4
Other (WRITE IN)

_____ 5
Don't know ------------------------ 6

(47)

Q11 Is this property leasehold or freehold?

(48)

Leasehold -------- 1
Freehold --------- 2

(48)

ASK ALL

Q12 ASK IF NECESSARY OTHERWISE CODE. Respondent is ....

(49)

Married/living as married ---- 1 GO TO Q15a
Single/widowed etc. --------- 2 ASK Q13

(49)

Q13 How long have you lived at this address?

(50)

Under 1 year --------------------- 1
1 year but less than 2 years ------ 2
2 years but less than 5 years ----- 3 ASK Q14
5 years but less than 10 years ---- 4
10 years but less than 20 years
-------------------------- 5
20 years or longer --------------- 6 GO TO
All life ------------------------- 7 Q17

(50)

- 4 -

Q14 SHOWCARD C Where were you living before?   (51)

                    Living with parents/relatives ----+-------- 1 NOW
                    Owned/buying own home -------------------- 2 GO
                    Rented from council/housing association -- 3 TO   (51)
                    Rented from private landlord ------------- 4 Q17
                    Other ------------------------------------ 5

ASK ALL MARRIED/LIVING AS MARRIED

Q15a How long have you lived at this address?

Q15b How long has your partner lived at this address?

                                         Respondent   Partner
                                            (52)   (53)
                    Under 1 year --------------- 1 ----------- 1
                    1 year but less than 2 years 2 ----------- 2
                    2 years but less than
                      5 years ------------------ 3 ----------- 3   (52/
                    5 years but less than   53)
                      10 years ----------------- 4 ----------- 4
                    10 years but less than
                      20 years ----------------- 5 ----------- 5
                    20 years or longer --------- 6 ----------- 6
                    All life ------------------- 7 ----------- 7

ASK ALL CODED 1-5 AT Q15a/Q15b

Q16a SHOWCARD C Where were you living before moving here?

Q16b SHOWCARD C Where was your partner living before moving here?

                                         Respondent   Partner
                                            (54)   (55)
                    Living with parents --------- 1 ---------- 1
                    Owned/buying own house ------ 2 ---------- 2
                    Rented from council/housing
                      association --------------- 3 ---------- 3   (54/
                    Rented from private landlord- 4 ---------- 4   55)
                    Other ----------------------- 5 ---------- 5

ASK ALL
Q17 Do you think you are likely to move from here in the next two years?
                                                        (56)
                    Yes ------------------- 1 ASK Q18
                    No -------------------- 2 GO TO
                    Don't know ----------- 3 Q19   (56)

Q18 Why do you think you will move away from this home in the next two years?
     CODE ALL THAT APPLY.   (57-59)
                    Home too small ---------------- 1
                    Home too large ---------------- 2
                    Want better quality home ------ 3
                    Change of work/retirement ------ 4
                    Time for change --------------- 5   (57/
                    To make profit ---------------- 6   59)
                    Want to buy ------------------- 7
                    Be near family ---------------- 8
                    Other (WRITE IN AND RING)

                    _____ 9

<u>ASK ALL</u>
I would now like to ask about heating your home.

Q19a What do you use as your <u>main</u> form of heating in the living room in winter?
CODE ONE ONLY BELOW

Q19b What else do you use to heat your living room? CODE ALL THAT APPLY BELOW.

Q19c What do you use to heat your kitchen and hall? CODE ALL THAT APPLY BELOW.

Q19d What do you use as your <u>main</u> form of heating in <u>your</u> bedroom in winter?
CODE ONE ONLY BELOW.

Q19e What do you use to heat your other bedrooms? CODE ALL THAT APPLY BELOW.

Q19f What do you use to heat your bathroom? CODE ALL THAT APPLY BELOW.

	Q19a (60)	Q19b (61)	Q19c (62)	Q19d (63)	Q19e (64)	Q19f (65)	
Central heating	1	1	1	1	1	1	
Storage heater	2	2	2	2	2	2	
Mains gas fire/convector	3	3	3	3	3	3	
Bottled gas heater	4	4	4	4	4	4	(60/65)
Paraffin heater	5	5	5	5	5	5	
Oil filled electric radiator	6	6	6	6	6	6	
Electric fire/convector/heater	7	7	7	7	7	7	
Solid fuel - open grate	8	8	8	8	8	8	
- enclosed grate/stove	9	9	9	9	9	9	
Other WRITE IN AND RING)	0	0	0	0	0	0	
No heating	X	X	X	X	X	X	
Room does not exist	Y	Y	Y	Y	Y	Y	

<u>IF USES CENTRAL HEATING OR TWO OR MORE STORAGE HEATERS ASK Q20. OTHERS GO TO Q23a</u>

Q20 What fuel does your central heating use?
(66)
Mains gas ----------------------------- 1
Bottled gas --------------------------- 2
Fuel oil ------------------------------ 3
Electricity - normal tariff ---------- 4
- off peak --------------- 5
Solid fuel - smokeless --------------- 6
- non-smokeless ----------- 7
Communal/district supply (all fuels) - 8
Other (WRITE IN AND RING) _____
9
Don't know --------------------------- 0
(66)

Q21 Can you turn your central heating on and off?
(67)
Yes -------------- 1
No -------------- 2
(67)

Q22 Does your central heating have any of these controls? READ OUT EACH IN TURN.

	Yes	No	Don't know	
Manual control valves on radiators or vents	1	2	3	(68)
Thermostat valves on radiators or vents	1	2	3	(69)
Room thermostat	1	2	3	(70)
Time switch/programmer	1	2	3	(71)

(68/
71)

ASK ALL

Q23a SHOWCARD D Thinking about weekdays, at what times do you usually heat your living room during the winter? CODE ALL THAT APPLY.

Q23b SHOWCARD D Thinking now about weekends, at what time do you usually heat your living room at weekends during the winter? CODE ALL THAT APPLY BELOW.

Q23c SHOWCARD D Thinking again about weekdays, at what time do you usually heat your bedroom during the winter? CODE ALL THAT APPLY BELOW.

	Q23a (72-74)	Q23b (75-77)	Q23c (78-80)
Breakfast time/early morning	1	1	1
Later morning	2	2	2
Afternoon	3	3	3
Evening/bedtime	4	4	4
Night	5	5	5
Daily - but no regular pattern	6	6	6
Only occasionally heated	7	7	7
Never heated	8	8	8
Room does not exist	9	9	9

(72/
80)

NEW CARD
DUP COLS
1 - 13
②(14)

SKIP COL 15

Q24 SHOWCARD E Overall how satisfied are you with your heating?

(16)
Very satisfied	1 GO TO Q26a
Fairly satisfied	2
Fairly dissatisfied	3 ASK Q25
Very dissatisfied	4
Don't know	5

(16)

Q25 What is it about your heating that you are not satisfied with? CODE ALL THAT APPLY.

(17-19)
Expensive to run	1
Can't afford to use heating	2
Not enough heat	3
Not enough radiators/only partial heating	4
Too old	5
Can't control heat	6
Too hard to set controls	7
Want central heating	8
Other (WRITE IN AND RING) _____	
_____	9

(17/
19)

Q26a What is your main way of heating water in the winter?

Q26b What is your main way of heating water in the summer?

	Q26a (20)	Q26b (21)
Central heating system	1	1
Electric immersion heather - off peak	2	2
- normal tariff	3	3
Electric instantaneous heater	4	4
Gas instantaneous heater (Ascot)	5	5
Gas fired back boiler (not central heating)	6	6
Solid fuel back boiler (not central heating)	7	7
Other (WRITE IN AND RING) _____		
_____	8	8
No hot water tap	9	9

(20/21)

Q27 What is the main fuel you use for cooking? CODE ONE ONLY (HOB) (22)

Mains gas	1
Bottled gas	2
Electricity	3
Coal/solid fuel	4
Oil	5

(22)

ASK ALL

Q28 Do you have any problems with condensation or damp in your home?

(23)

Yes	1 ASK Q29
No	2 GO TO FILTER BEFORE Q32

(23)

Q29 SHOWCARD F What sort of problems do you have? Any others?

(24-26)

Steamed-up windows/walls	1
Damage to paint on windows	2
Damage or mould growth to wall decoration	3
Damage to floors, carpets or furniture	4
Other (WRITE IN) _____	
_____	5

(24/26)

Q30 Which rooms does this affect? Any others? (27-30)

Kitchen	1
Bathroom	2
Living room	3
Dining room	4
Hall	5
Respondents bedroom	6
Other bedroom(s)	7
Other	8

(27/30)

Q31 Overall how much does the problem of condensation or damp affect you?
     READ OUT:
                                                                    (31)
                         It's no trouble --------------------- 1
                         It causes some inconvenience --------- 2
                         It causes some discomfort ------------ 3   (31)
                         You're distressed by it -------------- 4
                         (Don't know) ------------------------- 5

        IF RESPONDENT LIVES IN WHOLE HOUSE/TOP FLAT ASK Q32. OTHERS GO TO Q35.

Q32 Is your loft or roof insulated?
                                              (32)
                         Yes ----------------- 1 ASK Q33
                         No ------------------ 2 GO TO Q34   (32)
                         Don't know ---------- 3 GO TO Q35

Q33 When was the insulation put in?
                                                          (33)
                         Less than 2 years ago ----------------- 1
                         2 years but less than 5 years ago ---- 2 NOW
                         5 years but less than 8 years ago ---- 3 GO   (33)
                         8 years but less than 12 years ago --- 4 TO
                         12 years ago or more ----------------- 5 Q35
                         Don't know --------------------------- 6

Q34 Why have you not put in any insulation?
                                                          (34-36)
                         Too expensive/can't afford it -------- 1
                         Not my responsibility ---------------- 2
                         Not got round to it ------------------ 3   (34/
                         Never thought about it --------------- 4   36)
                         No space for insulation -------------- 5
                         Other (WRITE IN AND RING)

                         _____ 6
                         Don't know --------------------------- 7

        ASK ALL

Q35 Are any of your walls insulated? Is that all of them or only some of them?
                                                          (37)
                         All -------------- 1
                         One only --------- 2 ASK
                         Two only --------- 3 Q36
                         Three only ------- 4   (37)
                         None insulated --- 5 GO TO
                         Don't know ------- 6 Q37

Q36 What form of wall insulation is it?
                                                          (38)
                         Cavity wall insulation --- ----------- 1
                         Insulation to internal surface ------- 2   (38)
                         Insulation to external surface ------- 3
                         Other (WRITE IN AND RING)

                         _____ 4
                         Don't know --------------------------- 5

ASK ALL

Q37 Are any of your windows double glazed - that is with two panes of glass
or rigid plastic?

(39)

Yes --------------- 1 ASK Q38
No --------------- 2 GO TO Q39   (39)

Q38 Which rooms have double-glazed windows?   (40-42)

All of house/flat -------------------- 1
Kitchen ------------------------------ 2
Bathroom ----------------------------- 3
Living room -------------------------- 4   (40/
Dining room -------------------------- 5   42)
Hall --------------------------------- 6
Respondent's bedroom ----------------- 7
Other bedroom(s) --------------------- 8
Other -------------------------------- 9

ASK ALL

Q39 Do you have any form of draught excluder on your doors or windows?
PROBE AS NECESSARY.   (43)

Yes - on all --------------- 1
- on most ------------- 2
- on some ------------- 3   (43)
No ----------------------- 4

Q40 Do you have a hot water tank or cylinder?

(44)

Yes --------------- 1 ASK Q41
No --------------- 2 GO TO FILTER
BEFORE Q42   (44)

Q41 Is your hot water tank or cylinder insulated? IF YES: How?   (45)

Yes - Jacket ----------------------- 1
- Integral Foam Coating ---------- 2
- Other -------------------------- 3   (45)
No ---------------------------------- 4
Don't know -------------------------- 5

IF IN TEMPERATURE SUB-SAMPLE ASK Q42. OTHERS GO TO FILTER BEFORE Q.50

READ OUT

I would now like to ask you about how you pay your fuel bills and what your fuel costs are.

Q42 SHOWCARD G Which of these apply to you? Any others?   (46-48)

Pay bills direct to gas board --------------	1
Pay bills direct to electricity board ------	2
Pay for electricity through slot meter -----	3
Pay for gas through slot meter -------------	4
Buy fuel (coal, bottled gas etc) from supplier ---------------------------------	5
Fuel bills included in rent ----------------	6
Fuel bills paid, direct by DHSS ------------	7

(46/48)

IF PAY BILLS DIRECT TO GAS/ELECTRICITY BOARD ASK Q43. IF NOT GO TO FILTER BEFORE Q44.

Q43 Would you be prepared to give your permission for the Electricity Board or the Gas Board to tell the Department your fuel bills? The details would just be used solely for research purposes and would remain confidential.

(49)

Give permission --------	1 ASK RESPONDENT TO SIGN FORM (S)
Not give permission ----	2 GO TO FILTER BEFORE Q44

(49)

IF USES SLOT METER AT Q42 ASK Q44. OTHERS GO TO FILTER BEFORE Q45.

Q44 In the winter, how much on average do you think you put each week in the:

a)   electricity slot meter
b)   gas slot meter

IF NOT APPLICABLE WRITE IN XX

Electricity = £ [ ][ ] . [ ][ ] p   (50/53)
                (50) (51)   (52) (53)

Gas   = £ [ ][ ] . [ ][ ] p   (54/57)
                (54) (55)   (56) (57)

IF BUYS FUEL FROM SUPPLIER AT Q42 ASK Q45. OTHERS GO TO Q47.

Q45 SHOWCARD H Which of these types of fuel do you buy? Any others?

ASK Q46 ABOUT EACH FUEL BOUGHT.

Q46 How much do you spend on average on this fuel in winter?

	Q45 BUY	Q46 SPEND PER MONTH
	(58-60)	
Fuel oil -------------------- 1		£ [ ][ ] (61/2)
Smokeless fuel -------------- 2		£ [ ][ ] (63/4)
Coal (Coke/Anthracite) ------ 3		£ [ ][ ] (65/6)
Paraffin -------------------- 4		£ [ ][ ] (67/8)
Bottled gas ----------------- 5		£ [ ][ ] (69/70)
Logs/wood ------------------- 6		£ [ ][ ] (71/2)
None ------------------------ 7		

(58/72)

Q47 To help the Department assess different heating patterns, I would like to take two temperature readings in the house. Is that alright?

(73)

Yes --------	1 ASK Q48	(73)
No --------	2 GO TO Q50	

Q48 CODE ROOM TEMPERATURE MEASURED.

	1st (74)	2nd (75)	
Living room -------------------	1	1	
Dining room -------------------	2	2	(74/ 75)
Kitchen -----------------------	3	3	
Hall --------------------------	4	4	
Other (WRITE IN AND RING) _____			
_____	5	5	

Q49 Has the heating been on in ... today? For how long?

	1st (76)	2nd (77)	
Not on today -------------------	1	1	
Less than one hour -------------	2	2	(76/ 77)
1 but less than 2 hours --------	3	3	
2 but less than 3 hours --------	4	4	
3 but less than 4 hours --------	5	5	
4 but less than 5 hours --------	6	6	
5 but less than 6 hours --------	7	7	
7 hour or more -----------------	8	8	
Don't know ---------------------	9	9	

FIRST	SECOND	OUTSIDE	NEW CARD DUP COLS 1 - 13
(16)	(17)	(18)	③ (14)
PLUS -------- 1	PLUS -------- 1	PLUS -------- 1	SKIP COL 15
MINUS ------- 2	MINUS ------- 2	MINUS ------- 2	

TEMPERATURE:

□ □ . □	□ □ . □	□ □ . □	(16/ 27)
(19) (20) (21)	(22) (23) (24)	(25) (26) (27)	

ASK COUNCIL AND PRIVATE RENTERS ONLY. OWNER-OCCUPIERS GO TO Q52

Q50 SHOWCARD I Do you know of any major repairs or improvements done by the
council/your landlord to your home in the last five years - I mean things
like installing central heating, putting in double-glazing or retiling the
roof?

(28)

Yes ----------------- 1 NOTE BRIEF DETAILS BELOW

No ------------------ 2 GO TO Q51   (28)

1. _____
2. _____
3. _____
4. _____
5. _____
6. _____

IF ANY JOBS LISTED COMPLETE LANDLORD JOB SHEET FOR EACH ONE. IF NONE ASK Q51

Q51 SHOWCARD I (Apart from these) do you know of any other repairs or
improvements done by the council/ your landlord to your home in the last
12 months, including minor repairs or improvements?

(29)

Yes ----------------- 1 NOTE DETAILS BELOW

No ------------------ 2 GO TO Q52   (29)

1. _____
2. _____
3. _____
4. _____
5. _____
6. _____

FOR OFFICE USE ONLY

(30)(31) (32)(33) (34)(35) (36)(37) (38)(39)

(30/39)

ASK ALL

Q52 SHOWCARD I Have you had any major repairs or improvements done to this house/flat in the last five years which you paid for yourself or got a grant for? I mean things which would cost £400 or more to have done professionally?

(40)

		NOTE
Yes	------------------	1 DETAILS BELOW
No	------------------	2 GO TO Q55

(40)

1. _____

2. _____

3. _____

4. _____

5. _____

6. _____

IF ONLY ONE JOB COMPLETE RESPONDENT JOB SHEET FOR THAT JOB. IF MORE THAN ONE ASK Q53. IF NONE ASK Q55.

Q53 Thinking about the major jobs you have just mentioned, did you pay for each one separately, or were there some where you paid for more than one at the same time.

(41)

		COMPLETE RESPONDENT JOB
All separately	------------------	1 SHEET FOR EACH ONE
Some paid for at same time	------	2 ASK Q54

(41)

Q54 Which jobs did you pay for at the same time? FOR EACH GROUP OF JOBS WRITE IN DETAILS FROM Q52.

JOB GROUP A - _____

JOB GROUP B - _____

JOB GROUP C - _____

JOB GROUP D - _____

JOB GROUP E - _____

COMPLETE RESPONDENT JOB SHEET FOR EACH JOB GROUP. COMPLETE ONE RESPONDENT JOB SHEET FOR EACH SINGLE JOB NOT PART OF JOB GROUP.

Q55 SHOWCARD I (Apart from this) have you done any minor repairs or improvements to this house/flat in the last 12 months which you paid for yourself or got a grant for?

(INCLUDE ALL REPAIRS OR IMPROVEMENTS HOWEVER SMALL)

(42)

	NOTE
Yes ------------------	1 DETAILS BELOW
No -------------------	2 GO TO Q57

(42)

1. _____

2. _____

3. _____

4. _____

5. _____

6. _____

Q56 Overall, how much money would you say you have spent on these minor jobs over the last 12 months? PROBE FOR BEST ESTIMATE.

£ [ ][ ][ ][ ][ ]
  (43) (44)(45)(46)(47)

(43/47)

ASK ALL

Q57 SHOWCARD L Overall how would you rate the current state of repair of this house/flat?

(48)
Very good ------------------------------ 1
Fairly good ----------------------------- 2
Fairly poor ----------------------------- 3
Very poor ------------------------------- 4
Don't know ------------------------------ 5

(48)

FOR OFFICE USE ONLY

[ ][ ] [ ][ ] [ ][ ] [ ][ ] [ ][ ]
(49)(50) (51)(52) (53)(54) (55)(56) (57)(58)

(49/58)

Q58 Overall do you think the general state of repair of your home is worse than it was 5 years ago, or better than it was, or about the same?

(59)

```
Worse  ------------------------ 1 ASK Q59
Better ------------------------ 2
Same   ------------------------ 3 GO TO Q61      (59)
Don't know ------------------- 4
```

Q59 In what way is it in a worse state of repair? Any others?

(60-63)

_____

_____   1 2 3 4
5 6 7 8
_____   9 0 X Y

_____

Q60 Is there any particular reason why you have not done anything about the ——— state of repair?

(64-65)

```
Waiting for council to do it --------- 1
Can't afford to ---------------------- 2
Not bothered about it ---------------- 3          (64/
Waiting for grant/approval ----------- 4           65)
Doing something now ------------------ 5
Not my responsibility ---------------- 6
Other (WRITE IN)
```

_____ 7

ASK ALL

Q61 SHOWCARD M Which of these statements is closest to your own views?

(66)

```
I am constantly repairing/improving my home ---- 1
I always do maintenance jobs promptly to prevent
 problems developing --------------------------- 2
I get maintenance jobs done when they are
 essential but I don't look for work ----------- 3       (66)
I tend to get behind with maintenance jobs in
 the house ------------------------------------- 4
I just don't bother about the house though I feel
 it is my responsibility ----------------------- 5
I don't regard the house as my responsibility -- 6
```

IF RESPONDENT HAS RECEIVED A GRANT (CHECK JOB SHEETS) ASK Q63. OTHERS ASK Q62.

Q62 (Can I just check) have you ever asked the council for a grant for repairs, improvements or insulation on this property?

(67)

```
Yes ------- 1 ASK Q64
No. ------- 2 GO TO Q67      (67)
```

IF RECEIVED GRANT

Q63 (Can I just check) have you ever asked the council for <u>any other</u> grant for repairs, improvements or insulation on this property?

(68)

```
Yes ------- 1 ASK Q64
No ------- 2 GO TO Q67       (68)
```

IF YES AT Q62 OR Q63

Q64   What was this for?

_____

_____

_____

Q65   Did you complete written application forms from the council for this grant?

(69)

Yes ------- | 1 ASK Q66
No -------- | 2 GO TO Q67
Don't know- | 3 ASK Q66

(69)

IF YES/DON'T KNOW

Q66   Did you actually get a grant?

(70)

Yes ------- | 1 NOW GO TO Q68
No -------- | 2 ASK Q67

(70)

IF NO AT Q62/Q63/Q65/Q66

Q67   Is there any particular reason why not?

(71-72)

Don't need any repairs/improvements -- 1
Didn't know about them --------------- 2
Didn't think was eligible ------------ 3
Told not eligible -------------------- 4
Council ran out of money ------------- 5
Put on waiting list ------------------ 6
Waiting list too long ---------------- 7
Not worth it ------------------------- 8
Never got round to it ---------------- 9
Other (WRITE IN AND RING) _____

_____ 0
Don't know -------------------------- X

(71/ 72)

OFFICE USE ONLY

(73)(74) (75)(76) (77)(78) (79)(80)

(73/ 80)

NEW CARD
DUP COLS
1-13
④ (14)

I'd now like to ask you about the people in your household.

ASK Q68-70 ABOUT ALL HOUSEHOLD MEMBERS

Q68 Is .... male or female?

	HOH	2	3	4	5	6	7	8
	(15)	(21)	(28)	(35)	(42)	(49)	(56)	(69)
Male	1	1	1	1	1	1	1	1
Female	2	2	2	2	2	2	2	2

Q69 How old was ... last birthday?

(16)(17)	(22)(23)	(29)(30)	(36)(37)	(43)(44)	(50)(51)	(57)(58)	(64)(65)

Q70 How is .... related to the head of the household?

	(24)	(31)	(38)	(45)	(52)	(59)	(66)
Spouse	1	1	1	1	1	1	1
Mother/father	2	2	2	2	2	2	2
Child	3	3	3	3	3	3	3
Other relative	4	4	4	4	4	4	4
Non-relative	5	5	5	5	5	5	5

ASK Q71 FOR EACH HOUSEHOLD MEMBER AGED 16+

Q71 Is ....

	(18)	(25)	(32)	(39)	(46)	(53)	(60)	(67)
Single	1	1	1	1	1	1	1	1
Married	2	2	2	2	2	2	2	2
Widowed	3	3	3	3	3	3	3	3
Divorced	4	4	4	4	4	4	4	4
Separated	5	5	5	5	5	5	5	5

ASK Q72 AND Q73 FOR EACH MALE AGED 16-64 AND EACH FEMALE AGED 16-59.

Q72 SHOWCARD N Which of these best describes .....?

	(19)	(26)	(33)	(40)	(47)	(54)	(61)	(68)
Full-time	1	1	1	1	1	1	1	1
Part-time	2	2	2	2	2	2	2	2
YTS	3	3	3	3	3	3	3	3
Unemployed	4	4	4	4	4	4	4	4
Retired	5	5	5	5	5	5	5	5
Temporarily sick	6	6	6	6	6	6	6	6
Long-term sick/disabled	7	7	7	7	7	7	7	7
Maternity leave	8	8	8	8	8	8	8	8
Look after disabled person	9	9	9	9	9	9	9	9
Look after family	0	0	0	0	0	0	0	0
Student/at school	X	X	X	X	X	X	X	X
Other	Y	Y	Y	Y	Y	Y	Y	Y

Q73 SHOWCARD O Does .... receive any of these?

	(20)	(27)	(34)	(41)	(48)	(55)	(62)	(69)
Severe Disablement Allowance	1	1	1	1	1	1	1	1
Unemployment benefit	2	2	2	2	2	2	2	2
Supplementary benefit	3	3	3	3	3	3	3	3
Maternity benefit	4	4	4	4	4	4	4	4
None of these	5	5	5	5	5	5	5	5

IF HOH UNEMPLOYED ASK Q74. OTHERS GO TO Q75.

Q74 How long has .... (HOH) been unemployed?

	(70)
Under 3 months	1
3 but less than 6 months	2
6 but less than 12 months	3
1 but less than 2 years	4
2 years or more	5

ASK ALL

Q75 What is/was the occupation of ... (HOH)? IF NOT WORKING ASK ABOUT LAST
    MAIN JOB.   (71)
                              HOH never worked ------------ 1 GO TO Q76   (71)

  a) What is/was the job called? _____

  b) What does/did the work involve? _____
      _____

  c) Is/was this as an employee or self-employed?

                                                        (72)
                          Employee ---------------------------- 1
                          Self-employed ---------------------- 2   (72)

  d) Does/did the job involve supervising other people? How many?
                                                        (73)
                          No ---------------------------------- 1   (73)
                          Yes - 1 ---------------------------- 2
                                2 - 4 --------------------------- 3
                                5 - 9 --------------------------- 4
                                10 or more -------------------- 5
                                Don't know -------------------- 6

  e) What does his/her employer make or do? _____
      _____

  f) How many people work at the establishment where .... (HOH) works/
      worked?   (74)
                          1 - 4 --------------------------- 1
                          5 - 9 --------------------------- 2
                          10 - 99 ----------------------- 3   (74)
                          Over 100 ---------------------- 4
                          Don't know -------------------- 5

Q76 SHOWCARD P Where was... (HOH) born?
                                                        (75)
                          UK (inc. N. Ireland) ------------------ 1
                          Eire --------------------------------- 2   (75)
                          Other Europe ----------------------- 3
                          Africa ------------------------------- 4
                          India/Pakistan/Bangladesh ----------- 5
                          Other Asia --------------------------- 6
                          West Indies -------------------------- 7
                          North/South America ----------------- 8
                          Other (WRITE IN AND RING) _____
                          _____
                                                        9

                    ┌─────────────────────────┐
                    │   FOR OFFICE USE ONLY   │
                    │   ┌────┬────┐   │
                    │   │   │   │   │
                    │   └────┴────┘   │
                    │   (76)(77)   │
                    │   │
                    └─────────────────────────┘

ASK ALL OWNER-OCCUPIERS (INCLUDE SHARED OWNERSHIP). RENTERS GO TO Q96.

NEW CARD
DUP COLS
1 - 13
⑤(14)

Q77 On what date did you/your partner buy this property? PROBE FOR BEST
ESTIMATE, IF MONTH NOT KNOWN CODE 99.

MONTH [ ][ ]   19 [ ][ ]

(15)(16)   (17) (18)

IF BOUGHT IN LAST 10 YEARS ASK Q78 - IF LONGER GO TO Q83

Q78 What was the purchase price of this property? USE LEADING ZEROS.

DON'T KNOW = 99999

REFUSED   = 88888   £ [ ][ ][ ][ ][ ]   (19/
                           (19) (20)(21)(22)(23)   23)

Q79 SHOWCARD Q From which of the sources on this card did you (or your
partner) get the money to buy this property? CODE ALL THAT APPLY.

	(24)	
Building society mortgage/loan --------	1	
Bank mortgage/loan -------------------	2	
Local authority mortgage/loan ---------	3	ASK
Insurance/Finance company mortgage/ loan -------------------------------	4	Q80
Private loan from parents ------------	5	
Other private loan ------------------	6	
Gift --------------------------------	7	
Sale of previous property ------------	8	
Savings -----------------------------	9	GO TO
Another way -------------------------	0	Q87
Don't know --------------------------	X	
Refused -----------------------------	Y	

(24)

ASK IF CODED ANY OF 1-6 AT Q79

Q80 Was the money you borrowed at this time just to cover the cost of the
house/flat itself or was it also to cover the cost of repairs or
improvements?

(25)

Just for house/flat -------------------- 1 GO TO Q82
For repairs/improvements as well -------- 2 ASK Q81   (25)

Q81 How much did you borrow?

a)   for the property itself?   £ [ ][ ][ ][ ][ ]   (26/
                                 (26) (27) (28) (29) (30)   35)

b)   for repairs or improvements? £ [ ][ ][ ][ ][ ]   NOW GO
                                 (31) (32) (33) (34) (35) TO Q84

Q82 How much did you borrow?

                                 £ [ ][ ][ ][ ][ ]   NOW GO   (36/
                                 (36) (37) (38) (39) (40) TO Q84   40)

Q83 Do you have a mortgage or loan outstanding on your home?

(41)

Yes ------- | 1 ASK Q84
No ------- | 2 GO TO Q87   (41)

IF YES

Q84 For how many years have you had this mortgage/loan?

Q85 And how many years does the mortgage have left to run?

	Q84 (42)	Q85 (43)	
Mortage/loan fully repaid		1	GO TO Q87
Under 5 years	2	2	
5 but less than 10 years	3	3	
10 years but less than 15 years	4	4	ASK Q86
15 years but less than 20 years	5	5	(42/43)
20 years or more	6	6	
Don't know	7	7	

IF STILL HAVE MORTGAGE

Q86 How much are your repayments each month?

USE LEADING ZEROS

DON'T KNOW = 9999

REFUSED   = 8888

£ [ ][ ][ ][ ]
(44) (45) (46) (47)

(44/47)

ASK ALL OWNER-OCCUPIERS

Q87 After any rate rebate how much do you pay in rates?

USE LEADING ZEROS

DON'T KNOW = 9999

REFUSED   = 8888

DOESN'T PAY RATES = 0000

£ [ ][ ][ ][ ]
(48) (49) (50) (51)

(49/51)

Q88 What period does this cover?

(52)

Week ------------------------------------ 1
2 weeks --------------------------------- 2
Month ----------------------------------- 3
Tenth of year --------------------------- 4
Quarter --------------------------------- 5
Six months ------------------------------ 6
Year ------------------------------------ 7
Other ----------------------------------- 8

(52)

Q89 Do you pay water rates on this accommodation?

(53)

Yes -------------- | 1 ASK Q90
No -------------- | 2 GO TO
Don't know ------- | 3 Q92   (53)

Q90 How much are your water rates?

USE LEADING ZEROS

DON'T KNOW = 999

REFUSED   = 888   £ [ ][ ][ ]   (54/
                      (54) (55) (56)   56)

Q91 What period does this cover?   (57)
                          Week ----------------------------------- 1
                          2 weeks -------------------------------- 2
                          Month ---------------------------------- 3
                          Tenth of year ------------------------- 4   (57)
                          Quarter -------------------------------- 5
                          Six months ----------------------------- 6
                          Year ----------------------------------- 7
                          Other ---------------------------------- 8

Q92 SHOWCARD R Do you pay any of these additional charges? CODE ALL THAT APPLY
                                                          (58)
                          Ground rent ------------------- 1 GO TO
                          Maintenance charges ----------- 2 Q94
                          Service charges --------------- 3 ASK Q93
                          Hot water charge -------------- 4   (58)
                          Heating charge ---------------- 5 GO TO Q94
                          Other (WRITE IN AND RING)

                                                          6
                          None -------------------------- 7 GO TO FILTER
                                                            BEFORE Q96

ASK ALL PAYING SERVICE CHARGES

Q93 SHOWCARD S Does your service charge cover any maintenance or repairs
     listed on this card?   (59)
                          Decoration of halls/communal areas --- 1
                          Repairs to building eg. walls, roof -- 2
                          Electrical work within your property - 3
                          Plumbing/heating within your property- 4   (59)
                          Painting exterior of building -------- 5
                          Other (WRITE IN AND RING) _____

                          _____ 6
                          No, none ---------------------------- 7
                          Don't know -------------------------- 8

ALL PAYING ADDITIONAL CHARGES

Q94 How much are these charges in total? SHOWCARD R.

USE LEADING ZEROS

DON'T KNOW = 9999

REFUSED   = 8888   £ [ ][ ][ ][ ]   (60/
                      (60) (61) (62) (63)   63)

Q95 What period does this cover?   (64)
                          Week ------------------------- 1
                          2 weeks ---------------------- 2
                          Month ------------------------ 3 NOW
                          Tenth of year ---------------- 4 GO TO   (64)
                          Quarter ---------------------- 5 FILTER BEFORE
                          Six months ------------------- 6 Q96
                          Year ------------------------- 7
                          Other ------------------------ 8

ASK ALL RENTERS - INCLUDING SHARED OWNERS. OWNER-OCCUPIERS GO TO Q110.

Q96 How do you pay for your rent? READ OUT:

(65)

Do you pay your rent to the landlord/
the Council ---------------------- 1 ASK Q97
Or do you live in rent free
accommodation -------------------- 2
Or does the DHSS pay your rent direct
to the Council -------------------- 3 GO TO Q109
Or something else (WRITE IN AND RING)

(65)

4

Q97 After any rent rebate or allowance, how much does your household pay in rent?

USE LEADING ZEROS

DON'T KNOW = 9999

REFUSED   = 8888   £ [ ][ ][ ][ ]

(66) (67) (68) (69)

(66/
69)

Q98 What period does this cover?

(70)

Week	1
2 weeks	2
Month	3
Tenth of year	4
Quarter	5
Six months	6
Year	7
Other	8

(70)

ASK ALL RENTERS - SHARED OWNERS GO TO Q110.

Q99 Does your rent include your rates?

(71)

Yes ------------------ 1 GO TO Q 102
No ------------------ 2 ASK
Don't know ---------- 3 Q 100

(71)

Q100 After any rate rebate, how much do you pay in rates?

USE LEADING ZEROS

DON'T KNOW = 9999

REFUSED   = 8888   £ [ ][ ][ ][ ]

(72) (73) (74) (75)

(72/
75)

Q101 What period does this cover?

(76)

Week	1
2 weeks	2
Month	3
Tenth of year	4
Quarter	5
Six months	6
Year	7
Other	8

(76)

Q102 Does your rent include water rates?

(77)

Yes ----------------- 1 GO TO Q105
No ----------------- 2 ASK   (77)
Don't know ---------- 3 Q103

Q103 After any rebate, how much are your water rates?

USE LEADING ZEROS

DON'T KNOW = 9999

REFUSED = 8888

£ | | | | |
  (15) (16) (17) (18)

NEW CARD
DUP COLS
1 - 13
⑥ (14)

Q104 What period does this cover?

(19)

Week --------------------------------------- 1
2 weeks ------------------------------------ 2
Month -------------------------------------- 3
Tenth of year ------------------------------ 4   (19)
Quarter ------------------------------------ 5
Six months --------------------------------- 6
Year --------------------------------------- 7
Other -------------------------------------- 8

Q105 Do you have to pay a service charge as well as your rent?

(20)

Yes ----------------- 1 ASK Q106
No ----------------- 2 GO TO   (20)
Don't know ---------- 3 Q109

Q106 How much is your service charge?

USE LEADING ZEROS

DON'T KNOW = 9999

REFUSED = 8888

£ | | | | | (21/24)
  (21) (22) (23) (24)

Q107 What period does this cover?

(25)

Week -------------------------------- 1
2 weeks ----------------------------- 2
Month ------------------------------- 3
Tenth of year ----------------------- 4   (25)
Quarter ----------------------------- 5
Six months -------------------------- 6
Year -------------------------------- 7
Other ------------------------------- 8

Q108 SHOWCARD S Does your service charge cover any maintenance or repairs listed on this card?

(26-28)

Decoration of halls/communal areas --- 1
Repairs to the building eg.walls, roof 2
Electrical work within your property - 3   (26/28)
Plumbing/heating within your property- 4
Painting exterior of builidng ------- 5
Other (WRITE IN AND RING) _____

_____ 6
No, none --------------------------- 7
Don't know ------------------------- 8

Q109 Does your rent include the cost of heating or hot water?

(29)

Heating only --------------------------- 1
Hot water only ----------------------- 2   (29)
Both ----------------------------------- 3
Neither ------------------------------- 4

ASK ALL

Q110 I would finally like to ask you some questions about income from work
and other sources. Can I just check, are you ...? READ OUT.

(30)

Working as an employee ---------------- 1 GO TO Q112
Self-employed ------------------------- 2 ASK Q111a)
or not working ------------------------ 3 GO TO FILTER
                                          BEFORE Q115

Q111 a)   Do you receive an income on a regular basis from this work?

(31)

Yes ----------------- 1 GO TO Q112
No ------------------ 2 GO TO Q 111b)   (31)

IF NO

Q111 b)   Can you give me an estimate of how much you have received in the last
year?

Amount | | | | | | NOW GO TO Q113   (32/
       (32) (33)(34)(35)(36)   36)

Q112 What is your usual pay, before any deductions for tax and National
Insurance? (Accept "net" pay if gross cannot be given).

a)   Amount: | | | | | | DON'T KNOW = 99999   (37/
                  (37)(38)(39)(40) (41)   REFUSED   = 38888   41)

(42)

b)   Period: Day ------------------------------- 1
                  Week ------------------------------ 2
                  Two weeks ------------------------ 3
                  Four weeks ------------------------ 4   (42)
                  Month ----------------------------- 5
                  Year ------------------------------ 6
                  Other (WRITE IN)

                  _____ 7

(43)

c)   Accuracy: Exact consulted pay slip --------------- 1   (43)
                  Exact but not consult pay slip --------- 2
                  Estimate ------------------------------- 3

(44)

d)   Amount: Gross ---------------------------------- 1   (44)
                  Net ------------------------------------ 2

Q113 Do you have a second job, apart from the one we have just talked about?

(45)

Yes ----------------- 1 ASK Q114
No ------------------ 2 GO TO FILTER   (45)
                        BEFORE Q115

Q114 What is your <u>usual</u> pay from this second job before any deductions for tax and National Insurance? (Accept 'net' pay if gross cannot be given).

a) Amount: ▢▢▢▢▢   DON'T KNOW = 99999   (46/
    (46)(47)(48)(49)(50) REFUSED = 88888   50)
                                                 (51)

b) Period:
    Day ----------------------------------- 1
    Week ---------------------------------- 2
    Two weeks ----------------------------- 3   (51)
    Four weeks ---------------------------- 4
    Month --------------------------------- 5
    Year ---------------------------------- 6
    Other (WRITE IN)

    _____ 7
                                        (52)
c) Accuracy:
    Exact consulted pay slip --------------1
    Exact but not consult pay slip --------2   (52)
    Estimate ------------------------------3
                                        (53)
d) Amount:
    Gross ---------------------------------1
    Net ---------------------------------- 2   (53)

IF MARRIED/LIVING AS MARRIED ASK Q115 - OTHERS GO TO Q120

                                                  (54)
Q115 Is your partner ... READ OUT:
    Working as an employee --------------- 1 GO TO Q117
    Self-employed ------------------------ 2 ASK Q116a)
    or not working ----------------------- 3 GO TO Q120

    ## IE YES

Q116 a) Does he/she receive a regular income from this work?

                                        (55)
    Yes ---------------- 1 ASK Q117
    No ----------------- 2 GO TO Q116b   (55)

    ## IF NO

Q116 b) Can you give me an estimate of how much he/she received in the last year?

    Amount ▢▢▢▢▢ NOW GO TO Q118   (56/
          (56)(57)(58)(59)(60)   60)

Q117 What is his/her usual pay <u>before</u> any deductions for tax and National
Insurance? (Accept net if <u>gross</u> cannot be given).

a) Amount: ☐☐☐☐☐   DON'T KNOW = 99999   (61/
                REFUSED = 88888   65)
(61)(62)(63)(64) (65)

                                           (66)

b) Period: Day ------------------------------------- 1
              Week ------------------------------------ 2
              Two weeks ------------------------------ 3   (66)
              Four weeks ------------------------------ 4
              Month ----------------------------------- 5
              Year ------------------------------------ 6
              Other (WRITE IN)

              _____ 7

                                            (67)

c) Accuracy: Exact consulted pay slip --------------1
                 Exact but not consult pay slip --------2   (67)
                 Estimate ------------------------------3

                                          (68)

d) Amount: Gross --------------------------------- 1   (68)
             Net ----------------------------------- 2

Q118 Does he/she have a second job, apart from the one you have just told
me about?

                                         (69)
                      Yes ----------------- | 1 ASK Q119
                      No ------------------ | 2 GO TO Q120 | (69)

Q119 What is his/her usual pay from this second job <u>before</u> any deductions for
tax and National Insurance? (Accept net if <u>gross</u> cannot be given).

a) Amount: ☐☐☐☐☐   DON'T KNOW = 99999   (70/
                REFUSED = 88888   74)
(70)(71)(72) (73)(74)

                                           (75)

b) Period: Day ------------------------------------- 1
              Week ------------------------------------ 2
              Two weeks ------------------------------ 3   (75)
              Four weeks ------------------------------ 4
              Month ----------------------------------- 5
              Year ------------------------------------ 6
              Other (WRITE IN)

              _____ 7

                                           (76)

c) Accuracy: Exact consulted pay slip --------------1
                 Exact but not consult pay slip --------2   (76)
                 Estimate ------------------------------3

                                          (77)

d) Amount: Gross --------------------------------- 1   (77)
             Net ----------------------------------- 2

ASK ALL

Q120 a) I finally want to talk about income from sources other than work SHOWCARD T. At present are you (or your partner) receiving any of the benefits or incomes listed on this card? Any others? PROBE UNTIL NO. FOR EACH ONE CODED   ASK b-d (EXCEPT FOR FAMILY ALLOWANCE).

  b) How much was the last payment of .... (benefit/income). IF BOTH RESPONDENT AND PARTNER RECEIVE ADD TWO TOGETHER. CODE TO NEAREST POUND DO NOT CODE PENCE.

  Refused = 999   Don't know = 888

  c) What period did that cover?

  d) IF LIVING WITH SPOUSE/PARTNER   IF NOT LIVING WITH SPOUSE/PARTNER

  Do you or does your partner receive   Ring Code 1 for who received
  this benefit?

NEW CARD
DUP COLS
1-13
⑦(14)

	Received	Last payment (Pounds only)	Weeks 1	2	3	Months 1	2	3	6	12	DK	Who received Resp only	Part only	Both
Unemployment	(15) 1	☐☐☐ (16)(17)(18)	1	2	3	4	5	6	7	8	9 (19)	1	2	3 (20)
Old Age Pension	(21) 1	☐☐☐ (22)(23)(24)	1	2	3	4	5	6	7	8	9 (25)	1	2	3 (26)
Sickness	(27) 1	☐☐☐ (28)(29)(30)	1	2	3	4	5	6	7	8	9 (31)	1	2	3 (32)
Child Benefit	(33) 1	DO NOT ASK b) - d) FOR CHILD BENEFIT												
Family Income Supp	(34) 1	☐☐☐ (35)(36)(37)	1	2	3	4	5	6	7	8	9 (38)	1	2	3 (39)
Supp. Benefit	(40) 1	☐☐☐ (41)(42)(43)	1	2	3	4	5	6	7	8	9 (44)	1	2	3 (45)
Widows	(46) 1	☐☐☐ (47)(48)(49)	1	2	3	4	5	6	7	8	9 (50)	1	2	3 (51)
Industrial Injury	(52) 1	☐☐☐ (53)(54)(55)	1	2	3	4	5	6	7	8	9 (56)	1	2	3 (57)
Industrial Disablement	(58) 1	☐☐☐ (59)(60)(61)	1	2	3	4	5	6	7	8	9 (62)	1	2	3 (63)
Invalidity	(64) 1	☐☐☐ (65)(66)(67)	1	2	3	4	5	6	7	8	9 (68)	1	2	3 (69)
Other (WRITE IN) _____	(70) 1	☐☐☐ (71)(72)(73)	1	2	3	4	5	6	7	8	9 (74)	1	2	3 (75)
Allowances	(15) 1	☐☐☐ (16)(17)(18)	1	2	3	4	5	6	7	8	9 (19)	1	2	3 (20)
Non-state pension	(21) 1	☐☐☐ (22)(23)(24)	1	2	3	4	5	6	7	8	9 (25)	1	2	3 (26)
Annuities	(27) 1	☐☐☐ (28)(29)(30)	1	2	3	4	5	6	7	8	9 (31)	1	2	3 (32)
Rent	(33) 1	☐☐☐ (34)(35)(36)	1	2	3	4	5	6	7	8	9 (37)	1	2	3 (38)
Lodgers	(39) 1	☐☐☐ (40)(41)(42)	1	2	3	4	5	6	7	8	9 (43)	1	2	3 (44)

NEW CARD
⑧(14)

Q121 <u>SHOWCARD U</u> At the moment do you (or your partner) have any money saved
or <u>invested</u> in any of the places mentioned on this card?

(45)

Yes ---------------- 1 ASK Q122
No ---------------- 2 CLOSE INTERVIEW   (45)

Q122 <u>SHOWCARD V</u> How much do you (and your partner) have saved altogether? Please
<u>tell me</u> the letter on this card for the group in which you would place
your <u>total</u> savings.

(46)

A -------------------------- 1
B -------------------------- 2
C -------------------------- 3
D -------------------------- 4   (46)
E -------------------------- 5
F -------------------------- 6
G -------------------------- 7
H -------------------------- 8
I -------------------------- 9
Don't know ----------------- 0
Refused -------------------- X

**NB. IF IN TEMPERATURE SUB-SAMPLE REMEMBER TO TAKE OUTSIDE TEMPERATURE
AND RECORD AT Q49.**

1986

ENGLISH HOUSE CONDITION SURVEY

Address of Sample Dwelling

L

NOTE:
Probable tenure of
dwelling
P = Private
L = Local Authority
N = New Town
H = Housing Association

1. Please answer this questionnaire in respect of the above dwelling.

2. The questions relate to the period 1 November 1981 - 1 November 1986.

3. Read the accompanying notes before answering each question.

4. Complete the questionnaire by ringing the number(s) beside your answer and, if necessary, writing your reply in the space provided.

5. If you have any queries relating to the questionnaire contact the English House Condition Unit on 01-388-3191.

When you have completed the questionnaire, please check to ensure you have answered all the necessary questions. Return this form, with the other questionnaires, in the reply paid envelopes provided.

PLEASE ANSWER ALL THE QUESTIONS ON THIS PAGE.

THESE WILL THEN TELL YOU WHICH FURTHER

SECTIONS ARE TO BE COMPLETED.

NOTES ON COMPLETION	QUESTIONS

NOTES ON COMPLETION

1. Include all action (works, programmes, use of powers, assistance) by local authority. Also include action by other 'public' bodies (eg. housing association) where known to authority and/or is part of authority's housing strategy.

1a) Code 1 (Yes) if:
- sample dwelling included in Area/estate where action is taking place, even if no action on sample dwelling itself;
- in local authority (LA) estate on which works are part of estate-wide or part-of-estate programme;
- area clearance of any kind, for any purpose.

Include non-statutory areas such as 'repair area' or 'confidence area', and other areas adopted by Council resolution.

Code 2 (No) if action is only to sample dwelling (SD) or block containing SD, but no action to a wider area/estate; this type of action is covered in 1b below. See below for definition of block.

1b) Code 1 (Yes) only if action is on sample dwelling or block/group including sample dwelling (SD), even if SD/block is in area/estate.
Block means group of dwellings that are part of same structure eg block of flats, terraced block of houses.
Group scheme means simultaneous action on SD and other dwellings in same locality but not necessarily in same block.
If action on SD/block is part of area/estate programme, code 1 in 1(b) as well as in 1(a).
Assistance: include if given or applied for; exclude if application rejected.

2. Code 1 (Non-traditional): include all proprietary systems and other non-trads that are not system built i.e. include if known/probable that the building is prefabricated, of frame construction (including timber) or of in situ concrete.
Code 2 (Traditional) if known/probable that protective envelope and structural integrity of building are provided by the same component.

3. Code 2 (No) if there has been a change in ownership but the tenure remains the same.

Code 3 (Not known) if it is not possible to tell from local authority records whether tenure has changed.

QUESTIONS

1. On 1 November 1986, was the dwelling covered by any of the following kinds of action? (Include 'statutory' and 'non-statutory' action; include action that is current, proposed or has been completed since 1 November 1981.)

a) Area improvement, area clearance, or action on a local authority estate?

YES   1 ▶ ANSWER SECTION A

NO   2

b) Action on the sample dwelling or block containing the dwelling? (Include: enveloping/block/group schemes; 'compulsory' action; grant assistance/1985 Act Pt XVI assistance; action on local authority owned dwellings.)

YES   1 ▶ ANSWER SECTION B

NO   2

2. What was the construction method of the dwelling?

Non-traditional or probably non traditional   1 ▶ ANSWER SECTION C

Traditional or probably traditional   2
Not known   3

3. Did the tenure of the dwelling change between 1 November 1981 and 1 November 1986? (Include if change was made, transaction in progress, or change proposed in period.)

YES   1 ▶ ANSWER SECTION D

NO   2
NOT KNOWN   3

NOW COMPLETE THE APPROPRIATE SECTIONS, AS INDICATED BY YOUR ANSWERS ABOVE

NOTES ON COMPLETION	QUESTIONS

PLEASE ANSWER EVERY QUESTION IN THIS SECTION. IF NECESSARY, RING NOT APPLICABLE CODE.

A1 Identify separately:

    action completed (within the specified period)

    current action (at 1 Nov 1986)

    proposed action (at 1 Nov 1986).

Code 1 (Not Applicable) if any column does not apply.

A1 What was the main type of declaration/action on the area/estate (between 1 November 1981 and 1 November 1986)? COMPLETE EACH COLUMN. RING ONE ANSWER IN EACH COLUMN.

	Completed	Current	Proposed
Not applicable	1	1	1
AREA ACTION			
Area clearance	2	2	2
Housing Action Area	3	3	3
General Improvement Area	4	4	4
Conservation Area only	5	5	5
Other/non statutory area (GIVE DETAILS & CODE 6) _____	6	6	6
ESTATES			
Priority Estates Project or Estate Action scheme	7	7	7
Other LA scheme	8	8	8
Other (GIVE DETAILS AND CODE 9) _____	9	9	9

AREA ACTION

- Code as completed if area cleared, HAA terminated, GIA/non-statutory area effectively completed in the period.
- Code as current if council or its committees passed a resolution to declare area for clearance, or HAA, GIA, non-statutory area.
- Code as proposed if covered by approved programme for area action but not in progress by 1 November 1986.

ESTATES

- Code as completed if ALL work in estate programme was completed.
- Code as current if some work to estate was in progress, but scheme is being organised in phases.
- Code as proposed if scheme proposed but no work started.
- Code 08 (other LA scheme) for all LA schemes except Priority Estates Projects and Estate Action Schemes.

A2 If more than one scheme has taken place in the time period, code size of current scheme.

If no current scheme, code size of completed scheme.

If no completed scheme or current scheme, code size of proposed scheme.

A2 What is the approximate size of the above area/estate? RING ONE ANSWER

10 dwellings or less	1
11-49 dwellings	2
50-149 dwellings	3
150-300 dwellings	4
Over 300 dwellings	5

NOTES ON COMPLETION	QUESTIONS

<table>
<tr><td>

A3 Code all works that form part of area/estate programme, regardless of the extent of these works.

Code 03 <u>Improvements</u> for provision of amenities or modernization eg heating, insulation, kitchen/bathroom fittings, rewiring, re-plumbing.

Code 10 <u>Private Space</u>. Include works to boundary walls.

</td><td>

A3 What kind of works are involved (either completed, taking place or proposed)?

RING ALL THAT APPLY

None/Not applicable   <u>88</u>

<u>HOUSING</u>

Clearance/demolition   <u>01</u>
Conversion of dwellings   <u>02</u>
Improvements to dwellings   <u>03</u>
Major repairs   <u>04</u>
Improvements to security
  of dwellings   <u>05</u>
Works to common parts   <u>06</u>
New building   <u>07</u>

<u>ENVIRONMENT</u>

Landscaping/play provision
  on public space   <u>08</u>
Creation of private space   <u>09</u>
Works to private space
  (including curtilage)   <u>10</u>
Parking/traffic management
  works   <u>11</u>
Action on intrusive industry   <u>12</u>

<u>OTHER</u>
(Give details and code 13)   <u>13</u>

NOW GO TO NEXT APPROPRIATE SECTION

</td></tr>
</table>

SECTION B: ACTION ON SAMPLE DWELLING OR ON BLOCK CONTAINING DWELLING (BETWEEN 1 NOV 81 - 1 NOV 86)

NOTES ON COMPLETION	QUESTIONS

<table>
<tr><td>

</td><td>

PLEASE ANSWER EVERY QUESTION IN THIS SECTION. IF NECESSARY, RING NOT APPLICABLE CODE.

<u>BLOCK OR GROUP ACTION</u>

</td></tr>
<tr><td>

B1 Code 8 (Not applicable) if action is to sample dwelling only and there is no block/group action.

Code 1-5 only if adjacent activity is part of same specific scheme or 'contract'

Code 4 for LA scheme, even if action is part of action on estate identified in Section A

Code 2 for 'informal' enveloping schemes without formal DOE approval.

</td><td>

B1 What type of block action or group scheme (current, proposed or completed) occurred between 1 November 1981 and 1 November 1986?

RING ONE ANSWER

Not applicable/no block or
  group action   8

Enveloping scheme with/
  awaiting DOE approval   1
Other enveloping scheme   2
Block repair or improvement
  scheme involving grant
  assistance   3
Scheme on local authority
  built block   4
Other block or group
  scheme (GIVE DETAILS AND
  CODE 5)   5

</td></tr>
<tr><td>

PLEASE TURN OVER FOR REMAINDER OF SECTION B

</td><td></td></tr>
</table>

NOTE ON COMPLETION	QUESTIONS

NOTE ON COMPLETION

B2   Code 1 (completed) if all work completed since 1 November 1981.

Code 2 (current) if:
- there is completed and current work, or
- there is completed and proposed work, or
- there is current and proposed work.

Code 3 (proposed) if scheme proposed but no work started.

B4   Code 88 (Not applicable) if no action specific to sample dwelling.

Code 88 if 1985 Housing Act Pts XV and XVI (Assistance) are the only powers used. (Reference to 1985 Act includes earlier equivalent powers.)

Code 13 (Other) and specify for informal notice, voluntary grant aid (not Pt XV or XVI), funding to Housing Associations etc.

Code 01 (Action on LA dwelling) for any such action other than minor repairs; include even if action has also been identified in question A1 (estate) or B1 (block).

QUESTIONS

B2   On 1 November 1986, what was the status of the block or group scheme?   RING ONE ANSWER

Not applicable	8
Completed	1
In progress	2
Proposed	3

B3   What is the approximate size of the block or group?   RING ONE ANSWER

Not applicable	8
10 dwellings or less	1
11-24 dwellings	2
25-49 dwellings	3
50-149 dwellings	4
150-300 dwellings	5
Over 300 dwellings	6

POWERS USED ON THE DWELLING

B4   Under what compulsory or other powers was/is/will action on the dwelling (be) taken?   RING ALL THAT APPLY

Not applicable	88

1985 HOUSING ACT:

Action on dwelling built and owned by local authority (Pt II)	01
Pt IX Clearance Area	02
Pt IX Clearance - area added	03
Pt IX Closing/Demolition	04
Pt VI S189 Repairs Notice (unfit)	05
Pt VI S190 Repairs Notice (fit)	06
Pt VII Improvement Notice	07
Pt XI Works to HMO	08
Pt II Acquisition	09
Pt VIII Acquisition	10

OTHER POWERS:

Public Health Acts	11
Planning Acts	12
Other (GIVE DETAILS AND CODE 13)	13

_____

NON STATUTORY ACTION OR NOTICE
(Give details and code 14)   14

_____

NOTES ON COMPLETION	QUESTIONS

B5   Indicate status of action identified in B4.

Code 1 if demolition, closure, renovation etc, of dwelling completed in the specified period.

Code 2 if work in progress or there is a resolution to acquire dwelling, or any similar decision has been taken by an officer, Council or committee.

Code 3 if proposed or in programme of future action reported to Council or a committee. (Include dwellings in a 'clearance area' survey.)

B5   On <u>1 November 1986</u>, what was the status of the compulsory/other action?

Not applicable	8
Completed	1
In progress	2
Proposed	3

ASSISTANCE

B6   Do not include refused applications.

Code under '1st Application' the grant or assistance applied for or approved in the period 1 Nov 81 - 1 Nov 86.

Code under '2nd Application' any further application/approval in this period, even if simultaneous with first application. Otherwise code 8 (Not applicable)

If more than two applications, code those involving the most expenditure.

B6   What type of grant or assistance, under 1985 Housing Acts Pts XV and XVI, has been applied for or given? COMPLETE EACH COLUMN. RING ONE ANSWER IN EACH COLUMN.

	1st Application	2nd Application
Not applicable	8	8
PART XV GRANTS		
Improvement Grant	1	1
Intermediate Grant	2	2
Repairs Grant	3	3
Special Grant	4	4
Home Insulation Grant	5	5
PART XVI ASSISTANCE		
Reinstatement Grant	6	6
Repurchase	7	7
OTHER (Give details and code 9)	9	9

_____

_____

B7   Code 1 where assistance approved and payment has been made in full.

Code 2 if approved but payment not yet made in full.

Code 3 if application made but not yet approved/rejected.

B7   On <u>1 November 1986</u>, what was the status of this application(s)? COMPLETE EACH COLUMN. RING ONE ANSWER IN EACH COLUMN.

	1st Application	2nd Application
Not applicable	8	8
Assistance/grant given	1	1
Application approved	2	2
Application under consideration	3	3

PLEASE TURN OVER FOR REMINADER OF SECTION B

NOTE ON COMPLETION	QUESTIONS

QUESTIONS

DWELLING CONDITION AND WORKS TO THE DWELLING OR BLOCK/GROUP

B8 Identify whether unfit as defined in Pt XVIII of 1985 Housing Act.

B8 What was the condition of the dwelling before any action? **RING ONE ANSWER**

Unfit	1
Fit	2
Not known	3

B9 Identify separately works to Sample Dwelling only (resulting from action specified in B4 or B6) and works to block/group (resulting from action specified in B1).

If no work to Sample Dwelling or Block/Group code 88 (Not applicable).

Code Major Repairs if undertaken following compulsory action or grant assistance. For LA dwellings, code as major works if normally expended under capital account.

Code Minor Work etc (14) for small repair items in response to notice (eg. under Public Health Acts) such as repairs to guttering etc.

Code Closure/Change of Use (03) where change of use results from action identified in B4.

B9 What works are involved (completed, in progress or proposed)? **RING ALL THAT APPLY IN EACH COLUMN**

	Works to Sample Dwelling Only	Works to Block/ Group
Not applicable	88	88
DEMOLITION:		
Total clearance	01	01
Partial clearance	02	02
Closure/change of use	03	03
Short life patching	04	04
REPLANNING		
Conversion	05	05
New extensions	06	06
Internal rearrangement	07	07
Adaptations for elderly/ disabled	08	08
MAJOR REPAIRS TO:		
Roof coverings	09	09
Structure/external walls	10	10
External doors/windows	11	11
Damp proofing	12	12
Internal fabric	13	13
IMPROVEMENTS		
Heating arrangements	14	14
Insulation/condensation	16	15
Kitchen/bathroom fittings	16	16
Rewiring/replumbing	17	17
MINOR WORK IN RESPONSE TO STATUTORY OR INFORMAL NOTICE	18	18
OTHER WORKS		
Fire protection/escape	19	19
Asbestos treatment	20	20
Works to common parts	21	21
Curtilage works	22	22
Others (GIVE DETAILS AND CODE 23)	23	23

NOTES ON COMPLETION	QUESTIONS

B10 Who is/was or will probably be responsible for this work? **COMPLETE EACH COLUMN. RING ONE ANSWER IN EACH COLUMN**

	Works to Sample Dwelling	Works to Block/Group
Not applicable	88	88
PRIVATE AGENT:		
Owner-occupier	01	01
Private landlord/ developer	02	02
Tenant (any sector)	03	03
HOUSING ASSOCIATION	04	04
LOCAL AUTHORITY (LA):		
LA for private owner	05	05
LA alone	06	06
LA in association with DOE (Priority Estates Project or Estate Action schemes only)	07	07
LA in association with private sector (not PEP/EA schemes)	09	09
OTHER (Give details and code 10)	10	10

B11 Include cost of all work, relating to the Sample Dwelling, identified in Section B

If work not completed use contract or estimated cost.

If precise cost to Sample Dwelling is not known (eg block scheme) make an approximate apportionment by dividing total cost by number of dwellings involved.

Code 9 (Not known) if cost not known or apportionment not possible.

B11 Where work was/is/will be carried out on the sample dwelling, what is the approximate cost of all the work to this dwelling? **RING ONE ANSWER**

Not applicable/no work to sample dwelling	8
Less than £500	1
£500 - £2,000	2
£2,001 - £10,000	3
More than £10,000	4
Not known	5

B12 Give calendar year of final payment, contract, or estimate.

If only financial year of payment is known (eg 84/85) code earliest part of year (eg 84).

Code 88 (Not applicable) if no work to Sample Dwelling.

B12 To which year does this cost relate?

19 __ __

Not applicable	88
Not known	99

NOW GO TO NEXT APPROPRIATE SECTION

SECTION C: DWELLINGS OF NON TRADITIONAL CONSTRUCTION

| | NOTES ON COMPLETION | | QUESTIONS |

NOTES ON COMPLETION

QUESTIONS

PLEASE ANSWER EVERY QUESTION IN THIS SECTION.   IF NECESSARY, RING NOT APPLICABLE CODE.

C1   Specify in full (eg Cornish Unit Type 1). Name of system will suffice if precise construction type is not known (eg Cornish). Remember to Code 1, <u>as well as</u> writing in construction method.

C1   If a proprietary system, what is the name or description of the construction method of the dwelling or building containing the dwelling? **SPECIFY IN FULL AND RING CODE 1**

_____   1

_____

Not applicable/not a system   8
Not known   9

C2   <u>Boxwall/perimeter wall</u> (1) if loadbearing wall of any material (other than brick or block) which supports all upper floors and roof.
<u>Crosswall</u> (2) if walls which provide bearings for upper floors and roof structure are located at party walls (ie generally run between front and rear walls).
<u>Frame</u> (3) if any form of concrete, steel or timber frame which supports all other parts of the structure.
<u>Small Panel</u> (4) No frame; structure made up of small panels (which have probably been man-handled into position) and of pre-cast concrete construction.   Include narrow storey height panels.
<u>Large Panel</u> (5) No frame; structure made up of large panels (craned into position) normally of storey height, and of pre-cast concrete construction. If crosswall panels only, code 2 (crosswall).

C2   What is the predominant load-bearing structure of the dwelling or building containing the dwelling?   RING ONE ANSWER

Boxwall/Perimeter wall   1
Crosswall   2
Frame   3
Small panel   4
Large panel   5
Other (GIVE DETAILS & CODE 6) 6

_____

_____

_____

Not known   9

C3   Code only the material that forms part of the structure.   Do not include materials that merely form part of the non loadbearing elements (eg do not code if cladding or infill).

C3   What is the material of the main structural component?   RING ALL THAT APPLY.

Masonry (block, brick or
stone)   <u>1</u>
'No fines' in situ concrete   <u>2</u>
Other in situ concrete   <u>3</u>
Pre cast reinforced concrete   <u>4</u>
Timber   <u>5</u>
Aluminium   <u>6</u>
Steel   <u>7</u>
Other (DESCRIBE & CODE)   <u>8</u>

_____

_____

Not known   9

Record any major faults which affect structural integrity of building regardless of extent. Use space for notes to give further details eg extent, whether dormant or progressive.

Some items in C4 may be caused by other faults - record all faults present, whatever the cause.

Chimney Distortion (01): eg leaning, bulging or seriously cracked/defective pointing.

Foundation Problems (03): if inadequate or have failed.

Wall Distortion (04): eg bulging of untied flank walls; decaying timber in masonry walls; sulphate attack of mortar joints; unbonded party/external walls; snapped header brickwork.

Wall Settlement (06): record if any settlement between crosswalls and front or rear wall.

Crosswall separation (07): if evidence of separation between crosswalls and front or rear wall

Interstitial Condensation (09): ie condensation occurring within a structural element causing severe corrosion of embedded metal.

Water Penetration (10): if severe enough to have structural consequences.

Frame Spalling (11): record if evidence of spalling of surface concrete on exposed concrete frame members.

Panels Disjointed (13): record if evidence of defective panel fixings or movement in structure.

Private Balconies (15): record structural faults in any part of private balcony.

C4   On 1 November 1986 what structural faults were known to the authority? RING ALL THAT APPLY. WRITE NOTES ON FAULTS IN SPACE BELOW.

None present/none recorded	88
Chimney distortion	01
Roof distortion/spreading	02
Foundation problems	03
Walls: distorted	04
Walls: Severe cracks	05
Walls: Settlement	06
Crosswall separated from other wall(s)	07
Wall tie failure	08
Interstitial condensation	09
Water penetration	10
Frame spalling	11
Panel spalling/cracked	12
Panels disjointed	13
Severe systematic cracks in render	14
Private balcony defects	15
Other (GIVE DETAILS & CODE 16)	16

_____

_____

NOTES ON STRUCTURAL FAULTS (STATE FAULT AND GIVE FURTHER DETAILS)

_____

_____

_____

_____

_____

_____

_____

_____

_____

_____

_____

_____

_____

PLEASE TURN OVER FOR REMAINDER OF SECTION C

NOTES ON COMPLETION	QUESTIONS

NOTES ON COMPLETION

C5 Indicate how the information in C4 (even if no faults are recorded) is known to the authority).

If information in C4 is suggested from sample survey of dwellings similar to sample dwelling, code 3 (other) and give details.

QUESTIONS

C5 How is this information known to the authority? RING ONE ANSWER

Specialist structural/ engineering survey at dwelling/block	1
General house condition survey at dwelling/block	2
Other (GIVE DETAILS & CODE 3)	3

_____

_____

No survey/no information	9

C6 What is the date of the above survey or enquiry?

19 __ __

Not applicable	88
Not known	99

NOW GO TO NEXT APPROPRIATE SECTION.

SECTION D: CHANGE OF DWELLING TENURE (BETWEEN 1 NOV 81 - 1 NOV 86)

NOTES ON COMPLETION	QUESTIONS

NOTES ON COMPLETION

D1 Code one answer in each column, as applicable.

If tenure is private but it is not known whether rented or occupied, specify 'private' under "other" and code 6.

If more than one change has taken place between 1 Nov 81 and 1 Nov 86, give details of most recent change.

QUESTIONS

PLEASE ANSWER EVERY QUESTION IN THIS SECTION. IF NECESSARY, RING NOT APPLICABLE CODE.

D1 What change of tenure has taken place/is being transacted/is proposed? COMPLETE EACH COLUMN. RING ONE CODE IN EACH COLUMN

	TENURE CHANGED	
	FROM	TO
Local Authority	1	1
Owner Occupied	2	2
Private Rented	3	3
Housing Association	4	4
New Town	5	5
Other (DESCRIBE AND CODE 6)	6	6

D2 If not transferred from LA to another tenure, ring 8 - not applicable.

D2 Under what scheme is/was the transaction made? RING ONE ANSWER

Not applicable/none of below	8
1985 Housing Act (Pt V) Right to Buy	1
Other 'Right to Buy' scheme	2
Improvement for Sale scheme	3
Homesteading scheme	4

D3 On 1 November 1986, what stage had the transaction reached? RING ONE ANSWER.

Completed	1
Currently taking place	2
Proposed	3

DEPARTMENT OF THE ENVIRONMENT VALUATION SURVEY
----

48 SURVEY STREET ANYTOWN EH8 6CS	A2335306Z

Dwelling description

A privately rented mid-terrace house, built 1870-1899, with five rooms on three floors, inadequate street parking and no central heating .

Work required

Roof needs major repair.
80% of wall surface needs repointing/renewing.
60% windows need replacing.
Damp proof course needs installing.
Kitchen needs refitting.
Bathroom needs refitting.
Bath needs installing.
W.C. needs installing.
Electrical system needs rewiring.
Some internal repairs are needed.
Other less major work is also required.

Recent work done

No work has been carried out on this dwelling recently.

What would you estimate the market value to be

(As at 1 Nov 1986)? £10,000

What would you estimate the market value to be if all the

defects were rectified (As at 1 Nov 1986)?..........   £17,000

Are there any special circumstances that affect these

valuations? (ring the appropriate code).......... yes:- 1 no:-(2)

if yes, what are these circumstances?_____

Appendix B Changes to the method of physical survey

1.   The changes in the survey schedule were introduced to cope with the demands for more detailed information on housing conditions and to deal with shortcomings identified following the 1981 survey. These shortcomings stem both from the way the data were recorded and the method by which disrepair was measured. The 1981 survey required the surveyor to carry information on the whole property in his head until the completion of the survey when he was required to make overall assessments. Also, the scale against which the surveyor made assessments of repair required was coarse and not sufficiently sensitive where only modest works were required.

2.   The new physical survey schedule required the surveyor:

   (i)   to follow a clear procedure in completing the Form;

   (ii)   to carry out a more detailed survey, room by room internally and externally from at least two vantage points;

   (iii) to make finer and more precise judgements about the nature and scale of work required;

   (iv)   to make some assessment of the urgency of work and to identify major works not yet required but likely to be in the forseeable future;

   (v)   to record his findings at the time of observation and to make more explicit the connection between his observations of faults in the building and works required for their remedy.

3.   More descriptive information was collected than in earlier years. This included details of construction methods and materials, plan form and dimensions, and access arrangements for flats. Apart from the intrinsic value of such information, its inclusion was an integral part in the development of an alternative procedure for estimating repair costs (see Appendix F).

4.   Photographs of front and rear elevations were included in the survey for the first time in 1986 and have proved invaluable in the data processing and analysis.

Reconciliation of the main and longitudinal surveys

1.   There are two aspects to this reconciliation. First, the two surveys are grossed to national stock totals and, where they collected comparable information, should provide descriptions of the 1986 stock which are the same within the expected error ranges. Secondly, the two surveys determined the extent of disrepair in the stock by very different methods and it is necessary to identify how and why the results are different.

Comparison of basic statistics

2.   The Longitudinal survey seems to indicate more dwellings in poor condition than the Main survey and the discrepancies are well outside the confidence limits due to sampling error (Table C.1). The Longitudinal survey also indicates a higher proportion of older stock (Table C.2). Because of the strong correlation between the age of the stock and condition, any distortion in the survey which raises the proportion of older dwellings will also result in the condition of the stock appearing worse than it is.

Table C.1   Unfitness and lack of amenities: comparison of Main and Longitudinal surveys

thousands of dwellings

	Main Survey		Longitudinal Survey		
	Number	Sampling Confidence Interval	Number	Sampling Confidence Interval	Adjusted Number
Dwellings Unfit	909	+/−56	1,053	+/−72	952
Dwellings Lacking Amenities	463	+/−45	543	+/−73	491

Table C.2   Age of dwellings: comparison of Main and Longitudinal surveys

% of dwellings

	Main Survey	Longitudinal Survey
Pre-1919	26	29
1919−1944	24	22
Post-1944	50	49

3. This higher proportion of older housing is probably a result of the grossing that has to be used for the Longitudinal survey (Appendix D). If the number of older properties in the Longitudinal survey are scaled down to correspond more closely with the known national totals then the number of properties unfit or lacking amenities are also reduced. This adjustment, to compensate for the grossing error, results in acceptable agreement between the Longitudinal and Main surveys.

4. This apparent age bias of the Longitudinal sample does not affect the comparisons which are made between 1981 and 1986 as both these data sets were grossed in the same way. However, it does emphasise that the representation of condition of 1986 must be taken from the Main survey.

5. The comparison of repair costs is explained in Appendix F.

Appendix D Survey sample

Sample structure

1. The 1986 EHCS was made up of five separate surveys (Figure D1) each of which had its own sample. The sample structure was further complicated as the survey had two sampling frames:

    (i)   the addresses from the 1981 EHCS, which formed the basis of the Longitudinal survey;

    (ii)   a separate sample frame obtained from the Post Code Address file (held by the Office of Population Census and Surveys), and this formed the basis of the Main survey sample.

Longitudinal sample

2. The Longitudinal sample comprised those addresses which yielded some data in the 1981 EHCS. This list was amended using Inland Revenue data to update the list by excluding dwellings which were known to have been demolished or taken out of the domestic stock and by including new dwellings formed as a result of conversions.

Main sample

3. The base date of the new sample frame was 1985. It was updated using 1986 Inland Revenue data to exclude demolitions and include conversions. From this frame there was a selection process which provided a sample of local authority housing, stratified by region, and a sample for the private sector, stratified by region and age of dwelling.

4. All other samples were sub-samples of these two main samples and their sizes and structure are shown in Figure D.1.

Response rates

5. The response rate from the Longitudinal survey was higher than that for the Main survey (Table D.1). This is to be expected as households included in the longitudinal survey may have been visited in each of 4 years (1971, 1976, 1981 and 1986). These repeat visits will have tended to exclude those households who would automatically refuse to participate in any form of survey, with those remaining more likely to respond.

Fig D.1 Sample structure

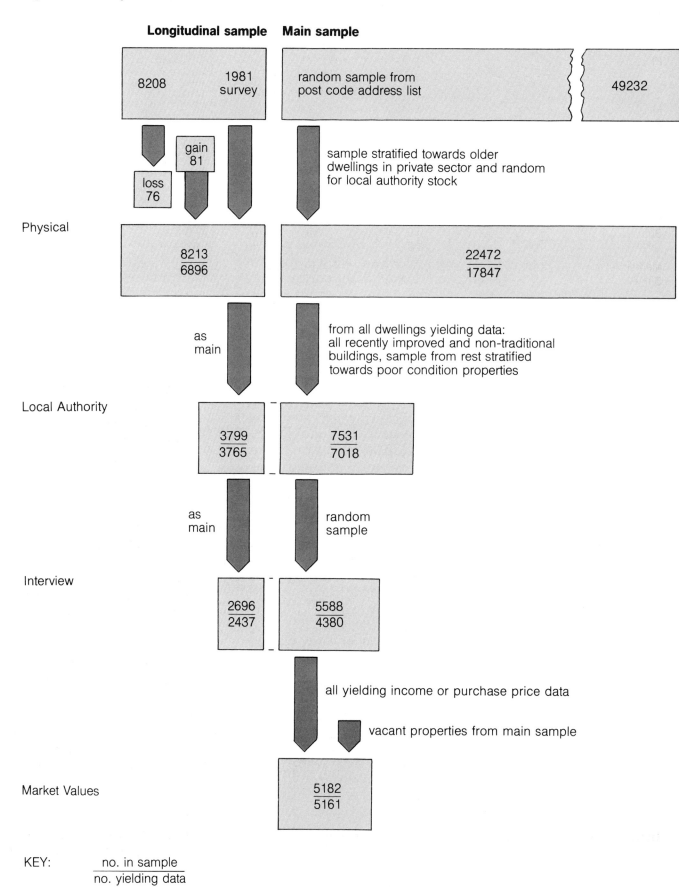

Longitudinal sample **Main sample**

8208 1981 survey

random sample from post code address list   } 49232

gain 81

loss 76

sample stratified towards older dwellings in private sector and random for local authority stock

Physical

$\frac{8213}{6896}$

$\frac{22472}{17847}$

as main

from all dwellings yielding data:
all recently improved and non-traditional buildings, sample from rest stratified towards poor condition properties

Local Authority

$\frac{3799}{3765}$

$\frac{7531}{7018}$

as main

random sample

Interview

$\frac{2696}{2437}$

$\frac{5588}{4380}$

all yielding income or purchase price data

vacant properties from main sample

Market Values

$\frac{5182}{5161}$

KEY: $\frac{\text{no. in sample}}{\text{no. yielding data}}$

(thousands of dwellings)

204

Table D.1 Response rates

Survey Component	Issued Addresses	Response		Response Rates (%)
Longitudinal Physical Survey	8,216	989	Refusals)	16
		331	Non-surveys (1))	
		1,624	Partial Surveys)	84
		5,272	Full Surveys)	
Main Physical Survey	22,472	3,446	Refusals)	21
		1,179	Non-Surveys)	
		15,348	Partial Surveys)	79
		2,499	Full Surveys)	
Postal Survey	11,330	527	Refusals)	5
		20	Not Returned)	
		10,783	Completed	95
Interview Survey	8,284	1,137	Refusals)	18
		372	Non-Surveys)	
		6,817	Full Interviews (2))	82
Market Value Survey	5,182	1	Not Returned)	0.4
		20	No Valuation)	
		5,162	Completed	99.6

(1) non-surveys due to dwellings being demolished, untraceable, etc.
(2) includes interviews with multi-households.

Grossing to national stock totals

6. To maximise the efficiency of data collection it has been necessary to use 'stratified' samples of dwellings which do not have a one to one relationship with the national stock. If such samples are to be used to draw conclusions about the stock they first have to be 'grossed'; that is, the weight to be attached to each dwelling to make the appropriate connection with the national total has to be established.

Basic procedure

7. In general the grossing procedure reproduces the steps used to obtain the sample, in order to allocate weights to each survey dwelling. Thus, if the sampling fraction for a particular category is 1 in 1,000 then each dwelling in that category receives a weight of 1,000. This procedure was followed for the main physical survey and also for the interview, postal and market value sub-samples. For the Longitudinal survey the process was more complex because it was made up of samples drawn in 1971 and 1976, so the procedure used in the sampling is no longer a good guide to grossing. For the 1981 survey a method was adopted which made reference to the published numbers of dwellings in given age bands within each region. This procedure was repeated for the 1986 Longitudinal physical survey. The interview and postal sub-samples of this survey were grossed by reproducing the steps used to draw the sample. For both the Main and the Longitudinal surveys, corrections were made to account for dwellings built or created since the samples were drawn.

Inclusion of new dwellings

8. New dwellings were distributed according to known characteristics of dwelling age, type tenure and regional distribution. It was assumed that new dwellings were fit, provided all basic amenities and did not require any repair. For all other variables the characteristics of new dwellings were distributed pro-rata as the rest of the stock.

Treatment of non-response

9.   The grossing procedure also takes account of non-response. For each sample, the variables associated with non-response were investigated and additional weighting factors were applied accordingly. For example, if a high proportion of dwellings in a particular category (such as region or type of dwelling) refused a survey, then the dwellings with surveys in that category received an extra weight.

10.   When grossed, different samples can produce different estimates for the same variable. This is to be expected because of sampling error (see paragraph 12 below). Further variation in estimates will occur if adjustments to weights cannot control all the variance introduced by differential response rates. In this survey different response rates were achieved in different tenure groups in the physical survey. A higher proportion of local authority dwellings had full surveys completed than did the private sector. This resulted in local authority dwellings being proportionately more likely to be selected for the interview and postal surveys and the grossing produces different totals for each tenure category compared with the physical survey. However, checks have confirmed that the overall effect of this difference does not affect any of the conclusions drawn.

11.   The Main and Longitudinal samples may also produce differences in estimates of the same variable. This is partly due to the different grossing procedures and in particular to the complexity of the sampling for the longitudinal survey (see Appendix C).

Sampling Error

12.   There are two possible sources of error in a sample:

(i)   bias: where, for example, dwellings with a particular characteristic have been disproportionately selected and this has not been accounted for in the grossing. No significant bias is evident in the sampling procedure (but see paragraph 9 above).

(ii)   sampling error: estimates of a particular variable may not equate exactly with the true value (eg number of unfit dwellings) because of chance factors in the selection of the sample which make it not truly representative of the stock. Thus survey estimates are inevitably subject to error. The smaller the sample size the larger, on average, will be the potential difference between true value and survey estimate. This is represented by error ranges around the survey estimate.

13.   Information about sampling errors is given in Tables D.2 to D.4. If a particular analysis relates only to the physical survey then Table D.2 (for the Main sample) and Table D.3 (for the Longitudinal sample) apply: if any data from the interview survey are included in the analysis then Table D.4 should be used. If a particular analysis based upon the Main physical survey relates only to pre-war dwellings then the first column of confidence limits should be used: if dwellings of all ages are included then the third column should be taken.

Table D.2 Approximate 95% confidence intervals
Main sample — physical survey

thousand dwellings

Estimates	Confidence Limits (+/−)		
	Pre-1945 and All Local Authority Dwellings	Post-1945 Dwellings Excluding Local Authority	Mixed Dwellings
5	4	6	5
10	6	9	6
25	9	14	10
50	13	20	15
100	18	28	20
250	29	44	32
500	40	61	45
1,000	56	82	63
2,500	82	111	96
5,000	100	96	125
10,000	80	n/a	141

14.   The use of the tables is best illustrated by an example. The estimate from the Main physical survey of number of unfit dwellings in the stock is 900,000. If it is known that most unfit dwellings were built in the early part of the century the first column of Table D.2 should be used. There the 95% confidence limit is given as about 53 (the range would be 56 on an estimate of 100,000). This means that there is a 5% chance that the true number of unfit dwellings is greater than 953,000 or less than 847,000. If the estimate were to be based on the longitudinal sample the range of confidence would be between 830,000 and 970,000 (Table D.3). (Note sampling is not the only factor contributing to the error in unfitness, see Appendix E).

Table D.3 Approximate 95% confidence intervals
Longitudinal sample — physical survey

thousand dwellings

Estimates	Confidence Limits (+/−)		
	Pre-1945 Dwellings	Post-1944 Dwellings	Mixed Dwellings
5	5	16	7
10	8	23	10
25	12	36	17
50	17	51	23
100	24	73	33
250	38	114	52
500	52	159	73
1,000	72	219	102
2,500	102	315	154
5,000	113	362	200
10,000	n/a	n/a	226

Table D.4 Approximate 95% confidence intervals interview survey

thousand dwellings

Estimates	Confidence Limits (+/−)		
	Main Sample	Longitudinal Sample	Both Samples
5	9	12	7
10	13	18	11
25	21	28	17
50	29	39	23
100	41	55	33
250	65	87	52
500	92	123	73
1,000	128	171	102
2,500	193	259	155
5,000	251	337	201
10,000	284	381	228

15.   Many of the tables in the Annex are based on sub-samples of the main data set. To enable sample errors to be calculated each table is given a sample size reference number. The key to these reference numbers is in Table D.5.

16.   Sample error is not the only source of error as other distortions can be introduced into the data through the non-availability of specific data items and the inherent inaccuracy of certain measurement techniques. These are dealt with in Appendix E.

Table D.5 Sample sizes for Annex tables

Main physical survey sample

Sample Code	Sample	Sample Size
Phy.1	All dwellings	22,472
Phy.2	All houses	17,089
Phy.3	All flats	5,383
Phy.4	All pre-1919 dwellings	5,939
Phy.5	All 1919–1944 dwellings	2,083
Phy.6	All post-1944 dwellings	5,352
Phy.7	All 1945–1964 dwellings	4,952
Phy.8	All post-1944 dwellings	4,145
Phy.9	All private-rented dwellings	1,560
Phy.10	All private-sector dwellings	14,603
Phy.11	All occupied dwellings	21,468
Phy.12	All multi-occupied dwellings	329
Phy.13	All non-temporary dwellings	22,445
Phy.14	All vacant dwellings	1,004
Phy.15	All purpose-built flats	3,712
Phy.16	All purpose-built occupied post-1944 flats	2,636
Phy.17	All dwellings with specific structural defects	3,793
Phy.18	All dwellings without central heating	4,903
Phy.19	All dwellings with central heating	9,630
Phy.20	All dwellings in poor condition	3,389
Phy.21	All non-traditional dwellings	1,958

Interview survey sample

Sample Code	Sample	Sample Size
I.1	All households	4,636
I.2	All owner occupiers	2,492
I.3	All local authority tenants	1,557
I.4	All private-rented tenants	476
I.5	All households (excluding housing association tenants)	4,525
I.6	All households whose landlords did work	789
I.7	All households who consider dwelling to have deteriorated	520
I.8	All households and landlords who undertook major work	1,835
I.9	All owner occupiers who undertook work	1,600
I.10	All tenants who undertook work	237

Longitudinal physical survey sample

Sample Code	Sample	Sample Size
L.1	1981 Physical survey — all dwellings	8,227
L.2	1981 Interview survey — all households	4,527
L.3	1986 Physical survey — all dwellings	8,311
L.4	1986 Interview survey — all households	2,219
L.5	Demolitions between 1981–1986	76
L.6	Dwellings no longer in residential use 1981–1986	51

Postal survey sample

Sample Code	Sample	Sample Size
Pos.1	Private-sector stock in 1981	2,907
Pos.2	Public-sector stock in 1981	596
Pos.3	Public-sector stock in 1986	2,157
Pos.4	Block or group repair schemes in the private sector	83
Pos.5	Block or group repair schemes in the public sector	354
Pos.6	Owner-occupied households	3,798
Pos.7	Powers used in the private sector	135
Pos.8	Area-based programmes in the private sector	335
Pos.9	Total grants given	300
Pos.10	Private sector: unsatisfactory stock in 1981	1,662
Pos.11	Private sector: completed action in 1986	575
Pos.12	Public sector: completed action by condition in 1986	435

Market value survey

Sample Code	Sample	Sample Size
Vol. 1	All dwellings	5,162

Appendix E Data quality

1. An extensive set of procedures was used to ensure that the data collected was as accurate as possible. Before any part of the survey was undertaken questionnaires and survey schedules were piloted to ensure that they were effective. Fieldwork for all parts of the survey began with briefing.

Briefing and fieldwork

2. The physical survey began with a five day session for each surveyor which included lectures, discussions and practice surveys using film or actual houses. All surveyors were provided with a comprehensive briefing manual. Four of the practice surveys towards the end of the session provided a comparison between surveyors. This allowed a measurement of the variability between surveyors as well as informing the individual of any adjustment he needed to make in his or her judgements. During the first week in the field a surveyor was accompanied for one or two days by a supervisor to identify and overcome any immediate problems. The same supervisor revisited a random 4% selection of surveyed dwellings to ensure that standards were being maintained throughout the survey.

3. One day briefing sessions were held for all interviewers who took part in the household interviews. This briefing was supplemented by an interviewers' instruction manual. Once in the field 10% of all interviewers were accompanied at some stage during the survey. In areas where there was a low response a second team of interviewers was employed to boost the contact rate. This yielded interviews in half the cases. A postal check was undertaken on 10% of all households interviewed by asking them a few questions about the survey.

4. For the postal survey of local authorities and the market value survey those responsible for providing the data were given a set of explanatory notes on how to fill in their forms. They were also provided with a Departmental contact who answered queries where difficulties arose.

Data checking

5. Completed forms from all parts of the survey were scrutinised for error. All forms were first double punched on data entry to minimise punching error. The physical survey forms were subjected to extensive computer validation to identify and rectify errors and inconsistencies in the data. Tests were also undertaken to identify major differences in assessment standards employed by individual surveyors.

6. A sub-sample of 400 dwellings from the Longitudinal survey were reinspected by surveyors using the Main survey schedule. This exercise, together with the practice surveys conducted during the briefing sessions, provided direct comparison between the 'old' and 'new' methods.

7. The initial questionnaires submitted by each interviewer were subjected to a 100% manual check and interviewers were notified of errors they were making. After this, only specific parts of the questionnaire were manually checked. All interview data was subjected to computer range, logic and consistency checks where appropriate. In addition each filter question was checked to ensure that only the intended groups of households had passed through each filter question.

8. The postal survey forms were checked for completeness and consistency. Where major gaps were seen to occur local authorities were contacted to supply the additional information. Market value data was also checked on the same basis.

Matching the sub-samples

9. Although each address had a unique code, which it retained whatever part of the survey it was included in, it was always possible that different people involved in the survey collected information from an address other than that specified. Checks were carried out to identify cases where different addresses had been visited. This was particularly important for the Longitudinal survey. Data were excluded from the survey where a mistake had been made and the wrong address visited.

Non-response

10. Complete non-response, such as when an occupant refused to be interviewed, was dealt with during the grossing procedure by applying weighting to compensate for any bias in the non-response. In individual cases when data were available but incomplete (usually because the surveyor could not gain access to the interior of a dwelling), the gaps were filled by reference to what was known about the dwelling. When this was not possible the gaps remained and at the tabulation stage an assumption was made that those dwellings with missing data were distributed amongst the cells of the table in precisely the same way as dwellings for which data were complete.

Assessment of condition

11. Particular difficulties of measurement are encountered in assessing the condition of dwellings, and these introduce uncertainty in the calculation of repair cost and in the determination of unfitness. The difficulties stem from variations among surveyors in the diagnosis and prognosis of defects found in dwellings, and from problems of definition and interpretation of standards of treatment. Any two surveyors inspecting a given dwelling will have different views of its condition. In a test in which a large number of surveyors was asked to survey the same dwelling which was in poor condition, one-third of the surveyors provided an assessment of disrepair whose calculated cost differed from the mean value by 30% or more (Figure E1). The impact of surveyor variability is diminished when large numbers of dwellings are treated in aggregate as they are in this survey.

Fig E.1 Surveyor variability in measuring repair on a single dwelling

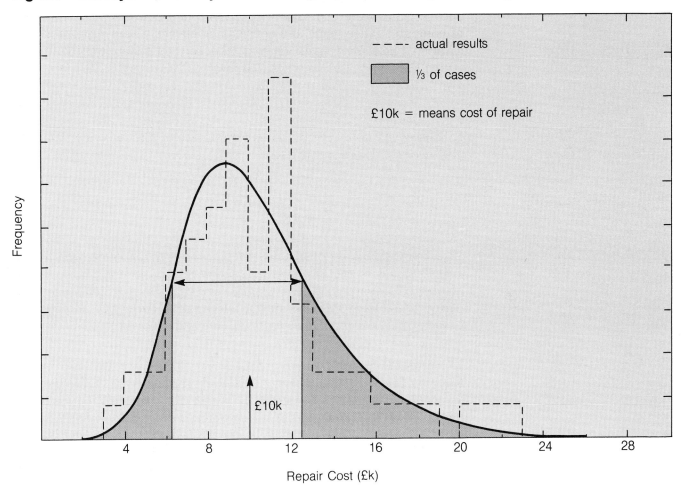

12. However, surveyor variability does make for particular difficulties in the determination of changes in disrepair over time. It also has a distorting effect on the overall distribution of repair cost within the stock: too many dwellings will be recorded as having very high, and too many very low, repair costs (Figure E2).

Fig E.2 The effect of surveyor variability on repair cost distribution

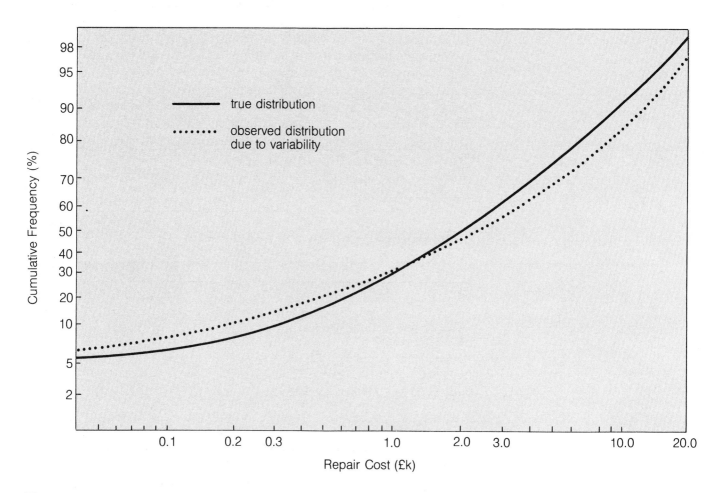

Treatment of unfitness

13. The distribution of serious defects within the stock is such that a slight change in the criterion adopted has a profound effect on the number of properties designated unfit. The subjectivity of the judgement of unfitness makes this a serious problem, particularly if the intention is to measure the trend between one survey and the next.

14. During the 1981 survey, data from 1981, 1976 and 1971 were analysed together in an attempt to reduce this problem. A preliminary examination of the relationship between the recorded defects in a dwelling and the likelihood of it being reported as unfit suggested that there had been sufficient change in the assessment standard since 1981 to require a similar exercise with the 1986 Longitudinal survey.

15. The analysis concentrated on those cases where the surveyor indicated his decision was borderline and on those in which there appeared to be inconsistencies within the 1986 data. Survey schedules from 1971, 1976 and 1986 (sometimes two from 1986 if a 'callback' survey had been carried out) were examined together with photographs from the 1986 survey by a panel of three survey supervisors[1] with support provided by a member of the Housing and Planning Inspectorate. The aim was to ensure consistency within the 1986 data and comparability between 1981 and 1986.

---

[1] This comprised two building professionals from the EHCS team and one independent Environmental Health Officer.

16. Survey forms from earlier years were also used to corroborate or add an unfitness rating in the 18% of cases in which data were incomplete. In the 16% of cases in which no data were obtained the problem was dealt with within the grossing (which included compensation for bias in the non-response).

17. The results of these exercises are shown in Table E.1. Adjustments to the amount of variability between surveyors reduced the rate of unfitness in 1986 by 0.4%. The treatment of missing data raised the figure by 0.7%. A very slight change was required to the 1981 standard to bring it into line with that used in 1986.

Table E.1 Estimation of rate of unfitness in 1981 and 1986

% of stock unfit

	1981	1986	Change 1981−86
'Raw' Data	6.0	5.3	
Adjustment Due to Imposing Consistency of 1981 Standard	+0.2	−	
Adjustment Due to Imposing Consistency of 1986 Standard	+0.1	−0.4	
Adjustment Due to Treatment of Missing Data	−	+0.7	
Following Adjustments	6.3	5.6	−0.7
Error of Measurement	+/−0.3	+/−0.3	+/−0.2
Sampling Error	+/−0.2	+/−0.2	+/−0.2
Total Error	+/−0.4	+/−0.4	+/−0.3

18. The sampling errors for the 1981 and 1986 results have been taken from Table D.3. The estimates of measurement errors are based on the magnitudes of the adjustments which were required to the 'raw' results. The errors in the two years are correlated since the two samples are identical and since the same adjustment procedures are applied to both data sets, and this is taken into account in deriving the error on the change in the rate of unfitness between the surveys.

19. The estimated reduction in the rate of unfitness between 1981 and 1986 is (0.7 +/−0.3)%. The conclusion that unfitness has reduced is just significant at the 95% confidence level.

Treatment of incomes
20. The survey collected information on the various components of income — regular salaries, irregular payments, benefits, allowances and pensions — for both the household head and partner. These provided the input to a computerised procedure which calculated tax and National Insurance contributions and estimated the net household income.

21. In the 23% of cases for which crucial data were not available estimates were made of the net household income based upon the relationships between it, the employment status of household head and partner and the socio-economic group of the head.

Treatment of remedial work undertaken

22. Information was collected on the nature and scale of improvement and repair activities over a five year period and on the expenditure involved. In a substantial number of cases the respondent was able to describe the work but could not recall, or perhaps had never known, its cost. For work undertaken by landlords, but described by tenants, no cost data were obtained. In both these cases a notional cost was established, based upon unit costs of individual items of work estimated, from those cases in which cost data were provided.

23. There is some evidence that remedial work was under-reported in the survey. When work recorded by tenants as having been carried out during 1986 by public sector landlords is costed and aggregated, the total sum falls short of the official estimates of expenditure by these bodies. Correspondingly information from local authorities themselves on the value of work undertaken also falls short of official estimates. Accordingly all costs of work by landlords have been scaled up by an appropriate factor. However, this approach may well have a distorting effect on the distribution of expenditure between different types of work, and almost certainly leaves underestimated the number of properties which benefitted from work by landlords.

24. The number of jobs reported as being undertaken each year by the occupants themselves increased dramatically between 1981 and 1986. Only a small part of this change can be explained by real changes in the quantity of work being undertaken or by the movement of occupants in the intervening years. This apparent lack of reported work suggests that occupants had forgotten that work had been undertaken and did not report it to the interviewer. Consequently, estimates of the absolute level of work have been derived only from that reported undertaken during 1986.

25. The uncertainty surrounding these data on remedial work affects the estimates which have been made of total expenditure. The overall estimate of expenditure on the stock in 1986 varies by around +/−£1bn.

Appendix F   Repair costs

The use made of repair costs in the report

1.   The expenditure required to carry out specified works provides a convenient measure of disrepair and allows different characteristics of disrepair to be summed on a common base. But the sums derived will vary not only with the level of disrepair but with the remedy proposed. Furthermore, prices vary from one locality to another, and with the prevailing economic climate. They may also depend upon whether the work is organised and supervised by a local authority, a housing association, or by a private owner. Therefore the estimated cost of repair generated by the survey can only be an indication of the actual price of any work required.

2.   In individual dwellings problems appear and get gradually worse until remedial action becomes either convenient or imperative, so at any point in time there will be an outstanding amount of repair which could be considered 'normal'. To provide a realistic assessment of disrepair some account has to be taken of the dynamic nature of the problem. This can prove difficult in any 'snapshot' survey but in 1986 an attempt was made for the first time to introduce 'time' into the definition of repair cost.

3.   The approach used was to ask each surveyor to identify all repairs required in a dwelling, but to distinguish between those which needed to be tackled immediately and those which needed to be tackled within five years. They were also asked to indicate how long it would be before the particular element of the building would need replacing given that the identified repairs were undertaken as specified.

4.   From this information it is possible to define several distinct estimates of the cost of repair. The main measure used in chapter 4 is 'repair' and this relates to all those repairs indicated by the surveyor as being required within five years. In addition, reference is made to 'urgent repairs' — those repairs which are required immediately, and to 'comprehensive repairs' — the package of activity which includes not only those repairs specified initially by the surveyor but also all replacements of building elements required within a ten year period.

5. The relationship between these three measures is shown in Figure F.1 in which are plotted the full frequency distributions obtained for the stock as a whole. It can be seen that on average, the estimated cost of 'urgent repairs' is approximately 50-60% of that for 'repair' and the estimated cost of 'comprehensive repair' is some 90% higher than the 'repair' figure.

Fig F.1   Repair Costs

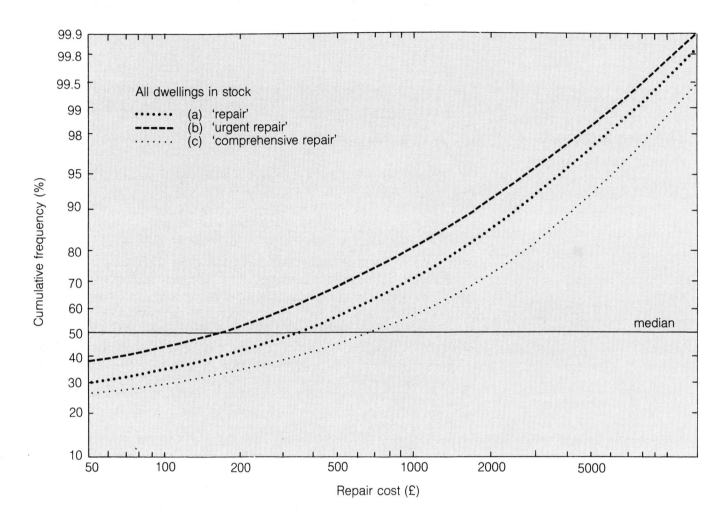

Method of estimating repair cost

6. The method of calculating repair costs in the 1986 survey differs fundamentally from that used in earlier years.

7. In earlier surveys disrepair was measured as the shortfall between the condition of the building surveyed and an equivalent new building. This began, for a particular building type, with an estimate of the total rebuilding cost which was then broken down between the major components of the building-roofs, walls, windows and so on. Surveyors reported the condition of each component as the proportion which needed rebuilding (or the equivalent), and it was this proportion which was applied to the rebuilding cost to give the repair cost for that element. The individual repair costs were aggregated to give the total repair cost for the dwelling.

8. Though this method provides a common measure of disrepair it bears little relationship to the way repairs are commissioned and the likely expenditure on those works in the real world. It relies on an abstract model which is difficult to relate to known labour and material costs. It requires each dwelling to be allocated to a stereotype class. It does not take adequate account of the variation in size of dwellings. It introduces certain distortions — in the case of dwellings with little work to be done (because of the insensitivity of the scale used in the schedule); and with those which require substantial work (since there is an imposed upper limit to the repair cost).

9. These procedures were employed in the longitudinal element of the 1986 survey to provide comparability with results obtained in 1981. The costs used in the model were not changed and therefore they are set at 1981 prices. As these figures are used only as a relative measure to make comparisons then the use of this historic price base has no material impact on the results.

10. The alternative procedure used in 1986 was to estimate the cost of each repair identified by the surveyor and aggregate these to provide estimates of the total cost of repair in any case. For each building element the works required and their quantities were recorded. During the data processing current prices[1] were applied to these quantities, with some allowance being made for economies of scale. To minimise the effort required of the surveyor he was not asked to measure the quantities requiring work but rather to make estimates of the proportions (tenths) of an element which were affected. He did however measure the overall dimensions of the building and described the plan form, and it was from this information that the computer was able to convert the proportions identified to square metres or linear metres which were required to estimate the cost of the work.

Comparison of the methods for estimating repair costs

11. Although the methods for estimating repair costs in the Longitudinal and Main survey differ, it is possible to compare the outcomes as both samples are grossed to stock totals. A more direct comparison of the methods is also available, since for a sub-sample of 400 dwellings (the 'overlap' sample), both survey schedules and both procedures for calculating repair costs were employed.

12. The two comparisons give consistent results, and show that the method developed in 1986 for the main survey yields estimates of the repair cost which are significantly lower than those given by the earlier method. (Figure F.2 and comparison of F.1 and F.4). The difference arises from a number of sources.

---

[1] Prices are based upon the Property Services Agency's "Schedule of Rates for Building Work — 1985" updated to November 1986 prices. They are exclusive of VAT and are average prices for the country as a whole.

Fig F.2 Comparison of repair costs from Main and Longitudinal survey schedules using different standards of repair

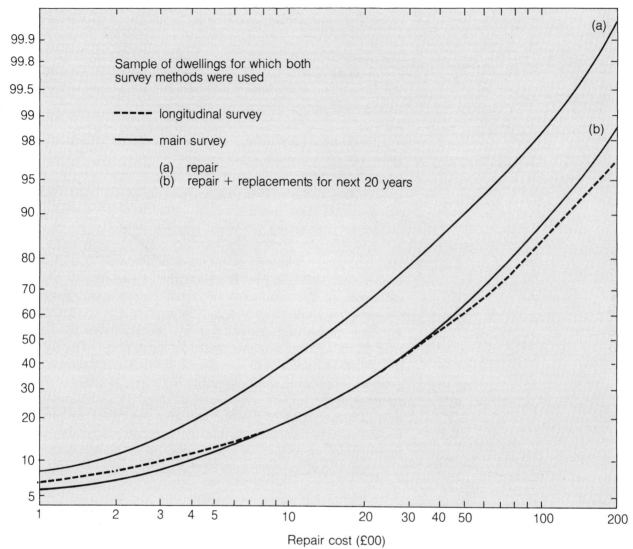

Repair cost (£00)

13. First, the costing procedure used in the Longitudinal Survey gives slightly different results to that developed for the 1986 Main Survey, given the same data from the survey schedule. It produces a higher proportion of dwellings with low repair costs, and a higher proportion with high repair costs while the average level of cost remains about the same (Figure F.3).

14. In addition, there tends to be a difference in the assessment of the condition of a dwelling according to which of the two survey schedules are used. Various factors are known to contribute to this result but their effects are not easily separated. The stricter control of the survey procedure required by the Main Survey schedule has an effect, as does the increased sensitivity and flexibility of the assessment scales used in this schedule. The introduction of the time dimension into the assessment of disrepair in the new schedule has also had an effect. The adoption of a 'thirty year life' criterion in earlier surveys is likely to have encouraged surveyors to have reported the need for replacement rather than short term repair. The Main survey schedule distinguishes between short term repairs and future replacements and these are recorded separately (Figure F.2).

Fig F.3   Effect of different costing procedures in the calculation of repair costs using data collected by the Main survey schedule

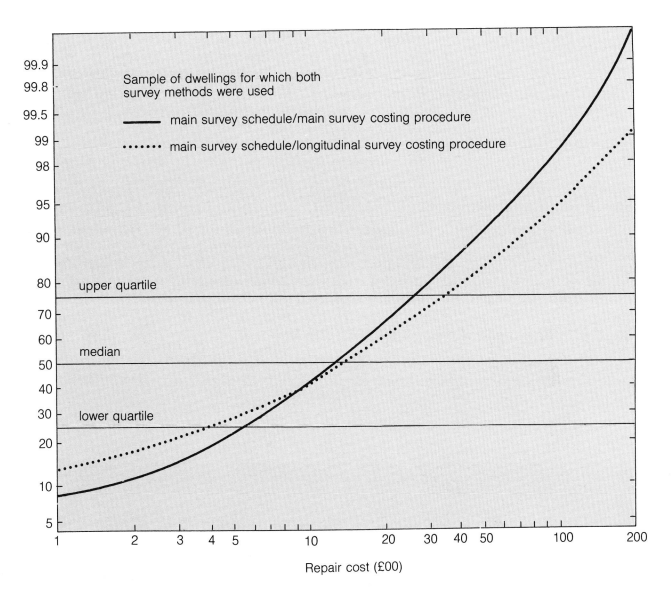

Treatment of missing data

15.   For some dwellings in the sample the data collected on the state of repair were not complete. This usually occurred when the surveyor was not able to gain access for an internal inspection.

16.   The problem was dealt with in the calculation of repair costs by assuming that those parts of the dwelling for which data were not available were similar in condition to the remainder (as long as at least half of the repair cost was directly measurable). When internal repair costs were not available they were estimated from external costs. When dwelling dimensions were not recorded they were assumed to be similar to the average for the particular type of building.

Estimation of changes in repair costs between 1981 and 1986

17. The Longitudinal survey was used to estimate trends. Data from the 1981 survey were reanalysed to ensure that exactly the same procedures were used for both data sets. Data on the building type were taken only from the 1986 survey to prevent any discrepancies between the two surveys causing a dwelling to be allocated to different building categories and hence to different pricing regimes. The costing method was basically that used for the 1981 survey using the 1981 price base. Inevitably the use of the 1986 definitions of building type and the 1986 method of distributing missing data produced "1981" figures which differed from those quoted in the 1981 report.

18. The assessment scales used in the Longitudinal survey are relatively insensitive and there is some uncertainty associated with their use (see paragraph 8 above). In order to indicate the range of uncertainty, repair costs have been calculated from the 1986 data using two extreme interpretations of the scales. The results are shown as frequency distributions in Figure F.4 together with the distributions calculated from the 1981 survey data. The most likely distribution for 1986 lies somewhere between the two lines given in the plot, with the lines being regarded as confidence limits.

Fig F.4   Comparison of repair cost 1981 and 1986

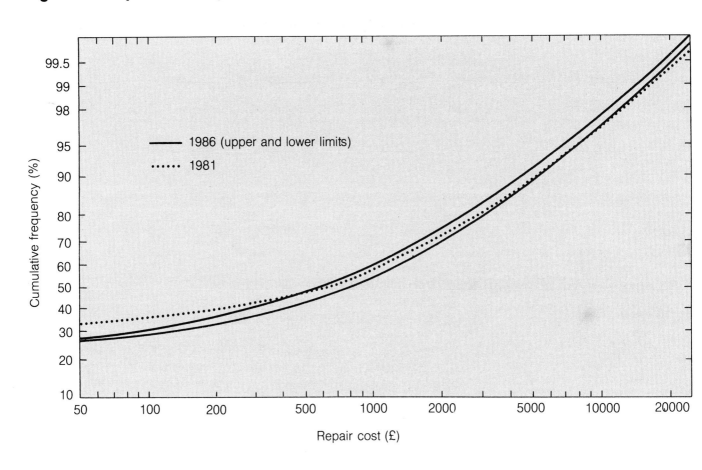

Appendix G 1986 EHCS additional tabulations service

1. The report contains only a small proportion of the total information which is available from this survey. Additional tabulations can be bought through the BRE Advisory Service.

2. Further details of this service and the prices of the tabulations can be obtained from:

BRE Advisory Service
Building Research Establishment
Bucknalls Lane
Garston
Watford

Tel: 0923-664664

Printed in the United Kingdom for Her Majesty's Stationery Office.
Dd.290591, 11/88, C30, 0434/1, 5673, 33660.